Philosophers on Religion

Philosophers on Religion

A historical reader

edited by
Patrick Sherry

Geoffrey Chapman
London

A Geoffrey Chapman book published by
Cassell Publishers Limited
Artillery House, Artillery Row, London SW1P 1RT

Compilation © Geoffrey Chapman, a division of Cassell Publishers Limited, 1987

First published 1987

ISBN 0 225 66496 8

British Library Cataloguing in Publication Data
Philosophers on religion: a historical reader.
    Religion—Philosophy
    I. Sherry, Patrick
    200'.1   BL51

Printed and bound in Great Britain by
Biddles Ltd, Guildford and King's Lynn

Contents

Preface

The purpose of this book is to provide a short collection of representative samples of the work of Western philosophers and theologians writing about the philosophical problems raised by religious belief. Many of the extracts are concerned with the existence and nature of God. But I have also selected writings which deal with other central religious concerns, such as prayer, revelation, the soul and miracles. I have tried to include some representative examples from the first millennium of the Christian era, as well as giving two extracts from Plato and Aristotle; for Western philosophy of religion did not begin with St Thomas Aquinas, or even with St Anselm! On the other hand, I have provided only two examples of twentieth-century work, because there are already many excellent anthologies of contemporary philosophy of religion.

In most cases I have given complete chapters or articles; where the length of the original has necessitated some selection, I have indicated omissions and provided an interlinking commentary. Of course limitations of space have compelled me to omit many authors whom I would like to have included, for instance Spinoza, Hegel, Newman and Whitehead. I would like, too, to have been able to give longer extracts from those writers who are represented, for example further parts of Hume's *Dialogues on Natural Religion*. But my brief introductory remarks before each selection indicate where the reader may follow up what he or she has read here.

The only general comment which needs to be made now about the readings is that one should approach them with a sense of history. Obviously, philosophers have had different attitudes to the religion of their time: there have been among them devout believers, wistful agnostics and hostile sceptics. Less obviously, they have had varying views about the proper relationship between philosophy and religious belief: some philosophers have seen their task as including the establishment of religious truths, thus leading people to a religious vision of reality and way of life; others have had a more limited view, seeing philosophy's task as being to justify the preambles of faith (e.g. the existence of God), to explain Scripture and Church teaching, and to defend the articles of faith against the attacks of sceptics; others, again, have allotted philosophy an even more limited role here, for example to establish the conditions of the possibility of religion or to analyse religious beliefs and language (on this, see further Max Charlesworth, *Philosophy of Religion: the Historic Approaches*, London, 1972). This means that if one reads a philosopher's demonstration of God's existence, for instance, one must have due regard to its purpose and context. St Anselm in his monastery was in circumstances very different from a Rationalist philosopher like Leibniz six centuries later or a modern philosopher debating with an atheist on the BBC. Moreover, the purpose of such demonstrations may be to evoke awe and wonder, to confirm the believer's faith, to correct false or heretical beliefs and to show common ground with other religions (and not to refute atheism, or not just this). In later centuries such arguments were often lifted from their original religious contexts and treated as part of subsequent debates. A similar danger of anachronism exists when one reads a sceptical writer. The 'natural religion' which Hume attacked was very much the creation of philosophers of his and the previous century. Similarly, his essay on miracles was aimed at a view of revelation and an apologetical appeal to prophecy and miracles which were prevalent in his time (see the selection from Locke), but which are hardly typical of much later Christianity. The moral to be drawn, then, is that all the religious believers and sceptics represented in this and other such anthologies are not necessarily members of two teams playing in a single game!

I am grateful for advice about my selection of texts to Bill Austin, Brian Davies, Richard Bell, David Burrell, John Clayton, Michael Durrant, Paul Helm and Colin Lyas.

Acknowledgements

I am grateful to the following publishers for permission to use copyright material: to the Clarendon Press, Oxford, to use W. D. Ross, *The Works of Aristotle Translated into English*, Vol. VIII, and M. J. Charlesworth, *St Anselm's Proslogion*; to Longmans, to use *Ancient Christian Writers*, Vol. 19; to the SCM Press, to use J. Burnaby, *Augustine, Later Works*; to William Heinemann, to use the Loeb edition of the works of Boethius; to Eyre and Spottiswoode, to use the Blackfriars edition of St Thomas Aquinas, *Summa Theologiae*, Vols II and III; to the Cambridge University Press, to use J. Cottingham *et al.*, *The Philosophical Writings of Descartes*, Vol. II; to Penguin Books to use B. Pascal (trans.

J. M. Cohen) *The Pensées*; to Reidel, to use Leroy Loemker, *G. W. F. Leibniz, Philosophical Papers and Letters*; to The Macmillan Company, to use I. Kant (trans. Norman Kemp Smith), *Critique of Pure Reason*; to Bobbs Merrill, to use I. Kant (trans. Lewis White Beck), *Critique of Practical Reason*; to Collins, to use S. Kierkegaard (trans. A. Dru), *The Present Age*, and to Basil Blackwell, to use J. Wisdom, *Philosophy and Psycho-analysis*.

1

Plato
An Early Natural Theology

Plato was born about 428 B.C. He intended to make a career in politics in Athens, but was disillusioned at the putting to death of his mentor Socrates by the state in 399. He founded a school of philosophy, the Academy, in Athens about 387 and died there about 347. His works include *Gorgias*, *Phaedo*, *The Republic*, *The Symposium* and *Theaetetus*.

The Laws is generally considered to be a late work. It is a discussion about laws and government between three interlocutors, an Athenian Stranger, a Cretan, Cleinias, and a Spartan, Megillus. In Book 10 Plato discusses impiety, and seeks to answer those who do not believe in the gods at all, those who believe in them but think that they have no care for men, and those who believe that they can be bribed by prayers and sacrifices. This passage contains his answer to the first category of sceptics.

Athenian Stranger   Come, then, and if ever we are to call upon the Gods, let us call upon them now in all seriousness to come to the demonstration of their own existence. And so holding fast to the rope we will venture upon the depths of the argument. When questions of this sort are asked of me, my safest answer would appear to be as follows:—Someone says to me, 'O stranger, are all things at rest and nothing in motion, or is the exact opposite of this true, or are some things in motion and others at rest?'—To this I shall reply that some things are in motion and others at rest. 'And do not things which move move in a place, and are not the things which are at rest at rest in a place?' Certainly. 'And some move or rest in one situation and some in more than one?' You mean to say, we shall rejoin, that those things which rest at their centre move in one situation, just as the circumference goes round of circles, which are said to be at rest? 'Yes.' And we observe that, in the revolution, the motion which carries round the larger and the lesser circle at the same time is proportionally distributed to greater and smaller, and is greater and smaller in a certain proportion. Here is a wonder which might be thought an impossibility, that the same motion should impart swiftness and slowness in due proportion to larger and less circles. 'Very true.' And when you speak of

1

bodies moving in many situations, you seem to me to mean those which move from one place to another, and sometimes have one centre of motion as basis, and sometimes more than one because they turn upon their axis; and whenever they meet anything, if it be stationary, they are divided by it; but if they get in the midst between bodies which are approaching and moving towards the same spot from opposite directions, they unite with them. 'I admit the truth of what you are saying.' Also when they unite they grow, and when they are divided they waste away,—that is, supposing the constitution of each to remain, or if that fails, then there is a second reason of their dissolution. 'And when are all things created and how?' Clearly, they are created when the first principle receives increase and attains to the second dimension, and from this arrives at the one which is neighbour to this, and after reaching the third becomes perceptible to sense. Everything which is thus changing and moving is in process of generation; only when at rest has it real existence; when it has passed from that into another state it is destroyed utterly. Have we not mentioned all motions that there are, and comprehended them under their kinds and numbered them with the exception, my friends, of two?

Cleinias   Which are they?

Athenian Stranger   Just the two with which our present inquiry is concerned.

Cleinias   Speak plainer.

Athenian Stranger   I suppose that our inquiry has reference to the soul?

Cleinias   Very true.

Athenian Stranger   Let us assume that there is a motion able to move other things, but never to move itself;—that is one kind; and there is another kind which can always move itself as well as other things, working in composition and decomposition, by increase and diminution and generation and destruction,—that is also one of the many kinds of motion.

Cleinias   Granted.

Athenian Stranger   And we will assume that which moves other, and is changed by other, to be the ninth, and that which changes itself and others, and is coincident with every action and every passion, and is the true principle of change and motion in all that is,—that we shall be inclined to call the tenth.

Cleinias   Certainly.

Athenian Stranger   And which of these ten motions ought we to prefer as being the mightiest and most efficient?

Cleinias   I must say that the motion which is able to move itself is ten thousand times superior to all the others.

Athenian Stranger   Very good; but may I make one or two corrections in what I have been saying?

Cleinias   What are they?

Athenian Stranger   When I spoke of the tenth sort of motion, that was not quite correct.

Cleinias   What was the error?

Athenian Stranger   According to the true order, the tenth was really the first in generation and power; then follows the second, which was strangely enough termed the ninth by us.

Cleinias   What do you mean?

Athenian Stranger   I mean this: when one thing changes another, and that another, of such will there be any primary changing element? How can a thing which is moved by another ever be the beginning of change? Impossible. But when the self-moved changes other, and that again other, and thus thousands upon tens of thousands of bodies are set in motion, must not the beginning of all this motion be the change of the self-moving principle?

Cleinias   Very true, and I quite agree.

Athenian Stranger   Or, to put the question in another way, making answer to ourselves:—If, as most of these philosophers have the audacity to affirm, all things were at rest in one mass, which of the above-mentioned principles of motion must necessarily be the first to spring up among them? Clearly the self-moving; for there could be no change in them arising out of any external cause; the change must first take place in themselves. Then we must say that self-motion being the origin of all motions, and the first which arises among things at rest as well as among things in motion, is the eldest and mightiest principle of change, and that which is changed by another and yet moves other is second.

Cleinias   Quite true.

Athenian Stranger   At this stage of the argument let us put a question.

Cleinias   What question?

Athenian Stranger   If we were to see this power existing in any earthy, watery, or fiery substance, simple or compound—how should we describe it?

Cleinias   You mean to ask whether we should call such a self-moving power life?

Athenian Stranger   I do.

Cleinias   Certainly we should.

Athenian Stranger   And when we see soul in anything, must we not do the same—must we not admit that this is life?

Cleinias   We must.

Athenian Stranger   And now, I beseech you, reflect;—you would admit that we have a threefold knowledge of things?

Cleinias   What do you mean?

Athenian Stranger   I mean that we know the essence, and that we know the definition of the essence, and the name,—these are the three; and there are two questions which may be raised about anything.

Cleinias   How two?

Athenian Stranger   Sometimes a person may give the name and ask the definition; or he may give the definition and ask the name. I may illustrate what I mean in this way.

Cleinias   How?

Athenian Stranger   Number like some other things is capable of being divided into equal parts; when thus divided, number is named 'even', and the definition of the name 'even' is 'number divisible into two equal parts'?

Cleinias   True.

Athenian Stranger   I mean, that when we are asked about the definition and give the name, or when we are asked about the name and give the definition—in either case, whether we give name or definition, we speak of the same thing, calling 'even' the number which is divided into two equal parts.

Cleinias   Quite true.

Athenian Stranger   And what is the definition of that which is named 'soul'? Can we conceive of any other than that which has been already given—the motion which can move itself?

Cleinias   You mean to say that the essence which is defined as the self-moved is the same with that which has the name soul?

Athenian Stranger   Yes; and if this is true, do we still maintain that there is anything wanting in the proof that the soul is the first origin and moving power of all that is, or has become, or will be, and their contraries, when she has been clearly shown to be the source of change and motion in all things?

Cleinias   Certainly not; the soul as being the source of motion, has been most satisfactorily shown to be the oldest of all things.

Athenian Stranger   And is not that motion which is produced in another, by reason of another, but never has any self-moving power at all, being in truth the change of an inanimate body, to be reckoned second, or by any lower number which you may prefer?

Cleinias   Exactly.

Athenian Stranger   Then we are right, and speak the most perfect and absolute truth, when we say that soul is prior to body, and that body is second and comes afterwards, and is born to obey soul, which is the ruler?

Cleinias   Nothing can be more true.

Athenian Stranger Do you remember our old admission, that if soul was prior to body the things of soul were also prior to those of body?

Cleinias Certainly.

Athenian Stranger Then characters and manners, and wishes and reasonings, and true opinions, and foresight, and recollection are prior to length and breadth and depth and strength of bodies, if soul is prior to body.

Cleinias To be sure.

Athenian Stranger In the next place, must we not of necessity admit that the soul is the cause of good and evil, base and honourable, just and unjust, and of all other opposites, if we suppose her to be the cause of all things?

Cleinias We must.

Athenian Stranger And as soul orders and inhabits all things that move, however moving, must we not say that she orders also the heavens?

Cleinias Of course.

Athenian Stranger One soul or more? More than one—I will answer for you; at any rate, we must not suppose that there are less than two—one the author of good, and the other of evil.

Cleinias Very true.

Athenian Stranger Yes, very true; soul then directs all things in heaven, and earth, and sea by her movements, and these are described by the terms—will, consideration, attention, deliberation, opinion true and false, joy and sorrow, confidence, fear, hatred, love, and other primary motions akin to these; which again receive the secondary motions of corporeal substances, and guide all things to growth and decay, to composition and decomposition, and to the qualities which accompany them, such as heat and cold, heaviness and lightness, hardness and softness, blackness and whiteness, bitterness and sweetness, and all those other qualities which the soul uses, herself a goddess, when truly receiving the divine mind she disciplines all things rightly to their happiness; but when she is the companion of folly, she does the very contrary of all this. Shall we assume so much, or do we still entertain doubts?

Cleinias There is no room at all for doubt.

Athenian Stranger Shall we say then that it is the soul which controls heaven and earth, and the whole world?—that it is a principle of wisdom and virtue, or a principle which has neither wisdom nor virtue? Suppose that we make answer as follows:—

Cleinias How would you answer?

Athenian Stranger If, my friend, we say that the whole path and movement of heaven, and of all that is therein, is by nature akin to the movement and revolution and calculation of mind, and proceeds by kindred laws, then, as is plain, we must say that the best soul takes care of the world and guides it along the good path.

Cleinias   True.

Athenian Stranger   But if the world moves wildly and irregularly, then the evil soul guides it.

Cleinias   True again.

Athenian Stranger   Of what nature is the movement of mind?—To this question it is not easy to give an intelligent answer; and therefore I ought to assist you in framing one.

Cleinias   Very good.

Athenian Stranger   Then let us not answer as if we would look straight at the sun, making ourselves darkness at midday,—I mean as if we were under the impression that we could see with mortal eyes, or know adequately the nature of mind;—it will be safer to look at the image only.

Cleinias   What do you mean?

Athenian Stranger   Let us select of the ten motions the one which mind chiefly resembles, this I will bring to your recollection, and will then make the answer on behalf of us all.

Cleinias   That will be excellent.

Athenian Stranger   You will surely remember our saying that all things were either at rest or in motion?

Cleinias   I do.

Athenian Stranger   And that of things in motion some were moving in one place, and others in more than one?

Cleinias   Yes.

Athenian Stranger   Of these two kinds of motion, that which moves in one place must move about a centre like wheels made in a lathe, and is most entirely akin and similar to the circular movement of mind.

Cleinias   What do you mean?

Athenian Stranger   In saying that both mind and the motion which is in one place move in the same and like manner, in and about the same, and in relation to the same, and according to one proportion and order, and are like the motion of a globe, we invented a fair image, which does no discredit to our ingenuity.

Cleinias   It does us great credit.

Athenian Stranger   And the motion of the other sort which is not after the same manner, nor in the same, nor about the same, nor in relation to the same, nor in one place, nor in order, nor according to any rule or proportion, may be said to be akin to senselessness and folly?

Cleinias   That is most true.

Athenian Stranger   Then, after what has been said, there is no difficulty in distinctly stating, that since soul carries all things round, either the best soul or the contrary must of necessity carry round and order and arrange the revolution of the heaven.

Cleinias And judging from what has been said, stranger, there would be impiety in asserting that any but the most perfect soul or souls carries round the heavens.

Athenian Stranger You have understood my meaning right well, Cleinias, and now let me ask you another question.

Cleinias What are you going to ask?

Athenian Stranger If the soul carries round the sun and moon, and the other stars, does she not carry round each individual of them?

Cleinias Certainly.

Athenian Stranger Then of one of them let us speak, and the same argument will apply to all.

Cleinias Which will you take?

Athenian Stranger Everyone sees the body of the sun, but no one sees his soul, nor the soul of any other body living or dead; and yet there is great reason to believe that this nature, unperceived by any of our senses, is circumfused around them all, but is perceived only by mind; and therefore by mind and reflection only let us apprehend the following point.

Cleinias What is that?

Athenian Stranger If the soul carries round the sun, we shall not be far wrong in supposing one of three alternatives.

Cleinias What are they?

Athenian Stranger Either the soul which moves the sun this way and that, resides within the circular and visible body, like the soul which carries us about every way; or the soul provides herself with a body of fire or air, as some affirm, and from some point without violently propels body by body; or thirdly, she is without such a body, but guides the sun by some extraordinary and wonderful power.

Cleinias Yes, certainly; the soul can only order all things in one of these three ways.

Athenian Stranger And this soul of the sun, which is therefore better than the sun, whether riding in the sun as in a chariot to give light to men, or acting from without, or in whatever way, ought by every man to be deemed a god.

Cleinias Yes, by every man who has the least particle of sense.

Athenian Stranger And of the stars too, and of the moon, and of the years and months and seasons, must we not say in like manner, that since a soul or souls having every sort of excellence are the causes of all of them, those souls are gods, whether they are living beings and reside in bodies, and in this way order the whole heaven, or whatever be the place and mode of their existence;—and will anyone who

admits all this tolerate the denial that all things are full of gods?
Cleinias   No one, stranger, would be such a madman.

Athenian Stranger   And now, Megillus and Cleinias, let us offer terms to him who has hitherto denied the existence of the gods, and leave him.

Cleinias   What terms?

Athenian Stranger   Either he shall teach us that we were wrong in saying that the soul is the original of all things, and arguing accordingly; or, if he be not able to say anything better, then he must yield to us and live for the remainder of his life in the belief that there are Gods.—Let us see, then, whether we have said enough or not enough to those who deny that there are Gods.

Cleinias   Certainly,—quite enough, stranger.

• From *The Laws*, Book X, 893b–899d, in B. Jowett, *The Dialogues of Plato*, Vol. IV (4th ed.; Oxford, 1964), pp. 461–470.

2

Aristotle
The Prime Mover

Aristotle was born in Stagira in 384 B.C. He entered Plato's Academy in 367, where he studied and taught for many years. After Plato's death he left Athens; he spent three years as tutor to the young Alexander the Great. He returned to Athens in 335 and founded his own school, the Lyceum. He died in 322. His main works include the *Metaphysics*, *Nicomachean Ethics*, *On the Soul* and *Posterior Analytics*.

The *Metaphysics* is a series of treatises dealing with topics which do not belong to any particular science, such as the analysis of fundamental concepts like 'substance', 'cause', 'form' and 'matter'; it also deals with 'First Philosophy', which Aristotle defines as the theory of being *qua* being. Book Lambda (XII), which was written earlier than most other parts of the *Metaphysics*, deals with more theological topics.

6 Since there were three kinds of substance, two of them physical and one unmovable, regarding the latter we must assert that it is necessary that there should be an eternal unmovable substance. For substances are the first of existing things, and if they are all destructible, all things are destructible. But it is impossible that movement should either have come into being or cease to be (for it must always have existed), or that time should. For there could not be a before and an after if time did not exist. Movement also is continuous, then, in the sense in which time is; for time is either the same thing as movement or an attribute of movement. And there is no continuous movement except movement in place, and of this only that which is circular is continuous.

But if there is something which is capable of moving things or acting on them, but is not actually doing so, there will not necessarily be movement; for that which has a potency need not exercise it. Nothing, then, is gained even if we suppose eternal substances, as the believers in the Forms do, unless there is to be in them some principle which can cause change; nay, even this is not enough, nor is another substance besides the Forms enough; for if it is not to *act*, there will be no movement. Further, even if it acts, this will not be enough, if its

9

essence is potency; for there will not be *eternal* movement, since that which is potentially may possibly not be. There must, then, be such a principle, whose very essence is actuality. Further, then, these substances must be without matter; for they must be eternal, if *anything* is eternal. Therefore they must be actuality.

Yet there is a difficulty; for it is thought that everything that acts is able to act, but that not everything that is able to act acts, so that the potency is prior. But if this is so, nothing that is need be; for it is possible for all things to be capable of existing but not yet to exist.

Yet if we follow the theologians who generate the world from night, or the natural philosophers who say that 'all things were together',[1] the same impossible result ensues. For how will there be movement, if there is no actually existing cause? Wood will surely not move itself—the carpenter's art must act on it; nor will the menstrual blood nor the earth set themselves in motion, but the seeds must act on the earth and the *semen* on the menstrual blood.

This is why some suppose eternal actuality—e.g. Leucippus and Plato;[2] for they say there is always movement. But why and what this movement is they do not say, nor, if the world moves in this way or that, do they tell us the cause of its doing so. Now nothing is moved at random, but there must always be something present to move it; e.g. as a matter of fact a thing moves in one way by nature, and in another by force or through the influence of reason or something else. (Further, what sort of movement is primary? This makes a vast difference.) But again for Plato, at least, it is not permissible to name here that which he sometimes supposes to be the source of movement—that which moves itself; for the soul is later, and coeval with the heavens, according to his account.[3] To suppose potency prior to actuality, then, is in a sense right, and in a sense not; and we have specified these senses. That actuality is prior is testified by Anaxagoras (for his 'reason' is actuality) and by Empedocles in his doctrine of love and strife, and by those who say that there is always movement, e.g. Leucippus. Therefore chaos or night did not exist for an infinite time, but the same things have always existed (either passing through a cycle of changes or obeying some other law), since actuality is prior to potency. If, then, there is a constant cycle, something must always remain,[4] acting in the same way. And if there is to be generation and destruction, there must be something else[5] which is always acting in different ways. This must, then, act in one way in virtue of itself, and in another in virtue of something else—either of a third agent, therefore, or of the first. Now it must be in virtue of the first. For otherwise this again causes the motion both of the second agent and of the third. Therefore it is better to say 'the first'. For it was the cause of eternal uniformity; and something else is the cause of variety, and evidently both together are the cause of eternal variety. This, accordingly, is the character which the motions actually exhibit. What need then is there to seek for other principles?

7 Since (1) this is a possible account of the matter, and (2) if it were not true, the world would have proceeded out of night and 'all things together'[6] and out of non-being, these difficulties may be taken as solved. There is, then, something which is always moved with an unceasing motion, which is motion in a circle; and this is plain not in theory only but in fact. Therefore the first heaven[7] must be eternal. There is therefore also something which moves it. And since that which is moves and moved is intermediate, there is something which moves without being moved, being eternal, substance, and actuality. And the object of desire and the object of thought move in this way; they move without being moved. The primary objects of desire and of thought are the same. For the apparent good is the object of appetite, and the real good is the primary object of rational wish. But desire is consequent on opinion rather than opinion on desire; for the thinking is the starting-point. And thought is moved by the object of thought, and one of the two columns of opposites[8] is in itself the object of thought; and in this, substance is first, and in substance, that which is simple and exists actually. (The one and the simple are not the same; for 'one' means a measure, but 'simple' means that the thing itself has a certain nature.) But the beautiful, also, and that which is in itself desirable are in the same column; and the first in any class is always best, or analogous to the best.

That a final cause may exist among unchangeable entities is shown by the distinction of its meanings. For the final cause is (a) some being for whose good an action is done, and (b) something at which the action aims; and of these the latter exists among unchangeable entities though the former does not. The final cause, then, produces motion as being loved, but all other things move by being moved. Now if something is moved it is capable of being otherwise than as it is. Therefore if its actuality is the primary form of spatial motion, then in so far as it is subject to change, in *this* respect it is capable of being otherwise,—in place, even if not in substance. But since there is something which moves while itself unmoved, existing actually, this can in no way be otherwise than as it is. For motion in space is the first of the kinds of change, and motion in a circle the first kind of spatial motion; and this the first mover *produces*.[9] The first mover, then, exists of necessity; and in so far as it exists by necessity, its mode of being is good,[10] and it is in this sense a first principle. For the necessary has all these senses—that which is necessary perforce because it is contrary to the natural impulse, that without which the good is impossible, and that which cannot be otherwise but can exist only in a single way.

On such a principle, then, depend the heavens and the world of nature. And it is a life such as the best which we enjoy, and enjoy for but a short time (for it is ever in this state, which we cannot be), since its actuality is also pleasure. (And for this reason are waking, perception, and thinking most pleasant, and hopes and memories are so on account of these.) And thinking in itself deals with that which is best in itself, and that which is thinking in the fullest sense with that which is best in the fullest sense. And thought thinks on itself because it shares the nature of the object of thought; for it becomes an object of thought in coming into contact with and thinking its objects, so that thought and object of thought are the same. For that which is *capable* of receiving the object of thought, i.e. the essence, is thought. But it is *active* when it *possesses* this object. Therefore the possession rather than the receptivity is the divine element which thought seems to contain, and the act of contemplation is what is most pleasant and best. If, then, God is always in that good state in which we sometimes are, this compels our wonder; and if in a better this compels it yet more. And God *is* in a better state. And life also belongs to God; for the actuality of thought is life, and God is that actuality; and God's self-dependent actuality is life most good and eternal. We say therefore that God is a living being, eternal, most good, so that life and duration continuous and eternal belong to God; for this *is* God.

Those who suppose, as the Pythagoreans and Speusippus do, that supreme beauty and goodness are not present in the beginning, because the beginnings both of plants and of animals are *causes*, but beauty and completeness are in the *effects* of these, are wrong in their opinion. For the seed comes from other individuals which are prior and complete, and the first thing is not seed but the complete being; e.g. we must say that before the seed there is a man,—not the man produced from the seed, but another from whom the seed comes.

It is clear then from what has been said that there is a substance which is eternal and unmovable and separate from sensible things. It has been shown also that this substance cannot have any magnitude, but is without parts and indivisible (for it produces movement through infinite time, but nothing finite has infinite power; and, while every magnitude is either infinite or finite, it cannot, for the above reason, have finite magnitude, and it cannot have infinite magnitude because there is no infinite magnitude at all). But it has also been shown that it is impassive and unalterable; for all the other changes are posterior to[11] change of place.

1 Anaxagoras, *Fragment* 1.
2 Cf. *Timaeus* 30a.
3 Cf. *Phaedrus* 245c, *Laws* 894e [p. 3 above], *Timaeus* 34b.
4 i.e. the sphere of the fixed stars.
5 i.e. the sun.
6 Anaxagoras, *Fragment* 1.
7 i.e. the outer sphere of the universe, in which the fixed stars are set.
8 Aristotle is referring to a list of opposites, e.g. limited and unlimited, good and evil, male and female, which he mentions earlier, in Book Alpha (I), Chapter 5.
9 The first mover produces the first movement and therefore cannot share in it; for if it did, we should have to look for something prior to it which imparted this motion to it.
10 i.e. it is necessary in the sense that it does not admit of being otherwise.
11 i.e. impossible without.

• From W. D. Ross, *The Works of Aristotle Translated into English*, Vol. VIII (Oxford, 1928), pp. 1071 b2–1073 a12.

3

St Clement of Alexandria
Philosophy and Christian Faith

St Clement (Titus Flavius Clemens) was probably born in Athens about A.D. 150. He settled later in Alexandria, but left there about 202 because of persecution and moved to Asia Minor, where he died about 212. He was well acquainted with Greek philosophy and literature, and used them in defending Christianity. He regarded all true knowledge and wisdom, from whatever source, as a preparation for Christianity and as reaching its fulfilment in it.

The *Miscellanies* (*Stromateis*) is a loosely connected treatment of various topics in eight books. Book I is concerned mainly with the relationship between secular learning, especially philosophy, and Christian faith.

Chapter 5

Philosophy the handmaid of theology

Accordingly, before the advent of the Lord, philosophy was necessary to the Greeks for righteousness. And now it becomes conducive to piety; being a kind of preparatory training to those who attain to faith through demonstration. 'For thy foot', it is said, 'will not stumble, if thou refer what is good, whether belonging to the Greeks or to us, to Providence.'[1] For God is the cause of all good things; but of some primarily, as of the Old and the New Testament; and of others by consequence, as philosophy. Perchance, too, philosophy was given to the Greeks directly and primarily, till the Lord should call the Greeks. For this was a schoolmaster to bring 'the Hellenic mind', as the law, the Hebrews, 'to Christ'.[2] Philosophy, therefore, was a preparation, paving the way for him who is perfected in Christ.

'Now', says Solomon, 'defend wisdom, and it will exalt thee, and it will shield thee with a crown of pleasure.'[3] For when thou hast strengthened wisdom with a cope by philosophy, and with right expenditure, thou wilt preserve it unassailable by sophists. The way of truth is therefore one. But into it, as into a perennial river, streams flow from all sides. It has been therefore said by inspiration: 'Hear, my son, and receive my words; that thine may be the many ways of life. For I teach thee the ways of wisdom; that the fountains fail thee not',[4] which gush forth from the earth itself. Not only did He enumerate several ways of salvation for any one righteous man, but He added many other ways of many righteous, speaking thus: 'The paths of the righteous shine like the light'.[5] The commandments and the modes of preparatory training are to be regarded as the ways and appliances of life.

'Jerusalem, Jerusalem, how often would I have gathered thy children, as a hen her chickens!'[6] And Jerusalem is, when interpreted, 'a vision of peace'. He therefore shows prophetically, that those who peacefully contemplate sacred things are in manifold ways trained to their calling. What then? He 'would', and could not. How often, and where? Twice; by the prophets, and by the advent. The expression, then, 'how often', shows wisdom to be manifold; and in every mode of quantity and quality, it by all means saves some, both in time and in eternity. 'For the Spirit of the Lord fills the earth . . . .'

Clement goes on to warn against misinterpreting some texts from Proverbs 5.

And when He says, 'Be not much with a strange woman',[7] He admonishes us to use indeed, but not to linger and spend time with, secular culture. For what was bestowed on each generation advantageously, and at seasonable times, is a preliminary training for the word of the Lord. 'For already some men, ensnared by the charms of handmaidens, have despised their consort philosophy, and have grown old, some of them in music, some in geometry, others in grammar, the most in rhetoric.'[8] 'But as the encyclical branches of study contribute to philosophy, which is their mistress; so also philosophy itself co-operates for the acquisition of wisdom. For philosophy is the study of wisdom, and wisdom is the knowledge of things divine and human; and their causes.' Wisdom is therefore queen of philosophy, as philosophy is of preparatory culture. For if philosophy 'professes control of the tongue, and the belly, and the parts below the belly, it is to be chosen on its own account. But it appears more worthy of respect and pre-eminence, if cultivated for the honour and knowledge of God'.[9] And Scripture will afford a testimony to what has been said in what follows. Sarah was at one time barren, being Abraham's wife. Sarah having no child, assigned her maid, by name Hagar, the Egyptian, to Abraham, in order to get children. Wisdom, therefore, who dwells with the man of faith (and Abraham was reckoned faithful and righteous), was still barren and without child in that generation, not having brought forth to Abraham aught allied to virtue. And she, as was proper, thought that he, being now in the time of progress, should have intercourse with secular culture first (by Egyptian the world is designated figuratively); and afterwards should approach to her according to divine providence, and beget Isaac.

And Philo interprets Hagar to mean 'sojourning'. For it is said in connection with this, 'Be not much with a strange woman'.[10] Sarah he interprets to mean 'my princedom'. He, then, who has received previous training is at liberty to approach to wisdom, which is supreme, from which grows up the race of Israel. These things show that that wisdom can be acquired through instruction, to which Abraham attained, passing from the contemplation of heavenly things to the faith and righteousness which are according to God. And Isaac is shown to mean 'self-taught'; wherefore also he is discovered to be a type of Christ. . . .

Clement gives some further exegesis of Genesis, based on Philo.

. . . We merely therefore assert here, that philosophy is characterized by investigation into truth and the nature of things (this is the truth of which the Lord Himself said, 'I am the truth'[11]); and that, again, the preparatory training for rest in Christ exercises the mind, rouses the intelligence, and begets an inquiring shrewdness, by means of the true philosophy, which the initiated possess, having found it, or rather received it, from the truth itself.

In Chapters 6–8 Clement goes on to commend the use of learning in coming to understand the faith and in refuting sophistry. He says that philosophy may be used for good or ill.

Chapter 9

Human knowledge necessary for the understanding of the scriptures

Some, who think themselves naturally gifted, do not wish to touch either philosophy or logic; nay more, they do not wish to learn natural science. They demand bare faith alone, as if they wished, without bestowing any care on the vine, straightway to gather clusters from the first. Now the Lord is figuratively described as the vine, from which, with pains and the art of husbandry, according to the word, the fruit is to be gathered.

We must lop, dig, bind, and perform the other operations. The pruning-knife, I should think, and the pick-axe, and the other agricultural implements, are necessary for the culture of the vine, so that it may produce eatable fruit. And as in husbandry, so also in medicine: he has learned to purpose, who has practised the various lessons, so as to be able to cultivate and to heal. So also here, I call him truly learned who brings everything to bear on the truth; so that, from geometry, and music, and grammar, and philosophy itself, culling what is useful, he guards the faith against assault. Now, as was said, the athlete is despised who is not furnished for the contest. For instance, too, we praise the experienced helmsman who 'has seen the cities of many men', and the physician who has had large experience; thus also some describe the empiric.[12] And he who brings everything to bear on a right life, procuring examples from the Greeks and barbarians, this man is an experienced searcher after truth, and in reality a man of much counsel, like the touchstone (that is, the Lydian), which is believed to possess the power of distinguishing the spurious from the genuine gold. And our much-knowing gnostic can distinguish sophistry from philosophy, the art of decoration from gymnastics, cookery from physic, and rhetoric from dialectics, and the other sects which are according to the barbarian philosophy, from the truth itself. And how necessary is it for him who desires to be partaker of the power of God, to treat of intellectual subjects by philosophising! And how serviceable is it to distinguish expressions which are ambiguous, and which in the Testaments are used synonymously! For the Lord, at the time of His temptation, skilfully matched the devil by an ambiguous expression. And I do not yet, in this connection, see how in the world the inventor of philosophy and dialectics, as some suppose, is seduced through being deceived by the form of speech which consists in ambiguity. And if the prophets and apostles knew not the arts by which the exercises of philosophy are exhibited, yet the mind of the prophetic and instructive spirit, uttered secretly, because all have not an intelligent ear, demands skilful modes of teaching in order to clear exposition. For the prophets and disciples of the Spirit knew infallibly their mind. For they knew it by faith, in a way which others could not easily, as the Spirit has said. But it is not possible for those who have not learned to receive it thus. 'Write', it is said, 'the commandments doubly, in counsel and knowledge, that thou mayest answer the words of truth to them who send unto thee.'[13] What, then, is the knowledge of answering? or what that of asking? It is dialectics. What then? Is not speaking our business, and does not action proceed from the Word? For if we act not for the Word, we shall act against reason. But a rational work is accomplished through God. 'And nothing', it is said, 'was made without Him'—the Word of God.[14]

And did not the Lord make all things by the Word? Even the beasts work, driven by compelling fear. And do not those who are called orthodox apply themselves to good works, knowing not what they do?

1 Prov 3:23.
2 Gal 3:24.
3 Prov 4:8f.
4 Prov 4:10f., 21.
5 Prov 4:18.
6 Mt 23:37; Lk 13:34.
7 Prov 5:20.
8 Philo, *On Seeking Instruction*, 435.
9 Quoted from Philo, with some alterations. The following interpretation of Genesis 16 draws on Philo.
10 Prov 5:20.
11 Jn 14:6.
12 The empirics were a class of physicians who stressed the importance of practice.
13 Prov 22:20f.
14 Jn 1:3.

- From *The Writings of Clement of Alexandria*, Vol. I, trans. W. Wilson (*The Ante-Nicene Christian Library*, Vol. 4; Edinburgh, 1867), pp. 366–370, 379–380.

4

Origen
Prayer

Origen was born of Christian parents in Alexandria about A.D. 186. He became the leading teacher of the Alexandrian school, though he spent his last years in Caesarea, where he was imprisoned and tortured during the Decian persecution. He survived but died soon afterwards, in about 255. He and St Irenaeus (c. A.D. 130–200) are usually regarded as the first Christian systematic theologians. His main works were a commentary on St John's Gospel, *On First Principles* and *Against Celsus* (a reply to the philosopher Celsus' attack on Christianity).

On Prayer is a shorter work, written about 233. It consists mainly of a commentary on the Lord's Prayer, but begins with a discussion of certain objections and difficulties with regard to the practice of prayer.

Chapter 5

Objections to prayer

If next we must expound, as you have asked us, the arguments—first, of those who think that prayer effects nothing and who therefore say that it is superfluous to pray, we shall do our best to carry out your wishes. In this connection we now use the term prayer in its most simple and ordinary meaning. . . .[1]

This view is not generally well-received and has no eminent protagonists, so much so that no one whatever who believes at all in Providence and God's supremacy in the universe can be found to reject prayer. It is a theory held either by those who are complete atheists and deny the existence of God, or by those who allow the existence of God in name but deny His Providence. But indeed only the influence of the Adversary, seeking to associate the most impious teachings with the name of Christ and the doctrine of the Son of God, could persuade certain men that they ought not to pray. The protagonists of this view are they who do away with all sense perception and practise neither Baptism nor the Eucharist. They quibble about the Scriptures as not even recommending the prayer of which we speak, but as teaching something else quite different from it.

2. Here then, approximately, are the arguments of those who reject prayer (I deal only with those who posit a God over all and allow that there is a Providence; for it is not my purpose here to examine the arguments of those who deny God and Providence altogether): God sees all things before they come to be, and there is nothing that, when it comes to be, becomes known to Him for the first time by its coming to be, in such a way as not to have been known by Him before. What then is the use of praying to Him who knows what we need even before we pray? *For the* heavenly *Father knoweth what is needful for us, before we ask him.*[2] It is only reasonable that, being the Father and Creator of everything, *loving all things that are and hating none of the things which He has made,*[3] He should arrange—as a father would—everything in security for each one without his praying for it, watching over His children, and not waiting until they ask. Indeed, they may not even be able to ask, or through ignorance may often wish to get something which is the opposite of what is suitable and profitable to them. And indeed we human beings share less the mind of God than little children the mind of their parents.

3. We can say not only that God foreknows what things are going to be, but also that He prearranges them, and that nothing happens contrary to His prearrangement. And so if a man prayed for the sun to rise, he would be regarded as simple in claiming that, what would happen even without his praying, happened because of it. In the same way a man who thinks that things, which would in any case happen even without his praying for them, happened because of it, has no sense. And again just as the man who, made uncomfortable and scorched by the sun at the summer solstice, thinks that by his prayer he can call the sun back to the constellations of spring and thus enjoy the balminess of the air, goes beyond all lunacy, so any man who thinks that by praying he can avoid what has been prearranged as of necessity happening to the human race, is mad beyond compare.

4. And if *sinners are alienated from the womb,*[4] and the just man *is chosen from his mother's womb,*[5] [and] *neither has yet been born or performed good or evil (so that the chosen design of God should depend not on deeds but upon His election),* and it is said that *the elder shall serve the younger:*[6] in vain do we seek remission of sins or the strength of the Spirit so that we may have power *to do all things* in Christ *who strengtheneth us.*[7] For if we are *sinners,* we *are alienated from the womb.* And if we are *chosen from our mother's womb,* we shall fare excellently without ever having prayed. What prayer did Jacob make before he was born so that it is prophesied that *he shall overcome* Esau and that his brother *shall serve* him?[8] What impiety has Esau committed so as

to be hated before he is born? And why does Moses pray, as we find in Psalm 90, if God is his *refuge* ... *before the mountains were made, or the earth and the world was formed?* ....⁹

5. It is in regard to all those who are to be saved that it is written in the Epistle to the Ephesians: *The Father* ... *chose them in Him,* in Christ *before the foundation of the world, that they should be holy and unspotted in His sight in charity. Who hath predestinated them unto the adoption of children through Jesus Christ unto Himself.*¹⁰ A man is then either of the number of them that have been chosen *before the foundation of the world,* and it is impossible for him to fall from the election and consequently he has no need of prayer; or he has not been chosen nor predestinated and he prays in vain. Even if he pray ten thousand times, his prayer will not be heard. *For whom He foreknew, He also predestinated to be made conformable to the image of the glory of His Son.* ... *And whom He predestinated, them He also called. And whom He called, them He also justified. And whom He justified, them He also glorified.*¹¹

Why does Josias trouble or why is he anxious in his prayer as to whether or no it will ever be heard? Had he not been prophesied by name many generations before? And as to what he should do, had he not only been known of beforehand, but heralded in advance, in the hearing of many men? And why does Judas pray so that even *his prayer becomes a sin,* seeing that from the time of David it had been announced of him that he would lose his office and that another would get it in his place?¹² Obviously then, since God cannot be changed in His intention, and has anticipated all things, and abides by His prearrangement, it is absurd to pray in the belief that one can change by prayer His prearrangement, or—as though He has not prearranged all things, but awaits each one's prayer—to intercede that He may dispose things suitably for him who prays according to his prayer: in which case He would only then be disposing of things as they seemed reasonable on examination without His having previously considered them.

6. The matter can be put for the moment in the very words which you used in your letter to me: 'First, if God foresees everything that will happen, and these things must happen, prayer is useless. Second, if everything happens according to the will of God, and His decisions are firm, and nothing that He wills can be changed, prayer is useless'. It is well, I think, when solving the difficulties that tend to produce apathy for prayer, to treat first of the following considerations.

Chapter 6

Objections answered

Of things that are moved, some have their movement from outside, as for example, (1) inanimate things and things that are kept together only by their being disposed in a certain way; and, (2) things that can move because of some natural principle or soul. These last, however, are to be considered here not as being such, but only as being on occasion like those things that are kept together merely by their being disposed in a certain way. Stones, for instance, that have been taken from a quarry and logs of wood that have ceased to grow—things which are kept together merely by their being disposed in a certain way—have their movement from outside; but the bodies of animals and plants that can be transplanted, if they are changed from one place to another by someone, are moved not as living things and plants move, but as if they were stones or logs that have ceased to grow. And even though these do move for the reason that all are perishable bodies and are in a state of flux, their movement is only a circumstance attending their decay.

In addition, there is a second class of things which are moved by an intrinsic principle or soul. They are described by those who are precise in their terminology as moving *out of* themselves.

A third kind of movement is that found in animals, which is termed movement *from* themselves.

I believe that the movement of rational beings is movement *by* themselves.

If we take away from the animal movement *from* itself, it can no longer be considered an animal, but will be similar either to a plant which is moved by an intrinsic principle only, or to a stone which is moved by some outside agent. But if something responds to its own principle of motion, so that it will then be said to move *by* itself, this thing must be rational.

2. Those then who hold that we have no freedom of will, must come to conclusions that are quite absurd: first, that we are not animals; second, that we are not rational beings: we are as it were moved by an external agent, do not move at all of ourselves, and really do what we are thought to do through his instrumentality. Let a man moreover reflect upon his own individual experience and convince himself that he cannot without recklessness say that it is not *he* that wills, that it is not *he* that eats, not *he* that walks, not *he* that assents to and accepts certain views, nor *he* that rejects others as false. Just as it is impossible to make a man believe certain teachings, even if you present your arguments most skilfully in ten thousand ways and

employ the most plausible reasonings, in the same way it is impossible to make a man believe that in the matter of human actions his will is not free. Is there anyone who believes that we can understand nothing? Is there anyone who lives on the basis of suspending judgment on everything? Does a man not punish his servant when he catches sight of him doing some wrong? And who does not find fault with a son who does not pay proper respect to his parents, or does not blame and condemn a woman who has committed adultery as having done a shameful act? Truth compels and forces us, no matter how many and ingenious the arguments to the contrary, to act, to commend, and to condemn. We believe that our wills are free and consequently subject to commendation or condemnation.

3. If we are satisfied about our freedom of will, which manifests innumerable tendencies to virtue or vice, or again to one's duty or the opposite of one's duty, it follows that God necessarily knew what form it would take before it took that form along with all the other things that were to be *from the creation and foundation of the world*.[13] And in all the things which God prearranges according as He has foreseen each of our free actions, He prearranged according to the requirements of each of our free actions both that which was to happen as a result of His Providence and that which was to happen in the sequence of events that were to be. Yet the foreknowledge of God is not a *cause* of everything that is to be and of the effects of our free actions resulting from our own impulses. For even if we suppose that God did not know what was to be, we could for all that still choose and do this or that. But as a result of His foreknowledge the free actions of every man *fit in* with that disposition of the whole which is necessary for the existence of the universe.

4. If then God knows the free will of every man, therefore, since He foresees it, He arranges by His Providence what is fair according to the deserts of each, and provides what he may pray for, the disposition of such and such thus showing his faith and the object of his desire. Providing for this, and following some such line in His disposition, He will have made arrangements somewhat in this way: 'I will give ear to this man who prays with understanding on account of the prayer itself which he will utter; but this other man I will not hear, because he will be unworthy to be heard, or because he asks for things as would be neither good for him to receive nor fitting for me to give. If the prayer of such and such is like the latter case, for example, I shall not hear him; but if like the former, I shall'. (And if someone is disturbed that, because God's foreknowledge of what is to be is infallible, everything happens of necessity, we must say to him that God has a firm knowledge on this point precisely that such and such a man does not firmly and fixedly will what is good, or will so desire what is bad that it will be

impossible to convert him to what is good.) And again: 'I will do such and such a thing for this man who prays, for it is fitting for me to do this since both his prayer will be beyond reproach and his address without blame. And to this other man, when he shall pray for a certain thing, I will give this and that *more abundantly than he desires or understands*.[14] For it is fitting that I should overcome such a one in doing good, and that I should give him more than he could ask for. To this other man who will be of such and such a character, I will send a particular guardian angel to work with him at his salvation from such and such a time, and to remain with him up to a certain time. And to another I will send another angel, one, for example, of higher rank, because this man will be better than the former. And in the case of another, who, having devoted himself to lofty teachings, becomes weak and returns to material things, I will deprive him of his more powerful helper; and when he departs, a certain evil power—as he deserves—will seize the opportunity of profiting by his weakness, and will seduce him, now that he has shown his readiness to sin, to commit such and such sins'.

5. Thus, as it were, will He speak who prearranges all things: 'Amon will beget Josias, who will not emulate his father's failings but, taking the way that leads to virtue, because of those that will be with him, he will be an upright man and good, and will raze the altar iniquitously built by Jeroboam. And I know that when my Son will live among men, Judas, who will be upright and good at first, will change later and fall into human sins. And for these it will be right that he should suffer certain punishments'. (Perhaps this foreknowledge of all things was possessed also by the Son of God, as it certainly was with regard to Judas and other mysteries. In His observation of the unfolding of things to come, He saw Judas and the sins that he would commit. Thus, even before Judas was born, He could say with full knowledge by the mouth of David: *O God, be not thou silent in my praise*,[15] and so on.)

'And since I foreknow the future and what great religious zeal Paul will have, I shall choose him in myself before the founding of the universe and as I set about the beginning of its creation, and shall give him at his birth in charge to these powers— his co-workers in the salvation of men—*separating him from his mother's womb*.[16] I shall allow him in the beginning of his youthful zeal to persecute in ignorance and under the pretext of religion those who believe in Christ, and to keep the garments of them that stone my servant and martyr Stephen, so that when he has put his hot-headed youth behind him, he may later start anew, and turning to what is best, may *not glory in my sight* but say: *I am not worthy to be called an apostle, because I persecuted the church of God*.[17] Seeing all the goodness that I shall show him after the aberrations of his youth made under the pretext of religion, he will say, *But by the grace of God I am what I am;*[18] and, prevented by his consciousness of what in his youth he had done against Christ, he will not be *exalted by the greatness of the revelations*[19] which in my goodness will be manifested to him.'

Chapter 7

Further, regarding the objection to prayer which asks for the sun to rise,[20] this much must be said. The sun has a certain freedom of will too, inasmuch as it and the moon praise God. *Praise ye Him, O sun and moon*, says Scripture. And it is clear that this holds also for the moon and consequently for all the stars: *Praise Him, all ye stars and light.*[21] Just as we have said that God makes use of the free will of every man on earth and arranges it for some purpose, fitting in with the requirements of what is on the earth, so we must suppose that through the freedom of will of the sun and moon and stars, being harmonious and firm, fixed, and wise, He has arranged *the whole order of heaven*[22] and the march and movement of the stars that fits in with all the universe. And if my prayer be not amiss when offered on behalf of what depends on the free will of another man, so much more likely am I to succeed when my prayer is offered for what depends on the free will of the stars that dance in the heavens for the good of the universe. And further, regarding the inhabitants of the earth one must say that various kinds of impressions which have their source in what surrounds us, induce our weakness or our inclination towards the good either to do or to say this or that. But where the heavenly bodies are concerned, what impression can arise to divert or move each of them from its course, so beneficial to the universe, possessing as they do a soul strengthened by reason and removed from the influence of these impressions, and moreover using a body that is so ethereal and purified?[23]

1 About two lines are missing from the manuscript here.
2 Mt 6:8.
3 Wis 11:24.
4 Ps 58:3.
5 Gal 1:15.
6 Rom 9:11f.
7 Phil 4:13.
8 Gen 25:23.
9 Ps 90:1f.; a lacuna of about 1½ lines follows here.
10 Eph 1:3–5.
11 Rom 8:29f.

12 Cf. Acts 1:16, 20.
13 Mt 25:34; Rom 1:20.
14 Eph 3:20.
15 Ps 109:1.
16 Gal 1:15.
17 I Cor 1:29; 15:9.
18 I Cor 15:10.
19 II Cor 12:7.
20 See above, Chapter 5, §3 [p. 20].
21 Ps 148:3.
22 Dt 4:19.
23 Origen believed that the sun, moon and stars were living, rational beings.

• From *Ancient Christian Writers*, Vol. 19, trans. J. O'Meara (London, 1954), pp. 26–36.

5

St Gregory Nazianzen
God as Designer

St Gregory Nazianzen was, together with his friends the two brothers St Basil and St Gregory of Nyssa, one of the Cappadocian Fathers. He was born in Nazianzus about A.D. 329, and studied rhetoric, literature and philosophy in Athens. He became bishop of Sasima, and later of Constantinople, where he presided over the Ecumenical Council in 381. Because of objections to his presidency he withdrew from it and retired from the world for the last years of his life. He died about 390.

He wrote several orations, of which the so-called *Five Theological Orations* (directed against the Eunomians) are considered the most important. The second of these (no. 28), which was probably written in 380, deals with God's glory and his power in creation.

VI. Now our very eyes and the Law of Nature teach us that God exists and that He is the Efficient and Maintaining Cause of all things: our eyes, because they fall on visible objects, and see them in beautiful stability and progress, immovably moving and revolving if I may so say; natural Law, because through these visible things and their order, it reasons back to their Author. For how could this Universe have come into being or been put together, unless God had called it into existence, and held it together? For every one who sees a beautifully made lute, and considers the skill with which it has been fitted together and arranged, or who hears its melody, would think of none but the lutemaker, or the luteplayer, and would recur to him in mind, though he might not know him by sight. And thus to us also is manifested That which made and moves and preserves all created things, even though He be not comprehended by the mind. And very wanting in sense is he who will not willingly go thus far in following natural proofs; but not even this which we have imagined or represented, or which reason has sketched for us, is God. But if any one has got even to some extent a comprehension of this, how is God's Being to be demonstrated? Who ever reached this extremity of wisdom? Who was ever deemed worthy of so great a gift? Who has opened the mouth of his mind and drawn in the Spirit,[1] so as by Him that

searcheth all things, yea the deep things of God,[2] to take in God, and
no longer to need progress, since he already possesses the Extreme
Object of desire, and That to which all the social life and all the
intelligence of the best men press forward?

Gregory goes on to warn against false conceptions of God, and then returns to
his earlier theme.

XVI. . . . For what is it which ordered things in heaven and things in
earth, and those which pass through air, and those which live in water;
or rather the things which were before these, heaven and earth, air and
water? Who mingled these, and who distributed them? What is it that
each has in common with the other, and their mutual dependence and
agreement? For I commend the man, though he was a heathen, who
said, What gave movement to these, and drives their ceaseless and
unhindered motion?[3] Is it not the Artificer of them Who implanted
reason in them all, in accordance with which the Universe is moved
and controlled? Is it not He who made them and brought them into
being? For we cannot attribute such a power to the Accidental. For,
suppose that its existence is accidental, to what will you let us ascribe
its order? And if you like we will grant you this: to what then will you
ascribe its preservation and protection in accordance with the terms of
its first creation. Do these belong to the Accidental, or to something
else? Surely not to the Accidental. And what can this Something Else
be but God? Thus reason that proceeds from God, that is implanted in
all from the beginning and is the first law in us, and is bound up in all,
leads us up to God through visible things.

Gregory goes on to say that in this life we glimpse only a little of God's nature
and essence. Towards the end of the oration he appeals to the manifestations
of God's power and wisdom in the creation of mankind, animals, fishes and
birds.

XXVI. If this knowledge has come within your reach and you are
familiar with these branches of science, look at the differences of
plants also, up to the artistic fashion of the leaves, which is adapted
both to give the utmost pleasure to the eye, and to be of the greatest
advantage to the fruit. Look too at the variety and lavish abundance of
fruits, and most of all at the wondrous beauty of such as are most
necessary. And consider the power of roots, and juices, and flowers,
and odours, not only so very sweet, but also serviceable as medicines;
and the graces and qualities of colours; and again the costly value, and
the brilliant transparency of precious stones. Since nature has set
before you all things as in an abundant banquet free to all, both the

necessaries and the luxuries of life, in order that, if nothing else, you may at any rate know God by His benefits, and by your own sense of want be made wiser than you were. Next, I pray you, traverse the length and breadth of earth, the common mother of all, and the gulfs of the sea bound together with one another and with the land, and the beautiful forests, and the rivers and springs abundant and perennial, not only of waters cold and fit for drinking, and on the surface of the earth; but also such as running beneath the earth, and flowing under caverns, are then forced out by a violent blast, and repelled, and then filled with heat by this violence of strife and repulsion, burst out by little and little wherever they get a chance, and hence supply our need of hot baths in many parts of the earth, and in conjunction with the cold give us a healing which is without cost and spontaneous. Tell me how and whence are these things? What is this great web unwrought by art? These things are no less worthy of admiration, in respect of their mutual relations than when considered separately.

How is it that the earth stands solid and unswerving? On what is it supported? What is it that props it up, and on what does that rest? For indeed even reason has nothing to lean upon, but only the Will of God. And how is it that part of it is drawn up into mountain summits, and part laid down in plains, and this in various and differing ways? And because the variations are individually small, it both supplies our needs more liberally, and is more beautiful by its variety; part being distributed into habitations, and part left uninhabited, namely all the great height of Mountains, and the various clefts of its coast line cut off from it. Is not this the clearest proof of the majestic working of God?

XXVII. And with respect to the Sea even if I did not marvel at its greatness, yet I should have marvelled at its gentleness, in that although loose it stands within its boundaries; and if not at its gentleness, yet surely at its greatness; but since I marvel at both, I will praise the Power that is in both. What collected it? What bounded it? How is it raised and lulled to rest, as though respecting its neighbour earth? How, moreover, does it receive all the rivers, and yet remain the same, through the very superabundance of its immensity, if that term be permissible? How is the boundary of it, though it be an element of such magnitude, only sand? Have your natural philosophers with their knowledge of useless details anything to tell us, those men I mean who are really endeavouring to measure the sea with a wine-glass, and such mighty works by their own conceptions? Or shall I give the really scientific explanation of it from Scripture concisely, and yet more satisfactorily and truly than by the longest arguments? 'He hath fenced the face of the water with His command.'[4] This is the chain of fluid nature. And how doth He bring upon it the Nautilus that inhabits the dry land (i.e., man) in a little vessel, and with a little breeze (dost thou not marvel at the sight of this,—is not thy mind astonished?), that earth and sea may be bound together by needs and commerce, and that things so widely separated by nature should be thus brought together into one for man? What are the first fountains of springs? Seek, O man, if you can trace out or find any of these things. And who was it who cleft the plains and the mountains for the rivers, and gave them an unhindered course? And how comes the marvel on the other side, that the Sea never overflows, nor the Rivers cease to flow? And what is the nourishing power of water, and what the difference therein; for some things are irrigated from above, and others drink from their roots, if I may luxuriate a little in my language when speaking of the luxuriant gifts of God.

He continues in a similar vein extolling the glories of the sky, wind and clouds.

Now if you have in your thought passed through the air and all the things of air, reach with me to heaven and the things of heaven. And let faith lead us rather than reason, if at least you have learnt the feebleness of the latter in matters nearer to you, and have known reason by knowing the things that are beyond reason, so as not to be altogether on the earth or of the earth, because you are ignorant even of your ignorance.

XXIX. Who spread the sky around us, and set the stars in order? Or rather, first, can you tell me, of your own knowledge of the things in heaven, what *are* the sky and the stars; you who know not what lies at your very feet, and cannot even take the measure of yourself, and yet must busy yourself about what is above your nature, and gape at the illimitable? For, granted that you understand orbits and periods, and waxings and wanings, and settings and risings, and some degrees and minutes, and all the other things which make you so proud of your wonderful knowledge; you have not arrived at comprehension of the realities themselves, but only at an observation of some movement, which, when confirmed by longer practice, and drawing the observations of many individuals into one generalization, and thence deducing a law, has acquired the name of Science (just as the lunar phenomena have become generally known to our sight), being the basis of this knowledge. But if you are very scientific on this subject, and have a just claim to admiration, tell me what is the cause of this order and this movement. How came the sun to be a beacon-fire to the whole world, and to all eyes like the leader of some chorus, concealing all the rest of the stars by his brightness, more completely than some of them conceal others. The proof of this is that they shine against him, but he outshines them and does not even allow it to be perceived that they rose simultaneously with him, fair as a bridegroom, swift and great as a giant[5]—for I will not let his praises be sung from any other source than my own Scriptures—so mighty in strength that from one end to the other of the world he embraces all things in his heat, and there is nothing hid from the feeling thereof, but it fills both every eye with light, and every embodied creature with heat; warming, yet not burning, by the gentleness of its temper, and the order of its movement, present to all, and equally embracing all.

1 Ps 119:131.
2 I Cor 2:10.
3 Plato, *Laws* X, 896a ff. [pp. 4 ff. above].
4 Job 26:10.
5 Ps 19:5.

● From the *Second Theological Oration*, trans. C. G. Browne and J. E. Swallow, in H. Wace and P. Schaff (eds), *A Select Library of Nicene and Post-Nicene Fathers*, 2nd series, Vol. VII (Oxford, 1894), pp. 290 (amended), 294, 298–300.

6

St Augustine
Freedom and Grace

St Augustine of Hippo, the greatest of the Western Church Fathers, was born in North Africa, of a pagan father and a Christian mother (St Monica), in A.D. 354. His *Confessions* recounts his dissolute youth, his conversions to Manichaeism, to Neoplatonism, and finally to orthodox Christianity (partly under the influence of St Ambrose, bishop of Milan, where Augustine had taught rhetoric for a time). He was baptized in 387 and returned to Africa the following year. A few years later he became bishop of Hippo, and died in 430. Besides the *Confessions*, his main works include *The City of God* and *On the Trinity*.

On the Spirit and the Letter is a brief work, written in 412 as part of a polemic against Pelagius and his followers, who seemed to Augustine to have a deficient theology of grace, redemption and salvation. He stresses that we can be righteous and avoid sin only by God's grace, which repairs the flaws in our nature. In §§ 57–60 (towards the end of the work) he returns to the problem of the relationship between grace and human freedom, seeking to show that they are not incompatible with each other.

57 (xxxiii). There is, however, a further question to which we should give some consideration. Is the will by which we believe also the gift of God, or is it exerted by the freedom of choice which is implanted in us by nature? If we say it is not God's gift, there is a danger of our supposing that we have found an answer to the apostle's rebuke: 'What hast thou that thou hast not received? But if thou hast received it, why dost thou glory as though thou hadst not received it?'[1] We may retort that we have the will to believe, which we have not received, and that gives us room to glory because we have not received it. If on the other hand we say that this act of will is nothing but the gift of God, again there will be danger lest the infidel and the godless be thought to have good ground for excusing their own unbelief on the plea that God has refused to grant them the will. When it is said that 'it is God who worketh in us both to will and to work according to his good pleasure',[2] we are already in the sphere of grace, granted to faith, in order that man may have the good works, worked by faith through the

love which is shed abroad in our hearts by the Holy Spirit which is given to us. But in order that this grace may be granted we believe, and our belief is an act of will. It is of this will that we ask whence it comes. If by nature, then why not to all, since the same God is the Creator of all? If by the gift of God, still why not to all, since he will have all men to be saved and come to the knowledge of the truth?[3]
58. Here the first point to be made, as a possible solution of the difficulty, is that the freedom of choice which the Creator has conferred in the way of nature upon the rational soul is a neutral power, which can either be exerted to faith or sink into unbelief. Accordingly it cannot be said that in the act of will whereby a man believes God, he possesses what he has not received, since it arises at God's call from the freedom of choice which he received in the way of nature at his creation. God wills all men to be saved and to come to the knowledge of the truth; but not so as to deprive them of that freedom of choice, for the good or evil use of which they are subject to the judgment of absolute Justice. By that judgment, the unbelieving act against God's will when they disbelieve his gospel; yet what they do is not to defeat his will but to cheat themselves of a supreme good and fall into the distress of punishment: in which they must learn the power of him whose mercy in his gifts they have despised. Thus the will of God is ever undefeated: which would not be, had he no way of dealing with his despisers, or were there any escape for them from his sentence upon such. Suppose a master say: 'I will that all these my servants work in the vineyard, and after their labour rest and feast; provided that any who will not so work shall grind for ever in the mill'. It might appear that one who should despise the order is acting against his master's will; but he will only defeat it if in his master's despite he escapes also from the mill. And that under the power of God is altogether impossible. So it is written: 'God spoke once'—which we understand in the sense of 'unchangeably', though it might also be taken to mean a single utterance—and then we hear the matter of this unchangeable word: 'these two things have I heard, that power belongeth unto God, and that mercy is thine, O Lord, who wilt render to every man according to his works'.[4] The despiser of his mercy, which calls for belief, must bear under his power the sentence of condemnation. But whosoever believes, and trusts himself to God for the absolution of all his sins, for the healing of all his sicknesses, for kindling and illumination by the warmth and light of God, shall have by his grace those good works which lead to deliverance even in the body from the corruption of death, to crowning and satisfaction with the good things which are not temporal but eternal, above all that we ask or think.[5]
59. Such is the order set forth in the Psalm: 'Bless the Lord, O my

soul, and forget not all his rewardings, who forgiveth all thine iniquities, who healeth all thine infirmities, who redeemeth thy life from
corruption, who crowneth thee with compassion and mercy, who
satisfieth thy desire with good things'.[6] And lest we despair of all these
good things because of that deformity of old age which is our mortal-
ity, we hear the assurance: 'thy youth shall be renewed like that of an
eagle'—as much as to say: 'all this that thou hast heard belongs to the
new man and the new covenant'. Dwell on it all with me, I pray you,
and take your delight in the praise of mercy, which is the grace of God.
'Bless the Lord, O my soul, and forget not all his rewardings'—not
awardings but rewardings, because he rewards evil with good. 'Who
forgiveth all thine iniquities': that is done in the sacrament of baptism.
'Who healeth all thine infirmities': that takes effect for the man of
faith in this life, wherein the flesh lusteth against the spirit and the
spirit against the flesh, so that we do not the things we would, wherein
the other law in our members wars against the law of the mind,
wherein to will is present but to perform the good is not; these
infirmities of old age, if we persevere in going forward, are healed by
the daily increase of new life in the faith that works through love.
'Who redeemeth thy life from corruption': that comes to pass in the
final resurrection of the dead. 'Who crowneth thee with compassion
and mercy': that will be in the judgment; then, when the King of
righteousness sits upon his throne to render unto every man according
to his works, who shall boast that he has a pure heart or is clean from
sin?[7] Here, therefore, there was need to speak of the Lord's compassion and mercy, since in that judgment the exaction of debt and
rendering of desert might seem to leave no place for mercy. He will
crown with compassion and mercy; yet this too will be according to
men's works. For it will be those set apart on his right hand who will
hear him say: 'I was hungry and thou gavest me to eat'.[8] There is a
'judgment without mercy', but it is 'to him that showed not mercy',
and 'blessed are the merciful, for they shall obtain mercy'.[9] Then
those on the left hand shall go into everlasting burning, but the
righteous into life eternal; and according to the saying that 'this is life
eternal, that they may know thee the one true God and Jesus Christ
whom thou hast sent',[10] so with that knowledge, that vision, that
contemplation shall the desire of the soul be satisfied with good
things. That and that alone suffices it, it has nothing more to seek, to
long for, to require. It was the desire of that satisfaction that kindled
the disciple's heart, who said to the Lord Christ: 'Show us the Father,
and it sufficeth us'; and received the answer: 'He that hath seen me,
hath seen the Father'.[11] For eternal life itself is 'that they may know
the one true God, thyself, and Jesus Christ whom thou hast sent'. And
if to have seen the Son is to have seen the Father, no doubt to see the

Father and the Son is to see the Holy Spirit of the Father and the Son.

Thus freedom of choice is undisturbed; and yet our soul may bless the Lord, not forgetting all his rewardings: it seeks not in ignorance of God's righteousness to establish its own, but believes on him who justifies the ungodly, and lives by faith till it be admitted into sight, by that faith which works through love. And this love is shed abroad in our hearts, not by the sufficiency of our own will nor by the letter of the law, but by the Holy Spirit which is given to us.

60 (xxxiv). If this line of argument be thought sufficient as answer to the question raised, well and good. It may, however, be replied that there is a danger of making God responsible for the sin committed by freedom of choice, if the reason for ascribing to God's gift the will to believe (in accordance with the saying: 'What hast thou which thou hast not received?') be that it arises from that freedom of choice, which we received in our creation. But it should be observed that this is not the only reason. This act of will is attributable to the divine bounty, not only because it comes of the freedom of choice which was created with us in the way of nature. Besides that, God works for our willing and believing through the inducement of impressions which we experience: whether the impressions be external, as in the exhortations of the Gospel, in which case the law's commands have a certain effect, if by warning a man of his own weakness they make him seek refuge through believing with the grace that justifies; or internal, as in the ideas which enter the mind willynilly, though consent or refusal thereto is a matter of one's own will. In these ways does God work upon the reasonable soul to believe: indeed freedom of choice could produce no act of belief, were there no inducement or invitation to belief. Assuredly then it is God who brings about in a man the very will to believe, and in all things does his mercy anticipate us; yet to consent to the calling of God or to refuse it, as I have said, belongs to our own will. Which, so far from conflicting with the text, 'What hast thou which thou hast not received?', does even confirm it. For the soul cannot receive and possess the gifts there spoken of, but by consenting. What it is to possess, what it is to receive, pertains to God: the receiving and the possessing necessarily to him who receives and possesses. There remains indeed the profound mystery, why this suasion in one man is effective, in another not. If I am pressed to attempt its fathoming, I can think at the moment of only two answers that I should like to give: 'O the depth of the riches . . .' and, 'Is there any unrighteousness with God?'[12] He whom the reply contents not may look for more instructed counsellors; but let him beware of finding such as are over-confident.

1 I Cor 4:7.
2 Phil 2:13.
3 I Tim 2:4. Note that here Augustine does not try to explain away this text, as he did elsewhere (cf. *Enchiridion* 103).
4 Ps 62:11f.
5 Eph 3:20.
6 Ps 103:2ff.
7 Prov 20:8f.
8 Mt 25:35.
9 James 2:13; Mt 5:7.
10 Jn 17:3.
11 Jn 14:8f.
12 Rom 11:33; 9:14.

• From *On the Spirit and the Letter*, in *Augustine: Later Works*, trans. J. Burnaby (*The Library of Christian Classics*, Vol. VIII; London, 1955), pp. 241–245.

7

Boethius
Time, Eternity and Divine Foreknowledge

Anicius Manlius Torquatus Severinus Boethius was born about A.D. 480 and became a high official under the Gothic King Theodoric (who ruled Italy). He fell from favour, was accused of treason, and executed about 524. He translated some of Aristotle's works on logic. His most famous work, *The Consolation of Philosophy*, was written in prison in Pavia, and describes how reason may attain to belief in God and the purposiveness of the universe. Book 5 (from which the longer extract comes) deals with the question of freedom, determinism and divine foreknowledge. It is preceded by a shorter extract from one of his *Theological Tractates*, 'The Trinity is one God not three Gods', Chapter 4.

It is otherwise, of course, with God. 'He is everywhere' does not mean that He is in every place, for He cannot be in any place at all—but that every place is present to Him for Him to occupy, although He Himself can be received by no place, and therefore He cannot anywhere be in a place, since He is everywhere but in no place. It is the same with the category of time, as 'A man came yesterday; God is ever'. Here again the predicate of 'coming yesterday' denotes not something substantial, but something happening in terms of time. But the expression 'God is ever' denotes a single Present, summing up His continual presence in all the past, in all the present—however that term be used—and in all the future. Philosophers say that 'ever' may be applied to the life of the heavens and other immortal bodies. But as applied to God it has a different meaning. He is ever, because 'ever' is with Him a term of present time, and there is this great difference between 'now', which is our present, and the divine present. Our present connotes changing time and sempiternity; God's present, abiding, unmoved, and immoveable, connotes eternity. Add *semper* to *eternity* and you get the constant, incessant and thereby perpetual course of our present time, that is to say, sempiternity.

★   ★   ★

Consolation of Philosophy, Book 5, Chapter VI

'Since, then, as was shown a little while ago, everything which is known is known not according to its own nature but according to the nature of those comprehending it, let us now examine, so far as is allowable, what is the nature of the divine substance, so that we may be able to recognize what kind of knowledge his is. Now that God is eternal is the common judgement of all who live by reason. Therefore let us consider, what is eternity; for this makes plain to us both the divine nature and the divine knowledge. Eternity, then, is the whole, simultaneous and perfect possession of boundless life, which becomes clearer by comparison with temporal things. For whatever lives in time proceeds in the present from the past into the future, and there is nothing established in time which can embrace the whole space of its life equally, but tomorrow surely it does not yet grasp, while yesterday it has already lost. And in this day to day life you live no more than in that moving and transitory moment. Therefore whatever endures the condition of time, although, as Aristotle thought concerning the world, it neither began ever to be nor ceases to be, and although its life is drawn out with the infinity of time, yet it is not yet such that it may rightly be believed to be eternal. For it does not simultaneously comprehend and embrace the whole space of its life, though it be infinite, but it possesses the future not yet, the past no longer. Whatever therefore comprehends and possesses at once the whole fullness of boundless life, and is such that neither is anything future lacking from it, nor has anything past flowed away, that is rightly held to be eternal, and that must necessarily both always be present to itself, possessing itself in the present, and hold as present the infinity of moving time.

'And therefore those are not right who, when they hear that Plato thought this world neither had a beginning in time nor would have an end, think that in this way the created world is made co-eternal with the Creator. For it is one thing to be drawn out through a life without bounds, which is what Plato attributes to the world, but it is a different thing to have embraced at once the whole presence of boundless life, which it is clear is the property of the divine mind. Nor should God seem to be more ancient than created things by some amount of time, but rather by his own simplicity of nature. For this present nature of unmoving life that infinite movement of temporal things imitates, and since it cannot fully represent and equal it, it fails from immobility into motion, it shrinks from the simplicity of that present into the infinite quantity of the future and the past and, since it cannot possess at once the whole fullness of its life, in this very respect, that it in some way never ceases to be, it seems to emulate to some degree which it cannot fully express, by binding itself to the sort of present of this brief and fleeting moment, a present which since it wears a kind of likeness of that permanent present, grants to whatsoever things it touches that they should seem to be. But since it could not be permanent, it seized on the infinite journeying of time, and in that way became such that it should continue by going on a life the fullness of which it could not embrace by being permanent. And so if we should wish to give things names befitting them, then following Plato we should say that God indeed is eternal, but that the world is perpetual.

'Since then every judgement comprehends those things subject to it according to its own nature, and God has an always eternal and present nature, then his knowledge too, surpassing all movement of time, is permanent in the simplicity of his present, and embracing all the infinite spaces of the future and the past, considers them in his simple act of knowledge as though they were now going on. So if you should wish to consider his foreknowledge, by which he discerns all things, you will more rightly judge it to be not foreknowledge as it were of the future but knowledge of a never-passing instant. And therefore it is called not prevision (*praevidentia*) but providence (*providentia*), because set far from the lowest of things it looks forward on all things as though from the highest peak of the world. Why then do you require those things to be made necessary which are scanned by the light of God's sight, when not even men make necessary those things they see? After all, your looking at them does not confer any necessity on those things you presently see, does it?'

'Not at all.'

'But if the comparison of the divine and the human present is a proper one, just as you see certain things in this your temporal present, so he perceives all things in his eternal one. And therefore this divine foreknowledge does not alter the proper nature of things, but sees them present to him just such as in time they will at some future point come to be. Nor does he confuse the ways things are to be judged, but with one glance of his mind distinguishes both those things necessarily coming to be and those not necessarily coming to be, just as you, when you see at one and the same time that a man is walking on the ground and that the sun is rising in the sky, although the two things are seen simultaneously, yet you distinguish them, and judge the first to be voluntary, the second necessary. So then the divine perception looking down on all things does not disturb at all the quality of things that are present indeed to him but future with reference to imposed conditions of time. So it is that it is not opinion but a knowledge grounded rather upon truth, when he knows that something is going to happen, something which he is also aware lacks all necessity of happening.

'If at this point you were to say that what God sees is going to occur cannot not occur, and that what cannot not occur happens from necessity, and so bind me to this word "necessity", I will admit that this is a matter indeed of the firmest truth, but one which scarcely anyone except a theologian could tackle. For I shall say in answer that the same future event, when it is related to divine knowledge, is necessary, but when it is considered in its own nature it seems to be utterly and absolutely free. For there are really two necessities, the one simple, as that it is necessary that all men are mortal; the other conditional, as for example, if you know that someone is walking, it is necessary that he is walking. Whatever anyone knows cannot be otherwise than as it is known, but this conditional necessity by no means carries with it that other simple kind. For this sort of necessity is not caused by a thing's proper nature but by the addition of the condition; for no necessity forces him to go who walks of his own will, even though it is necessary that he is going at the time when he is walking. Now in the same way, if providence sees anything as present, that must necessarily be, even if it possesses no necessity of its nature. But God beholds those future events which happen because of the freedom of the will, as present; they therefore, related to the divine perception, become necessary through the condition of the divine knowledge, but considered in themselves do not lose the absolute freedom of their nature. Therefore all those things which God foreknows will come to be, will without doubt come to be, but certain of them proceed from free will, and although they do come to be, yet in happening they do not lose their proper nature, according to which, before they happened, they might also not have happened. What then does it matter that they are not necessary, since on account of the condition of the divine knowledge it will turn out in all respects like necessity? Surely as much as those things I put before you a moment ago, the rising sun and the walking man: while these things are happening, they cannot not happen, but of the two one, even before it happened, was bound to happen, while the other was not. So also, those things God possesses as present, beyond doubt will happen, but of them the one kind is consequent upon the necessity of things, the other upon the power of those doing them. So therefore we were not wrong in saying that these, if related to the divine knowledge, are necessary, if considered in themselves, are free from the bonds of necessity, just as everything which lies open to the senses, if you relate it to the reason, is universal, if you look at it by itself, is singular.

'But if, you will say, it lies in my power to change my intention, I shall make nonsense of providence, since what providence foreknows,

I shall perhaps have changed. I shall reply that you can indeed alter your intention, but since the truth of providence sees in its present both that you can do so, and whether you will do so and in what direction you will change, you cannot avoid the divine prescience, just as you could not escape the sight of an eye that was present, even though of your own free will you changed to different courses of action. What then will you say? Will the divine knowledge be changed by my disposition, so that, since I want to do this at one time and that at another, it too alternates from this kind of knowledge to that? Not at all. For the divine perception runs ahead over every future event and turns it back and recalls it to the present of its own knowledge, and does not alternate, as you suggest, foreknowing now this, now that, but itself remaining still anticipates and embraces your changes at one stroke. And God possesses this present instant of comprehension and sight of all things not from the issuing of future events but from his own simplicity. In this way that too is resolved which you suggested a little while ago, that it is not right that our future actions should be said to provide the cause of the knowledge of God. For the nature of his knowledge as we have described it, embracing all things in a present act of knowing, establishes a measure for everything, but owes nothing to later events. These things being so, the freedom of the will remains to mortals, inviolate, nor are laws proposing rewards and punishments for wills free from all necessity unjust. There remains also as an observer from on high foreknowing all things, God, and the always present eternity of his sight runs along with the future quality of our actions dispensing rewards for the good and punishments for the wicked. Nor vainly are our hopes placed in God, nor our prayers, which when they are right cannot be ineffectual. Turn away then from vices, cultivate virtues, lift up your mind to righteous hopes, offer up humble prayers to heaven. A great necessity is solemnly ordained for you if you do not want to deceive yourselves, to do good, when you act before the eyes of a judge who sees all things.'

• From Boethius, *The Theological Tractates*, trans. H. F. Stewart, E. K. Rand and S. J. Tester, and *The Consolation of Philosophy*, trans. S. J. Tester, Loeb ed. (W. H. Heinemann, London, 1973), pp. 21, 23, 423, 425, 427, 429, 431, 433 and 435.

8

St Anselm
An Ontological Argument

St Anselm was born in Aosta in northern Italy in 1033. He became abbot of Bec in Normandy and then archbishop of Canterbury, where he was involved in disputes about the investiture of bishops with William II and Henry I. He died in 1109. He is generally regarded as one of the most important of the early Scholastic thinkers. His works include the *Monologion, Cur Deus Homo?* and *Proslogion*. The last of these consists of a meditation on the idea of God, in which Anselm concludes that it is impossible to truly understand what God is and yet deny his existence. Anselm's argument is the ancestor of a type of argument put forward by Descartes, Spinoza, Leibniz and others, which was later termed the Ontological Argument. It should be noted, however, that Anselm's argument starts from an understanding of God reached in prayerful meditation, and is not a knock-down argument starting from a definition of God.

Proslogion

Chapter I

A rousing of the mind to the contemplation of God

Come now, insignificant man, fly for a moment from your affairs, escape for a little while from the tumult of your thoughts. Put aside now your weighty cares and leave your wearisome toils. Abandon yourself for a little to God and rest for a little in Him. Enter into the inner chamber of your soul, shut out everything save God and what can be of help in your quest for Him and having locked the door seek Him out [Matt. vi. 6]. Speak now, my whole heart, speak now to God: 'I seek Your countenance, O Lord, Your countenance I seek' [Ps. xxvi. 8].

Come then, Lord my God, teach my heart where and how to seek You, where and how to find You. Lord, if You are not present here, where, since You are absent, shall I look for You? On the other hand, if You are everywhere why then, since You are present, do I not see You? But surely You dwell in 'light inaccessible' [1 Tim. vi. 16]. And where is this inaccessible light, or how can I approach the inaccessible light? Or who shall lead me and take me into it that I may see You in it? Again, by what signs, under what aspect, shall I seek You? Never have I seen You, Lord my God, I do not know Your face. What shall he do, most high Lord, what shall this exile do, far away from You as he is? What shall Your servant do, tormented by love of You and yet cast off 'far from Your face' [Ps. i. 13]? He yearns to see You and Your countenance is too far away from him. He desires to come close to You, and Your dwelling place is inaccessible; he longs to find You and does not know where You are; he is eager to seek You out and he does not know Your countenance. Lord, You are my God and my Lord, and never have I seen You. You have created me and re-created me and You have given me all the good things I possess, and still I do not know You. In fine, I was made in order to see You, and I have not yet accomplished what I was made for.

Anselm goes on to bewail the separation of man from God brought about by the Fall, and prays that God may turn his countenance to us and enlighten us.

... Let me discern Your light whether it be from afar or from the depths. Teach me to seek You, and reveal Yourself to me as I seek, because I can neither seek You if You do not teach me how, nor find You unless You reveal Yourself. Let me seek You in desiring You; let me desire You in seeking You; let me find You in loving You; let me love You in finding You.

I acknowledge, Lord, and I give thanks that You have created Your image in me, so that I may remember You, think of You, love You. But this image is so effaced and worn away by vice, so darkened by the smoke of sin, that it cannot do what it was made to do unless You renew it and reform it. I do not try, Lord, to attain Your lofty heights, because my understanding is in no way equal to it. But I do desire to understand Your truth a little, that truth that my heart believes and loves. For I do not seek to understand so that I may believe; but I believe so that I may understand. For I believe this also, that 'unless I believe, I shall not understand' [Is. vii. 9].

Chapter II

That God truly exists

Well then, Lord, You who give understanding to faith, grant me that I may understand, as much as You see fit, that You exist as we believe

You to exist, and that You are what we believe You to be. Now we believe that You are something than which nothing greater can be thought. Or can it be that a thing of such a nature does not exist, since 'the Fool has said in his heart, there is no God' [Ps. xiii. 1, lii. 1]? But surely, when this same Fool hears what I am speaking about, namely, 'something-than-which-nothing-greater-can-be-thought', he understands what he hears, and what he understands is in his mind, even if he does not understand that it actually exists. For it is one thing for an object to exist in the mind, and another thing to understand that an object actually exists. Thus, when a painter plans beforehand what he is going to execute, he has [the picture] in his mind, but he does not yet think that it actually exists because he has not yet executed it. However, when he has actually painted it, then he both has it in his mind and understands that it exists because he has now made it. Even the Fool, then, is forced to agree that something-than-which-nothing-greater-can-be-thought exists in the mind, since he understands this when he hears it, and whatever is understood is in the mind. And surely that-than-which-a-greater-cannot-be-thought cannot exist in the mind alone. For if it exists solely in the mind even, it can be thought to exist in reality also, which is greater. If then that-than-which-a-greater-cannot-be-thought exists in the mind alone, this same that-than-which-a-greater-*cannot*-be-thought is that-than-which-a-greater-*can*-be-thought. But this is obviously impossible. Therefore there is absolutely no doubt that something-than-which-a-greater-cannot-be-thought exists both in the mind and in reality.

Chapter III

That God cannot be thought not to exist

And certainly this being so truly exists that it cannot be even thought not to exist. For something can be thought to exist that cannot be thought not to exist, and this is greater than that which can be thought not to exist. Hence, if that-than-which-a-greater-cannot-be-thought can be thought not to exist, then that-than-which-a-greater-cannot-be-thought is not the same as that-than-which-a-greater-cannot-be-thought, which is absurd. Something-than-which-a-greater-cannot-be-thought exists so truly then, that it cannot be even thought not to exist.

And You, Lord our God, are this being. You exist so truly, Lord my God, that You cannot even be thought not to exist. And this is as it should be, for if some intelligence could think of something better than You, the creature would be above its creator and would judge its creator—and that is completely absurd. In fact, everything else there is, except You alone, can be thought of as not existing. You alone, then, of all things most truly exist and therefore of all things possess existence to the highest degree; for anything else does not exist as truly, and so possesses existence to a lesser degree. Why then did 'the Fool say in his heart, there is no God' [Ps. xiii. I, lii. I] when it is so evident to any rational mind that You of all things exist to the highest degree? Why indeed, unless because he was stupid and a fool?

Chapter IV
How 'the Fool said in his heart' what cannot be thought

How indeed has he 'said in his heart' what he could not think; or how could he not think what he 'said in his heart', since to 'say in one's heart' and to 'think' are the same? But if he really (indeed, since he really) both thought because he 'said in his heart' and did not 'say in his heart' because he could not think, there is not only one sense in which something is 'said in one's heart' or thought. For in one sense a thing is thought when the word signifying it is thought; in another sense when the very object which the thing is is understood. In the first sense, then, God can be thought not to exist, but not at all in the second sense. No one, indeed, understanding what God is can think that God does not exist, even though he may say these words in his heart either without any [objective] signification or with some peculiar signification. For God is that-than-which-nothing-greater-can-be-thought. Whoever really understands this understands clearly that this same being so exists that not even in thought can it not exist. Thus whoever understands that God exists in such a way cannot think of Him as not existing.

I give thanks, good Lord, I give thanks to You, since what I believed before through Your free gift I now so understand through Your illumination, that if I did not want to *believe* that You existed, I should nevertheless be unable not to *understand* it.

In Chapter 5 Anselm argues that God is just, truthful, happy and whatever it is better to be than not to be. The rest of the work is mainly concerned with spelling out the nature of God's attributes.

A monk from Marmoutier, Gaunilo, published a *Response on behalf of the Fool*, in which he attacked the argument of the *Proslogion*, claiming that one could use reasoning similar to Anselm's to prove the existence of all kinds of unreal objects, for instance an island more excellent than all other lands. Anselm published a response.

Reply to Gaunilo

[III.] You claim, however, that this is as though someone asserted that it cannot be doubted that a certain island in the ocean (which is more fertile than all other lands and which, because of the difficulty or even the impossibility of discovering what does not exist, is called the 'Lost Island') truly exists in reality since anyone easily understands it when it is described in words. Now, I truly promise that if anyone should discover for me something existing either in reality or in the mind alone—except 'that-than-which-a-greater-cannot-be-thought' —to which the logic of my argument would apply, then I shall find that Lost Island and give it, never more to be lost, to that person. It has already been clearly seen, however, that 'that-than-which-a-greater-cannot-be-thought' cannot be thought not to exist, because it exists as a matter of such certain truth. Otherwise it would not exist at all. In short, if anyone says that he thinks that this being does not exist, I reply that, when he thinks of this, either he thinks of something than which a greater cannot be thought, or he does not think of it. If he does not think of it, then he does not think that what he does not think of does not exist. If, however, he does think of it, then indeed he thinks of something which cannot be even thought not to exist. For if it could be thought not to exist, it could be thought to have a beginning and an end—but this cannot be. Thus, he who thinks of it thinks of something that cannot be thought not to exist; indeed, he who thinks of this does not think of it as not existing, otherwise he would think what cannot be thought. Therefore 'that-than-which-a-greater-cannot-be-thought' cannot be thought not to exist.

[IV.] You say, moreover, that when it is said that this supreme reality cannot be *thought* not to exist, it would perhaps be better to say that it cannot be *understood* not to exist or even to be able not to exist. However, it must rather be said that it cannot be *thought*. For if I had said that the thing in question could not be *understood* not to exist, perhaps you yourself (who claim that we cannot understand—if this word is to be taken strictly—things that are unreal) would object that nothing that exists can be understood not to exist. For it is false [to say that] what exists does not exist, so that it is not the distinguishing characteristic of God not to be able to be understood not to exist. But, if any of those things which exist with absolute certainty can be understood not to exist, in the same way other things that certainly exist can be understood not to exist. But, if the matter is carefully considered, this objection cannot be made apropos [the term] 'thought'. For even if none of those things that exist can be *understood* not to exist, all however can be *thought* as not existing, save that which exists to a supreme degree. For in fact all those things (and they alone) that have a beginning or end or are made up of parts and, as I have already said, all those things that do not exist as a whole in a particular place or at a particular time can be thought as not existing. Only that being in which there is neither beginning nor end nor conjunction of parts, and that thought does not discern save as a whole in every place and at every time, cannot be thought as not existing.

Know then that you can think of yourself as not existing while yet you are absolutely sure that you exist. I am astonished that you have said that you do not know this. For we think of many things that we know to exist, as not existing; and [we think of] many things that we know not to exist, as existing—not judging that it is really as we think but imagining it to be so. We *can*, in fact, think of something as not existing while knowing that it does exist, since we can [think of] the one and know the other at the same time. And we *cannot* think of something as not existing if yet we know that it does exist, since we cannot think of it as existing and not existing at the same time. He, therefore, who distinguishes these two senses of this assertion will understand that [in one sense] nothing can be thought as not existing while yet it is known to exist, and that [in another sense] whatever exists, save that-than-which-a-greater-cannot-be-thought, can be thought of as not existing even when we know that it does exist. Thus it is that, on the one hand, it is the distinguishing characteristic of God that He cannot be thought of as not existing, and that, on the other hand, many things, the while they do exist, cannot be thought of as not existing. In what sense, however, one can say that God can be thought of as not existing I think I have adequately explained in my tract.

• From *St Anselm's Proslogion*, ed. and trans. M. J. Charlesworth (Oxford, 1965), pp. 111, 115, 117, 119, 121, 175, 177, 179.

9

St Thomas Aquinas
The Five Ways

St Thomas Aquinas, perhaps the greatest of mediaeval thinkers, was born at Roccasecca near Naples about 1225. He joined the Order of Preachers (founded by St Dominic in 1220–21) in 1244, and spent much of his life as a teacher at the university of Paris and at Dominican houses of studies in Rome, Naples and elsewhere. He died in 1274, on his way to the Council of Lyons. Besides commentaries on Scripture and Aristotle, he produced two massive summaries of Christian doctrine (the *Summa contra Gentiles* and the *Summa Theologiae*), *On Truth*, *On Power* and many other shorter works.

The *Summa Theologiae* is generally considered to be his greatest work. It has three parts, of which the first (consisting of 119 chapters or 'Questions' each subdivided into several articles) deals with the existence and nature of God, the Trinity and Creation. Each article begins with a question and a series of objections, then states a thesis (often supported by a quotation from Scripture) which is discussed in the main body of the article, and concludes with replies to the objections. The work begins with a Question on the nature of sacred teaching, and then in Question II it discusses the existence of God. In the first two articles of this Aquinas argues that although his existence is not self-evident to us, it can be demonstrated from creation; in the third (given here) he outlines five such demonstrations. Earlier versions of the arguments, more indebted to Aristotle's *Physics*, can be found at the beginning of the *Summa contra Gentiles*.

article 3. is there a God?

The third point: 1. It seems that there is no God. For if, of two mutually exclusive things, one were to exist without limit, the other would cease to exist. But by the word 'God' is implied some limitless good. If God then existed, nobody would ever encounter evil. But evil is encountered in the world. God therefore does not exist.

2. Moreover, if a few causes fully account for some effect, one does not seek more. Now it seems that everything we observe in this world can be fully accounted for by other causes, without assuming a God. Thus natural effects are explained by natural causes, and contrived

effects by human reasoning and will. There is therefore no need to suppose that a God exists.

On the other hand, the book of *Exodus* represents God as saying, *I am who am.*[1]

Reply: There are five ways in which one can prove that there is a God.

The first and most obvious way is based on change. Some things in the world are certainly in process of change: this we plainly see. Now anything in process of change is being changed by something else. This is so because it is characteristic of things in process of change that they do not yet have that towards which they move, though able to have it; whereas it is characteristic of something causing change to be in act already. For to cause change is to bring into being what was previously only able to be, and this can only be done by something that already is: thus fire, which is actually hot, causes wood, which is able to be hot, to become actually hot, and in this way causes change in the wood. Now the same thing cannot at the same time be both actually x and potentially x, though it can be actually x and potentially y: the actually hot cannot at the same time be potentially hot, though it can be potentially cold. Consequently, a thing in process of change cannot itself cause that same change; it cannot change itself. Of necessity therefore anything in process of change is being changed by something else. Moreover, this something else, if in process of change, is itself being changed by yet another thing; and this last by another. Now we must stop somewhere, otherwise there will be no first cause of the change, and, as a result, no subsequent causes. For it is only when acted upon by the first cause that the intermediate causes will produce the change: if the hand does not move the stick, the stick will not move anything else. Hence one is bound to arrive at some first cause of change not itself being changed by anything, and this is what everybody understands by God.

The second way is based on the nature of causation. In the observable world causes are found to be ordered in series; we never observe, nor ever could, something causing itself, for this would mean it preceded itself, and this is not possible. Such a series of causes must however stop somewhere; for in it an earlier member causes an intermediate and the intermediate a last (whether the intermediate be one or many). Now if you eliminate a cause you also eliminate its effects, so that you cannot have a last cause, nor an intermediate one, unless you have a first. Given therefore no stop in the series of causes, and hence no first cause, there would be no intermediate causes either, and no last effect, and this would be an open mistake. One is therefore forced to suppose some first cause, to which everyone gives the name 'God'.

The third way is based on what need not be and on what must be, and runs as follows. Some of the things we come across can be but need not be, for we find them springing up and dying away, thus sometimes in being and sometimes not.[2] Now everything cannot be like this,[3] for a thing that need not be, once was not; and if everything need not be, once upon a time there was nothing. But if that were true there would be nothing even now, because something that does not exist can only be brought into being by something already existing. So that if nothing was in being nothing could be brought into being, and nothing would be in being now, which contradicts observation. Not everything therefore is the sort of thing that need not be; there has got to be something that must be. Now a thing that must be, may or may not owe this necessity to something else. But just as we must stop somewhere in a series of causes, so also in the series of things which must be and owe this to other things. One is forced therefore to suppose something which must be, and owes this to no other thing than itself; indeed it itself is the cause that other things must be.[4]

The fourth way is based on the gradation observed in things. Some things are found to be more good, more true, more noble, and so on, and other things less. But such comparative terms describe varying degrees of approximation to a superlative; for example, things are hotter and hotter the nearer they approach what is hottest. Something therefore is the truest and best and most noble of things, and hence the most fully in being; for Aristotle says that the truest things are the things most fully in being.[5] Now *when many things possess some property in common, the one most fully possessing it causes it in the others: fire*, to use Aristotle's example, *the hottest of all things, causes all other things to be hot.*[6] There is something therefore which causes in all other things their being, their goodness, and whatever other perfection they have. And this we call 'God'.

The fifth way is based on the guidedness of nature. An orderedness of actions to an end is observed in all bodies obeying natural laws, even when they lack awareness. For their behaviour hardly ever varies, and will practically always turn out well;[7] which shows that they truly tend to a goal, and do not merely hit it by accident. Nothing however that lacks awareness tends to a goal, except under the direction of someone with awareness and with understanding; the arrow, for example, requires an archer. Everything in nature, therefore, is directed to its goal by someone with understanding, and this we call 'God'.

Hence: 1. As Augustine says, *Since God is supremely good, he would not permit any evil at all in his works, unless he were sufficiently almighty and good to bring good even from evil.*[8] It is therefore a mark of the limitless goodness of God that he permits evils to exist, and draws from them good.

2. Natural causes act for definite purposes under the direction of some higher cause, so that their effects must also be referred to God as the first of all causes. In the same manner contrived effects must likewise be referred back to a higher cause than human reasoning and will, for these are changeable and can cease to be, and, as we have seen, all changeable things and things that can cease to be require some first cause which cannot change and of itself must be.

1 Ex 3:14.
2 One manuscript reads here 'thus they are able to be and not to be'.
3 Some manuscripts read here 'But it is impossible for such things to exist always'.
4 Some manuscripts add 'and this everyone calls God'.
5 *Metaphysics* II, 1, 993b 30.
6 *Metaphysics* II, 1, 993b 25.
7 Some manuscripts read here 'For they nearly always behave in the way which will obtain the best result'.
8 *Enchiridion* XI.

• From the Blackfriars edition of the *Summa Theologiae*, Vol. 2, trans. T. McDermott (London, 1964), pp. 13 (amended), 15, 17.

10

St Thomas Aquinas
God's Perfections

In Question III Aquinas argues that God is simple (i.e. not made up of matter and form, or composed in any other way), and is being itself, self-subsistent. In Question IV he discusses God's perfection, arguing both from his nature in himself and from the perfections found in creatures.

article 1. is God perfect?

The first point: 1. 'Perfect' does not seem a suitable term to apply to God, for etymologically it means 'thoroughly made'. Now since we would not say that God is made, we should not say that he is perfect.

2. Moreover, God is the first origin of things. But things have imperfect origins: plants and animals, for example, begin from seed. God therefore is imperfect.

3. Moreover, as we have shown, the nature of God is simply to exist. Now simply to exist is seemingly most imperfect: the lowest common denominator of all things. God then is not perfect.

On the other hand, we read in *Matthew: be ye perfect, as your heavenly Father is perfect.*[1]

Reply. Aristotle[2] tells us that certain ancient philosophers—the Pythagoreans and Speusippus—did not regard the first origin of things as the acme of goodness and perfection; the reason being that they only paid attention to the matter out of which things originated, and primordial matter is the most imperfect of all things. For matter as such is only potential, and primordial matter is therefore sheer potentiality and entirely imperfect.

We however hold God to be not primordial matter but the primary operative cause of things, and thus the most perfect of things. For just as matter as such is potential, so an acting thing as such is actual. Thus the first origin of all activity will be the most actual, and therefore the most perfect, of all things. For things are called perfect when they have achieved actuality, the perfect thing being that in which nothing required by the thing's particular mode of perfection fails to exist. Hence: 1. What is not made cannot properly be called perfect, but, as Gregory says, *stammering, we echo the heights of God as best we can.*[3] And so, because things that are made are called perfect when the potentiality of them has been actualized, we extend the word to refer to anything that is not lacking in actuality, whether made or not. 2. The imperfect matter from which the things around us originate, is not their ultimate origin, but is itself preceded by something perfect. For even when an animal is generated from seed, the original seed itself derives from some previous animal or plant. Anything potential must be preceded by something actual, since only the already actual can actualize a thing which exists potentially. 3. The most perfect thing of all is to exist, for everything else is potential compared to existence. Nothing achieves actuality except it exist, and the act of existing is therefore the ultimate actuality of everything, and even of every form. So it is that things acquire existence, and not existence things. For in the very phrases 'the existence of man' or 'of a horse' or 'of some other thing', it is existence that is regarded as an acquisition like a form, not the thing to which existence belongs.

article 2. is God's perfection all-embracing, containing, so to say, the perfection of everything else?

The second point: 1. God, it seems, does not contain the perfections of everything. For God, as we have seen, is simple, and the perfections of things are many and diverse. So God does not contain every perfection of things. 2. Moreover, opposites cannot exist together. Now the perfections of things are opposed to one another; for each species is perfected by that which differentiates it from other species in the same genus, and such constitutive differences are opposed to one another. So it seems that, because opposites cannot exist together in the same thing, God does not contain all the perfections of things. 3. Moreover, a living thing is more perfect than a merely existent thing, and one that is wise more perfect than one that is merely alive; so that to live is more perfect than to be, and to be wise more perfect than to live. Now it is the nature of God simply to be. Perfections like life and wisdom therefore are not to be found in him.

On the other hand, we have Dionysius saying that *all existent things are contained in a primordial unity in God.*[4]

Reply: The perfections of everything exist in God. For this reason we call his perfection 'all-embracing', for, as Averroes says, he lacks no excellence of any sort.[5] There are two ways of showing this.

Firstly, because any perfection found in an effect must be found also in the cause of that effect; and this either without modification when cause and effect are of the same sort (thus man begets man), or in a more perfect manner when cause and effect are not of the same sort (thus the sun's power produces things having a certain likeness to the sun). This is because effects obviously pre-exist potentially in their causes. Now to pre-exist potentially in a cause is to pre-exist in a more perfect, not in a less perfect, manner, even if to pre-exist potentially in matter is to pre-exist less perfectly; for although matter as such is imperfect, agents as such are perfect. Since God then is the primary operative cause of all things, the perfections of everything must pre-exist in him in a higher manner. And Dionysius is touching upon this argument when he refuses any description of God as *this and not that*, saying *God is everything, inasmuch as he is everything's cause.*[6]

Secondly, because as we have seen God is self-subsistent being itself, and therefore necessarily contains within himself the full perfection of being. For clearly a hot thing falls short of the full perfection of heat only because it does not fully partake of the nature of heat; to a self-subsistent heat nothing of the virtue of heat could be lacking. Nothing therefore of the perfection of existing can be lacking to God, who is subsistent existence itself. Now every perfection is a perfection of existing, for it is the manner in which a thing exists that determines the manner of its perfection. No perfection can therefore be lacking to God. And Dionysius is touching upon this argument when he says that *God does not exist in any qualified way, but possesses primordially in himself all being, without qualification and without circumscription.* And later he adds that *God is the being of all that subsists.*[7]

Hence: 1.   If the sun, as Dionysius says, *possesses in itself, primordially and without diversity, the divers qualities and substances of the things we can sense, while yet maintaining the unity of its own being and the homogeneity of its light, how much more must everything pre-exist in unity of nature in the cause of all?*[8] Perfections therefore which are diverse and opposed in themselves, pre-exist as one in God, without detriment to his simpleness.

2.   The above answer solves this argument also.

3.   In the same chapter Dionysius[9] tells us that, when considered as notionally separate, existence as such is more perfect than life as such, and life as such more perfect than wisdom as such. Nevertheless, living things, which both live and exist, are more perfect than things which merely exist; and one who is wise also exists and also lives. So, although being an existent thing does not involve being living or wise

(for nothing partaking of existence need partake every mode of existence), nevertheless, existence itself[10] does involve life and wisdom (for subsistent existence itself cannot lack any perfection of existence).

1 Mt 5:48.
2 *Metaphysics* XII, 7, 1072 b30.
3 St Gregory the Great, *Magna Moralia* 5:36.
4 Pseudo-Dionysius, *On the Divine Names* 5:9.
5 Ibn Roschd, *Commentary on Aristotle's Metaphysics* V.21.
6 Pseudo-Dionysius, *op. cit.* 5:8.
7 *Ibid.* 5:4.
8 *Ibid.* 5:8.
9 *Ibid.* 5:3.
10 i.e. the existence of God.

• From the Blackfriars edition of the *Summa Theologiae*, Vol. 2, trans. T. McDermott (London, 1964), pp. 49, 51, 53, 55.

11

St Thomas Aquinas
Analogy

In Questions V–XI Aquinas discusses goodness in general, and the goodness, infinity, presence, immutability, eternity and unity of God. He then discusses how God is known by us (Question XII) and how he is named (Question XIII). Aquinas thinks that God can be spoken of in many ways, e.g. in negative terms ('unchangeable') and in metaphors. But he is particularly interested in terms like 'good', 'living', and 'wise', which he thinks can be used properly and positively of God, though not in quite the same sense that they are used of creatures. He calls the use of such terms of God 'analogical'.

article 5. are words used univocally or equivocally of God and creatures?

The fifth point: 1. It seems that words used both of God and of creatures are used univocally:[1] the equivocal is based on the univocal as the many is based on the one. A word such as 'dog' may be used equivocally of a hound and a fish, but only because it is first used univocally—of hounds—otherwise there would be nowhere to start from and we should go back for ever. Now there are some causes that are called univocal because their effects have the same name and description as themselves—what is generated by a man, for example, is also a man. Some causes, however, are called equivocal, as is the sun when it causes heat, for the sun itself is only equivocally said to be hot. Since, therefore, the equivocal is based on the univocal it seems that the first cause upon which all others are based must be an univocal cause, hence what is said of God and of his creatures must be said univocally.

2. There is no resemblance between things that are only equivocally the same, but according to *Genesis* there is a resemblance between creatures and God; *Let us make man in our own image and likeness.*[2] So it seems that something can be said univocally of God and creatures.

3. Aristotle says that the measure must be of the same order as the

thing measured,[3] and he also describes God as the first measure of all beings. God, therefore, is of the same order as creatures; and so something can be said univocally of both.

On the other hand for two reasons it seems that such words must be used equivocally. First, the same word when used with different meanings is used equivocally, but no word when used of God means the same as when it is used of a creature. 'Wisdom', for example, means a quality when it is used of creatures, but not when it is applied to God. So then it must have a different meaning, for we have here a difference in the genus which is part of the definition. The same applies to other words; so all must be used equivocally.

And second, God is more distant from any creature than any two creatures are from each other. Now there are some creatures so different that nothing can be said univocally of them—for example when they differ in genus. Much less, therefore, could there be anything said univocally of creatures and God.

Reply: It is impossible to predicate anything univocally of God and creatures. Every effect that falls short of what is typical of the power of its cause represents it inadequately, for it is not the same kind of thing as the cause. Thus what exists simply and in a unified way in the cause will be divided up and take various forms in such effects—as the simple power of the sun produces many different kinds of lesser things. In the same way, as we said earlier,[4] the perfections which in creatures are many and various pre-exist in God as one.

The perfection words that we use in speaking of creatures all differ in meaning and each one signifies a perfection as something distinct from all others. Thus when we say that a man is wise, we signify his wisdom as something distinct from the other things about him—his essence, for example, his powers or his existence. But when we use this word about God we do not intend to signify something distinct from his essence, power or existence. When 'wise' is used of a man, it so to speak contains and delimits the aspect of man that it signifies, but this is not so when it is used of God; what it signifies in God is not confined by the meaning of our word but goes beyond it. Hence it is clear that the word 'wise' is not used in the same sense of God and man, and the same is true of all other words, so they cannot be used univocally of God and creatures.

Yet although we never use words in exactly the same sense of creatures and God we are not merely equivocating when we use the same word, as some have said,[5] for if this were so we could never argue from statements about creatures to statements about God—any such argument would be invalidated by the Fallacy of Equivocation. That this does not happen we know not merely from the teachings of the philosophers who prove many things about God but also from the teaching of St Paul, for he says, *The invisible things of God are made known by those things that are made.*[6]

We must say, therefore, that words are used of God and creatures in an analogical way, that is in accordance with a certain order between them. We can distinguish two kinds of analogical or 'proportional' uses of language. Firstly there is the case of one word being used of two things because each of them has some order or relation to a third thing. Thus we use the word 'healthy' of both a diet and a complexion because each of these has some relation to health in a man, the former as a cause, the latter as a symptom of it. Secondly there is the case of the same word used of two things because of some relation that one has to the other—as 'healthy' is used of the diet and the man because the diet is the cause of the health in the man.

In this way some words are used neither univocally nor purely equivocally of God and creatures, but analogically, for we cannot speak of God at all except in the language we use of creatures, and so whatever is said both of God and creatures is said in virtue of the order that creatures have to God as to their source and cause in which all the perfections of things pre-exist transcendently.

This way of using words lies somewhere between pure equivocation and simple univocity, for the word is neither used in the same sense, as with univocal usage, nor in totally different senses, as with equivocation. The several senses of a word used analogically signify different relations to some one thing, as 'health' in a complexion means a symptom of health in a man, and in a diet means a cause of that health.

Hence: 1. Even if it were the case that in speech the equivocal were based on the univocal, the same is not true of causality. A non-univocal cause is causal by reference to an entire species—as the sun is the cause that there are men. An univocal cause, on the other hand, cannot be the universal cause of the whole species (otherwise it would be the cause of itself, since it is a member of that same species), but is the particular cause that this or that individual should be a member of the species. Thus the universal cause which must be prior to the individual cause, is non-univocal. Such a cause, however, is not wholly equivocal, for then there would be no resemblance in any sense between it and its effects. We could call it an analogical cause, and this would be parallel to the case of speech, for all univocal predications are based on one non-univocal, analogical predicate, that of being.[7]

2. The resemblance of creatures to God is an imperfect one, for as we have said,[8] they do not even share a common genus.

3. God is not a measure that is proportionate to what is measured; so it does not follow that he and his creatures belong to the same order.

The two arguments in the contrary sense do show that words are not used univocally of God and creatures but they do not show that they are used equivocally.

1 A word is said to be used univocally when it has exactly the same meaning in different applications; it is used equivocally when it has different meanings in different applications, as with all puns. Thus 'tap' is used equivocally of a knock on the door and the thing on the barrel. In the following example Aquinas is referring to the dog-fish.

2 Gen 1:26.

3 *Metaphysics* X, 1, 1053a 24.

4 In the previous article.

5 Averroes and Maimonides.

6 Rom 1:20.

7 St Thomas means that whatever we say (affirmatively) of a thing, we say that it *is* such and such. In this sense every predication, in whatever category, is a predication of being. But 'being' itself is used non-univocally, for *being* a man and *being* upside down and *being* happy are not all being in the same sense.

8 In Question IV, article 3.

• From the Blackfriars edition of the *Summa Theologiae*, Vol. 3, trans. H. McCabe OP (London, 1964), pp. 61, 63, 65, 67.

12

Descartes
The Soul and Immortality

René Descartes was born in Touraine in 1596. He studied law in Poitiers, but then became a soldier for a time. He lived in Holland from 1628 until 1649, when he went to Sweden at the invitation of Queen Christina. He succumbed to the harsh climate there, and died in 1650. His main works include the *Discourse on Method, Principles of Philosophy, Meditations concerning First Philosophy* and *Passions of the Soul.* In his insistence on accepting only what is certain and in starting from his own immediate experience he may be regarded as the founder of two subsequent traditions in philosophy, Rationalism and Empiricism. He is also an important representative of Dualism, the view that the soul or mind is an immaterial, unextended and indivisible substance causally related to the body. Since this view holds that there is no reason to think that what destroys the body also destroys the soul, it holds that there is at least a strong presumption for belief in the immortality of the latter.

The *Meditations* were published in 1641. In the first one Descartes outlines his method of universal doubt and his principle of accepting only what is indubitable. In *Meditation II* he finds something of which he is certain, his own existence (in the *Discourse on Method* he expresses his argument pithily 'cogito ergo sum'—I think therefore I am).

Second Meditation

The nature of the human mind, and how it is better known than the body

So serious are the doubts into which I have been thrown as a result of yesterday's meditation that I can neither put them out of my mind nor see any way of resolving them. It feels as if I have fallen unexpectedly into a deep whirlpool which tumbles me around so that I can neither stand on the bottom nor swim up to the top. Nevertheless I will make an effort and once more attempt the same path which I started on yesterday. Anything which admits of the slightest doubt I will set aside just as if I had found it to be wholly false; and I will proceed in this way until I recognize something certain, or, if nothing else, until I at least recognize for certain that there is no certainty. Archimedes used to demand just one firm and immovable point in order to shift the entire earth; so I too can hope for great things if I manage to find just one thing, however slight, that is certain and unshakeable.

I will suppose then, that everything I see is spurious. I will believe that my memory tells me lies, and that none of the things that it reports ever happened. I have no senses. Body, shape, extension, movement and place are chimeras. So what remains true? Perhaps just the one fact that nothing is certain.

Yet apart from everything I have just listed, how do I know that there is not something else which does not allow even the slightest occasion for doubt? Is there not a God, or whatever I may call him, who puts into me the thoughts I am now having? But why do I think this, since I myself may perhaps be the author of these thoughts? In that case am not I, at least, something? But I have just said that I have no senses and no body. This is the sticking point: what follows from this? Am I not so bound up with a body and with senses that I cannot exist without them? But I have convinced myself that there is absolutely nothing in the world, no sky, no earth, no minds, no bodies. Does it now follow that I too do not exist? No: if I convinced myself of something[1] then I certainly existed. But there is a deceiver of supreme power and cunning who is deliberately and constantly deceiving me. In that case I too undoubtedly exist, if he is deceiving me; and let him deceive me as much as he can, he will never bring it about that I am nothing so long as I think that I am something. So after considering everything very thoroughly, I must finally conclude that this proposition, *I am, I exist*, is necessarily true whenever it is put forward by me or conceived in my mind.

But I do not yet have a sufficient understanding of what this 'I' is, that now necessarily exists. So I must be on my guard against carelessly taking something else to be this 'I', and so making a mistake in the very item of knowledge that I maintain is the most certain and evident of all. I will therefore go back and meditate on what I originally believed myself to be, before I embarked on this present train of thought. I will then subtract anything capable of being weakened, even minimally, by the arguments now introduced, so that what is left at the end may be exactly and only what is certain and unshakeable.

What then did I formerly think I was? A man. But what is a man? Shall I say 'a rational animal'? No; for then I should have to inquire what an animal is, what rationality is, and in this way one question would lead me down the slope to other harder ones, and I do not now have the time to waste on subtleties of this kind. Instead I propose to concentrate on what came into my thoughts spontaneously and quite naturally whenever I used to consider what I was. Well, the first thought to come to mind was that I had a face, hands, arms and the whole mechanical structure of limbs which can be seen in a corpse, and which I called the body. The next thought was that I was nourished, that I moved about, and that I engaged in sense-perception and thinking; and these actions I attributed to the soul. But as to the nature of this soul, either I did not think about this or else I imagined it to be something tenuous, like a wind or fire or ether, which permeated my more solid parts. As to the body, however, I had no doubts about it, but thought I knew its nature distinctly. If I had tried to describe the mental conception I had of it, I would have expressed it as follows: by a body I understand whatever has a determinable shape and a definable location and can occupy a space in such a way as to exclude any other body; it can be perceived by touch, sight, hearing, taste or smell, and can be moved in various ways, not by itself but by whatever else comes into contact with it. For, according to my judgement, the power of self-movement, like the power of sensation or of thought, was quite foreign to the nature of a body; indeed, it was a source of wonder to me that certain bodies were found to contain faculties of this kind.

But what shall I now say that I am, when I am supposing that there is some supremely powerful and, if it is permissible to say so, malicious deceiver, who is deliberately trying to trick me in every way he can? Can I now assert that I possess even the most insignificant of all the attributes which I have just said belong to the nature of a body? I scrutinize them, think about them, go over them again, but nothing suggests itself; it is tiresome and pointless to go through the list once more. But what about the attributes I assigned to the soul? Nutrition or movement? Since now I do not have a body, these are mere fabrications. Sense-perception? This surely does not occur without a body, and besides, when asleep I have appeared to perceive through the senses many things which I afterwards realized I did not perceive through the senses at all. Thinking? At last I have discovered it— thought; this alone is inseparable from me. I am, I exist—that is certain. But for how long? For as long as I am thinking. For it could be that were I totally to cease from thinking, I should totally cease to exist. At present I am not admitting anything except what is necessarily true. I am, then, in the strict sense only a thing that thinks; that is, I am a mind, or intelligence, or intellect, or reason—words whose meaning I have been ignorant of until now. But for all that I am a thing which is real and which truly exists. But what kind of a thing? As I have just said—a thing that thinks.

What else am I? I will use my imagination.[2] I am not that structure of limbs which is called a human body. I am not even some thin vapour which permeates the limbs—a wind, fire, air, breath, or whatever I depict in my imagination; for these are things which I have supposed to be nothing. Let this supposition stand; for all that I am still something. And yet may it not perhaps be the case that these very things which I am supposing to be nothing, because they are unknown to me, are in reality identical with the 'I' of which I am aware? I do not know, and for the moment I shall not argue the point, since I can make judgements only about things which are known to me. I know that I exist; the question is, what is this 'I' that I know? If the 'I' is understood strictly as we have been taking it, then it is quite certain that knowledge of it does not depend on things of whose existence I am as yet unaware; so it cannot depend on any of the things which I invent in my imagination. And this very word 'invent' shows me my mistake. It would indeed be a case of fictitious invention if I used my imagination to establish that I was something or other; for imagining is simply contemplating the shape or image of a corporeal thing. Yet now I know for certain both that I exist and at the same time that all such images and, in general, everything relating to the nature of body, could be mere dreams [and chimeras]. Once this point has been grasped, to say 'I will use my imagination to get to know more distinctly what I am' would seem to be as silly as saying 'I am now awake, and see some truth; but since my vision is not yet clear enough, I will deliberately fall asleep so that my dreams may provide a truer and clearer representation'. I thus realize that none of the things that the imagination enables me to grasp is at all relevant to this knowledge of myself which I possess, and that the mind must therefore be most carefully diverted from such things[3] if it is to perceive its own nature as distinctly as possible.

But what then am I? A thing that thinks. What is that? A thing that doubts, understands, affirms, denies, is willing, is unwilling, and also imagines and has sensory perceptions.

This is a considerable list, if everything on it belongs to me. But does it? Is it not one and the same 'I' who is now doubting almost everything, who nonetheless understands some things, who affirms that this one thing is true, denies everything else, desires to know more, is unwilling to be deceived, imagines many things even involuntarily, and is aware of many things which apparently come from the senses? Are not all these things just as true as the fact that I exist, even if I am asleep all the time, and even if he who created me is doing all he can to deceive me? Which of all these activities is distinct from my thinking? Which of them can be said to be separate from myself? The fact that it is I who am doubting and understanding and willing is so evident that I see no way of making it any clearer. But it is also the case that the 'I' who imagines is the same 'I'. For even if, as I have supposed, none of the objects of imagination are real, the power of imagination is something which really exists and is part of my think-ing. Lastly, it is also the same 'I' who has sensory perceptions, or is aware of bodily things as it were through the senses. For example, I am now seeing light, hearing a noise, feeling heat. But I am asleep, so all this is false. Yet I certainly *seem* to see, to hear, and to be warmed. This cannot be false; what is called 'having a sensory perception' is strictly just this, and in this restricted sense of the term it is simply thinking.

In the second half of *Meditation II* Descartes goes on to argue that his consciousness of himself is more distinct than his perceptions of objects, for such perceptions in fact depend on the understanding of the intellect. In *Meditations III–V* he gives some arguments for God's existence, and explains how we fall into error. In the last *Meditation* (no. VI) he discusses the existence of material things, arguing that God guarantees the veracity of our senses, and the relationship of body and mind.

But now, when I am beginning to achieve a better knowledge of myself and the author of my being, although I do not think I should heedlessly accept everything I seem to have acquired from the senses, neither do I think that everything should be called into doubt.

First, I know that everything which I clearly and distinctly under-stand is capable of being created by God so as to correspond exactly with my understanding of it. Hence the fact that I can clearly and distinctly understand one thing apart from another is enough to make me certain that the two things are distinct, since they are capable of being separated, at least by God. The question of what kind of power is required to bring about such a separation does not affect the judgement that the two things are distinct. Thus, simply by knowing that I exist and seeing at the same time that absolutely nothing else belongs to my nature or essence except that I am a thinking thing, I can infer correctly that my essence consists solely in the fact that I am a thinking thing. It is true that I may have (or, to anticipate, that I certainly have) a body that is very closely joined to me. But neverthe-less, on the one hand I have a clear and distinct idea of myself, in so far as I am simply a thinking, non-extended thing; and on the other hand I have a distinct idea of body,[4] in so far as this is simply an extended, non-thinking thing. And accordingly, it is certain that I[5] am really distinct from my body, and can exist without it.

Besides this, I find in myself faculties for certain special modes of thinking, namely imagination and sensory perception. Now I can clearly and distinctly understand myself as a whole without these faculties; but I cannot, conversely, understand these faculties without me, that is, without an intellectual substance to inhere in. This is because there is an intellectual act included in their essential definition; and hence I perceive that the distinction between them and myself corresponds to the distinction between the modes of a thing and the thing itself. Of course I also recognize that there are other faculties (like those of changing position, of taking on various shapes, and so on) which, like sensory perception and imagination, cannot be understood apart from some substance for them to inhere in, and hence cannot exist without it. But it is clear that these other faculties, if they exist, must be in a corporeal or extended substance and not an intellectual one; for the clear and distinct conception of them includes extension, but does not include any intellectual act whatsoever. . . .

Later on in *Meditation VI* Descartes suggests a further differentiation between mind and body.

The first observation I make at this point is that there is a great difference between the mind and the body, inasmuch as the body is by its very nature always divisible, while the mind is utterly indivisible. For when I consider the mind, or myself in so far as I am merely a thinking thing, I am unable to distinguish any parts within myself; I understand myself to be something quite single and complete. Although the whole mind seems to be united to the whole body, I recognize that if a foot or arm or any other part of the body is cut off, nothing has thereby been taken away from the mind. As for the faculties of willing, of understanding, of sensory perception and so on, these cannot be termed parts of the mind, since it is one and the same mind that wills, and understands and has sensory perceptions. By contrast, there is no corporeal or extended thing that I can think of which in my thought I cannot easily divide into parts; and this very fact makes me understand that it is divisible. This one argument would be enough to show me that the mind is completely different from the body, even if I did not already know as much from other considerations.

My next observation is that the mind is not immediately affected by all parts of the body, but only by the brain, or perhaps just by one small part of the brain, namely the part which is said to contain the 'common' sense.[6] Every time this part of the brain is in a given state, it presents the same signals to the mind, even though the other parts of the body may be in a different condition at the time. This is established by countless observations, which there is no need to review here.

1 '... or thought anything at all' (French version).
2 '... to see if I am not something more' (added in French version).
3 '... from this manner of conceiving things' (French version).
4 The Latin term *corpus* as used here by Descartes is ambiguous as between 'body' (i.e. corporeal matter in general) and 'the body' (i.e. this particular body of mine).
5 '... that is, my soul, by which I am what I am' (added in French version).
6 The supposed faculty which integrates the data from the five specialized senses (the notion goes back ultimately to Aristotle). 'The seat of the common sense must be very mobile, to receive all the impressions coming from the senses, but must be moveable only by the spirits which transmit these impressions. Only the *conarion* (pineal gland) fits these conditions' (letter to Mersenne, 21 April 1641).

• From *The Philosophical Writings of Descartes*, Vol. II, trans. J. Cottingham, R. Stoothoff and D. Murdoch (Cambridge, 1984), pp. 16–19, 54–55 and 59–60.

13

Pascal
A Wager for Sceptics

Blaise Pascal was born in Clermont-Ferrand in 1623. His early work was devoted to science and mathematics (his interest in the calculus of probabilities was partly motivated by his desire to explain the results achieved in gambling by his friend the Chevalier de Méré). He also organized the first omnibus service in Paris. But in November 1654 he had a powerful religious experience, the record of which was found sewn into his coat after his death in 1662: it begins 'FIRE. God of Abraham, God of Isaac, God of Jacob, not the God of philosophers and men of letters. Certitude, certitude. Feeling. Joy. Peace'. He devoted most of the rest of his short life to religious work and writing, in association with the Jansenist community at Port-Royal. His sympathies with Jansenism are evident in the *Provincial Letters*, an attack written in 1656–57 on Jesuit theories of grace and moral theology. His *Pensées* is an unfinished sketch of a Christian apologetic, in which Pascal criticizes the rationalistic type of apologetic stemming from Descartes and substitutes a much wider kind of argument, appealing to 'reasons of the heart'. It was published posthumously in 1670.

His 'Wager' forms only a small part of this long apologetic, and has a limited purpose. It should not be regarded as expressing Pascal's view of the nature of Christian faith, but rather as an *ad hominem* argument aimed at the kind of unbeliever who does not acknowledge any special revelation, sees the evidence for and against God's existence as finely balanced, and therefore remains in a state of suspended belief.

451. *Infinity—nothing.* Our soul is cast into the body, where it finds number, time, and dimensions. On these it reasons, calling them natural and necessary, and it can believe in nothing else.

A unit joined to infinity adds nothing to it, any more than one foot added to infinite length. The finite is annihilated in the presence of infinity, and becomes a pure zero. So is our intellect before God, so is our justice before divine justice. But there is not so much disproportion between our justice and God's as there is between unity and infinity.

God's justice must be vast, like His compassion. Now justice towards the reprobate is less vast, and must be less amazing than mercy towards the elect.

We know that there is an infinite, and do not know its nature. As we know it to be untrue that numbers are finite, it is therefore true that there is a numerical infinity. But we do not know its nature; it cannot be even and it cannot be odd, for the addition of a unit cannot change it. Nevertheless it is a number, and all numbers are either even or odd (this is certainly true of every finite number). So, we may well know that there is a God without knowing what He is.

Is there no substantial truth, seeing that there are so many truths that are not the truth itself?

We know then the existence and nature of the finite, because we too are finite and have extension. We know the existence of the infinite, and do not know its nature, because it has extension like us, but unlike us no limits. But we know neither the existence nor the nature of God, because He has neither extension nor limits.

But by faith we know that He exists; in glory we shall know His nature. Now I have already shown that we can very well know a thing exists without knowing its nature.

Let us now speak according to the light of nature.

If there is a God, He is infinitely incomprehensible, since, being undivided and without limits, He bears no relation to us. We are, therefore, incapable of knowing either what He is, or whether He exists. This being so, who will be so rash as to decide the question? Not we who bear no relation to Him.

Who, then, will blame Christians for being unable to give a reason for their belief, since they profess a religion which they cannot explain by reason? In proclaiming it to the world, they declare that it is a foolishness, *stultitiam*,—and then you complain that they do not prove it. If they proved it, they would be denying their own statement; their lack of proof shows that they are not lacking in sense.

'Yes, but although this excuses those who present religion in that way, and we cannot, therefore, blame them for doing so without advancing reasons, it does not excuse those who accept it.'

Let us then examine this point, and say: 'Either God is, or He is not'. But which side shall we take? Reason can decide nothing here; there is an infinite chaos between us. A game is on, at the other side of this infinite distance, and the coin will fall heads or tails. Which will you gamble on? According to reason you cannot gamble on either; according to reason you cannot defend either choice.

But do not blame those who have decided for making a wrong choice; you know nothing about the matter.

'No, I shall not blame them for the choice they have made, but for making any choice at all. For the man who calls heads and the man who calls tails have made the same mistake. They are both wrong: the proper thing is not to bet at all.'

Yes, but you must bet. There is no option; you have embarked on the business. Which will you choose, then? Let us see. Since you must choose, let us see which will profit you less. You have two things to lose: truth and good, and two things to stake: your reason and your will, your knowledge and your happiness. And your nature has two things to avoid: error and misery. Since you must necessàrily choose, it is no more unreasonable to make one choice than the other. That is one point cleared up. But your happiness? Let us weigh the gain and loss in calling heads, that God exists. Let us estimate the two chances; if you win, you win everything; if you lose, you lose nothing. Do not hesitate, then; gamble on His existence.

'This is splendid. Yes, I must make the bet; but perhaps I shall stake too much.'

Let us see. There being an equal chance of gain or loss, supposing you had two lives to gain for one, you might still gamble. But if you stood to gain three you would have to (being compelled to take part in the game). And since you have to play you would be foolish not to stake your one life for three in a game where the chances of gain and loss are equal. But here there is an eternity of life and happiness to be won. And this being so, even if there were an infinity of chances and only one in your favour, you would be right to stake one life against two; and it would be absurd, since you are compelled to play, to refuse to stake one life against three in a game in which one of an infinity of chances is in your favour, if what you stood to gain was an infinity of infinite happiness. But there *is* an infinity of infinite happiness to be gained, there is one chance of winning against a finite number of chances that you will lose, and what you are staking is finite. And so, since you are compelled to play, you would be mad to cling to your life instead of risking it for an infinite gain, which is as liable to turn up as a loss—of nothing.

For it is no use saying that our gain is uncertain, and that the infinite distance between the certainty of what we stake and the uncertainty of what we gain puts the finite good which we certainly risk on a level with the infinite, which is uncertain. This is not the case. Every gambler risks a certain sum to gain an uncertain one; and yet when he stakes a finite certainty to gain a finite uncertainty, he is not acting unreasonably. There is not an infinite difference between the certainty of the stake and the uncertainty of the gain; not at all. There is, indeed, an infinity between the certainty of gain and the certainty of loss. But the uncertainty of winning is proportionate to the certain amount of the stake, and the odds in favour of gain or loss.[1] If therefore there are as many chances on one side as on the other, the odds are equal; and the fixed sum at stake is equal to the uncertain gain; there is no infinity of difference between them. And so our argument is infinitely strong when only the finite is at stake in a game in which the chances of gain and loss are equal, and infinity is to be won. This is demonstrable; and if men are susceptible to any truth, here is one.

'I confess and admit it. But yet, is there no way of seeing the face of the cards?' . . .

Yes, Holy Scripture and other writings, etc.

'Yes. But my hands are tied and my mouth is gagged. I am forced to play, and I am not free. Something holds me back, for I am so made that I cannot believe. What would you have me do?'

What you say is true. But at least be aware that your inability to believe arises from your passions. For your reason urges you to it, and yet you find it impossible. Endeavour, therefore, to gain conviction, not by an increase of divine proofs, but by the diminution of your passions. You wish to come to faith, but do not know the way. You wish to cure yourself of unbelief, and you ask for remedies. Learn from those who have been hampered like you, and who now stake all their possessions. These are the people who know the road that you wish to follow; they are cured of the disease of which you wish to be cured. Follow the way by which they began: by behaving as if they believed, by taking holy water, by having masses said, etc. This will bring you to belief in the natural way, and will soothe your mind.

'But that is just what I am afraid of.'

And why? What have you to lose?

But to show you that this will lead you there, it is this that will lessen your passions, which are your great obstacles. (*End of this discourse.*) Now what harm will come of you if you follow this course? You will be faithful, honest, humble, grateful, generous, a sincere friend, and a truthful man. Certainly you will be without those poisonous pleasures, ambition and luxury. But will you not have others? I tell you that you will gain in this life, and that at every step you take on this road you will see such certainty of gain and such nothingness in your stake that you will finally realize you have gambled on something certain and infinite, and have risked nothing for it.

'Oh your words transport me, ravish me, etc.'

If this argument pleases you, and seems convincing, let me say that it is the utterance of a man who has knelt before and after, praying that infinite and undivided Being to whom he submits all he has that He may bring all your being likewise into submission, for your own good and His glory, and that thus strength may be brought into touch with weakness.

1 e.g. in buying a lottery ticket, we are buying a proportion of the total chances of winning, which is decided by the number of tickets sold.

- From Pascal, *The Pensées*, trans. J. M. Cohen (Harmondsworth, Middx, 1961), pp. 155–159.

14

Locke
Faith, Reason and Revelation

John Locke was born in Somerset in 1632. He lectured in Greek and Moral Philosophy at Oxford, but then qualified in medicine and practised for a time. He later got into the political world in the entourage of Lord Shaftesbury, and died in 1704. His main works are *An Essay concerning Human Understanding*, *Two Treatises on Civil Government* and *Letters on Toleration*.

The first of these works was published in 1690. Its main aim is to show that the human mind is a 'blank tablet' which acquires all its knowledge from experience and from reflection. Locke regards such an Empiricist standpoint as compatible with religious belief, for he thinks that it is possible to prove the existence of God from created existence, movement and intelligence (Book IV, Chapter 10). But he thinks that reason must judge the credentials of any putative revelation—a view which he later discussed in *The Reasonableness of Christianity, as Delivered in the Scriptures* (1695).

Chapter XVIII

Of faith and reason, and their distinct provinces

1. It has been above shown: (1) That we are of necessity ignorant and want knowledge of all sorts where we want *ideas*. (2) That we are ignorant and want rational knowledge where we want proofs. (3) That we want general knowledge and certainty, as far as we want clear and determined specific *ideas*. (4) That we want probability to direct our assent in matters where we have neither knowledge of our own nor testimony of other men to bottom our reason upon.

From these things thus premised, I think we may come to lay down the measures and *boundaries between faith and reason*: the want whereof may possibly have been the cause, if not of great disorders, yet at least of great disputes, and perhaps mistakes, in the world. For till it be resolved how far we are to be guided by reason, and how far by faith, we shall in vain dispute and endeavour to convince one another in matters of religion.

2. I find every sect, as far as reason will help them, makes use of it gladly; and where it fails them, they cry out, *It is matter of faith, and above reason*. And I do not see how they can argue with anyone, or ever convince a gainsayer who makes use of the same plea, without setting down strict boundaries between *faith* and *reason*, which ought to be the first point established in all questions where *faith* has anything to do.

Reason, therefore, here, as contradistinguished to *faith*, I take to be the discovery of the certainty or probability of such propositions or truths, which the mind arrives at by deduction made from such *ideas* which it has got by the use of its natural faculties, viz. by sensation or reflection.

Faith, on the other side, is the assent to any proposition, not thus made out by the deductions of reason, but upon the credit of the proposer as coming from God, in some extraordinary way of communication. This way of discovering truths to men we call *revelation*.

3. First, then, I say that *no man inspired by* God *can by any revelation communicate to others any new simple ideas* which they had not before from sensation or reflection. For, whatsoever impressions he himself may have from the immediate hand of God, this revelation, if it be of new simple *ideas*, cannot be conveyed to another, either by words or any other signs. Because words, by their immediate operation on us, cause no other *ideas* but of their natural sounds; and it is by the custom of using them for signs that they excite and revive in our minds latent *ideas*, but yet only such *ideas* as were there before. For words seen or heard recall to our thoughts those *ideas* only which to us they have been wont to be signs of, but cannot introduce any perfectly new and formerly unknown simple *ideas*. The same holds in all other signs, which cannot signify to us things of which we have before never had any *idea* at all.

Thus whatever things were discovered to St *Paul*, when he was rapt up into the third heaven, whatever new *ideas* his mind there received, all the description he can make to others of that place is only this, that there are such things *as eye hath not seen, nor ear heard, nor hath it entered into the heart of man to conceive*. And supposing God should discover to anyone supernaturally, a species of creatures inhabiting, for example, *Jupiter* or *Saturn* (for that it is possible there may be such, nobody can deny) which had six senses, and imprint on his mind the *ideas* conveyed to theirs by that sixth sense: he could no more, by words, produce in the minds of other men those *ideas* imprinted by that sixth sense, than one of us could convey the *idea* of any colour, by the sounds of words, into a man who, having the other four senses perfect, had always totally wanted the fifth, of seeing. For our simple *ideas*, then, which are the foundation and sole matter of all our notions and knowledge, we must depend wholly on our reason, I mean, our natural faculties; and can by no means receive them, or any of them, from *traditional revelation*, I say *traditional revelation* in distinction to *original revelation*. By the one, I mean that first impression which is made immediately by God on the mind of any man, to which we cannot set any bounds; and by the other, those impressions delivered over to others in words and the ordinary ways of conveying our conceptions one to another.

4. *Secondly*, I say that *the same truths may be discovered and conveyed down from revelation, which are discoverable to us by reason*, and by those *ideas* we naturally may have. So God might, by revelation, discover the truth of any proposition in *Euclid*; as well as men, by the natural use of their faculties, come to make the discovery themselves. In all things of this kind there is little need or use of *revelation*, God having furnished us with natural and surer means to arrive at the knowledge of them. For whatsoever truth we come to the clear discovery of, from the knowledge and contemplation of our own *ideas*, will always be certainer to us than those which are conveyed to us by *traditional revelation*. For the knowledge we have that this *revelation* came at first from God can never be so sure as the knowledge we have from the clear and distinct perception of the agreement or disagreement of our own *ideas*: v.g. if it were revealed, some ages since, that the three angles of a triangle were equal to two right ones, I might assent to the truth of that proposition upon the credit of the tradition that it was revealed; but that would never amount to so great a certainty as the knowledge of it upon the comparing and measuring my own *ideas* of two right angles and the three angles of a triangle. The like holds in matter of fact knowable by our senses: v.g. the history of the deluge is conveyed to us by writings which had their original from revelation; and yet nobody, I think, will say he has as certain and clear a knowledge of the flood as *Noah*, that saw it, or that he himself would have had, had he then been alive and seen it. For he has no greater an assurance than that of his senses, that it is writ in the book supposed writ by *Moses* inspired; but he has not so great an assurance that *Moses* wrote that book as if he had seen *Moses* write it. So that the assurance of its being a revelation is less still than the assurance of his senses.

5. In propositions, then, whose certainty is built upon the clear perception of the agreement or disagreement of our *ideas*, attained either by immediate intuition, as in self-evident propositions, or by evident deductions of reason in demonstrations, we need not the assistance of *revelation*, as necessary to gain our assent and introduce them into our minds. Because the natural ways of knowledge could settle them there, or had done it already; which is the greatest assurance we can possibly have of anything, unless where God immediately

reveals it to us; and there too our assurance can be no greater than our knowledge is, that it is a *revelation* from God. But yet nothing, I think, can under that title shake or overrule plain knowledge, or rationally prevail with any man to admit it for true in a direct contradiction to the clear evidence of his own understanding. For since no evidence of our faculties, by which we receive such *revelations*, can exceed, if equal, the certainty of our intuitive knowledge, we can never receive for a truth anything that is directly contrary to our clear and distinct knowledge: v.g. the *ideas* of one body and one place do so clearly agree, and the mind has so evident a perception of their agreement, that we can never assent to a proposition that affirms the same body to be in two distant places at once, however it should pretend to the authority of a divine *revelation*: since the evidence, *first*, that we deceive not ourselves in ascribing it to God; *secondly*, that we understand it right, can never be so great as the evidence of our own intuitive knowledge whereby we discern it impossible for the same body to be in two places at once. And therefore *no proposition can be received for divine revelation* or obtain the assent due to all such, *if it be contradictory to our clear intuitive knowledge.* Because this would be to subvert the principles and foundations of all knowledge, evidence, and assent whatsoever; and there would be left no difference between truth and falsehood, no measures of credible and incredible in the world, if doubtful propositions shall take place before self-evident, and what we certainly know give way to what we may possibly be mistaken in. In propositions therefore contrary to the clear perception of the agreement or disagreement of any of our *ideas*, it will be in vain to urge them as matters of *faith*. They cannot move our assent under that or any other title whatsoever. For *faith* can never convince us of anything that contradicts our knowledge. Because, though *faith* be founded on the testimony of God (who cannot lie) revealing any proposition to us: yet we cannot have an assurance of the truth of its being a divine revelation greater than our own knowledge: since the whole strength of the certainty depends upon our knowledge that God revealed it; which, in this case, where the proposition supposed revealed contradicts our knowledge or reason, will always have this objection hanging to it, (viz.) that we cannot tell how to conceive that to come from God, the bountiful Author of our being, which, if received for true, must overturn all the principles and foundations of knowledge he has given us; render all our faculties useless; wholly destroy the most excellent part of his workmanship, our understandings; and put a man in a condition wherein he will have less light, less conduct than the beast that perisheth. For if the mind of man can never have a clearer (and, perhaps, not so clear) evidence of anything to be a divine *revelation*, as it has of the principles of its own reason, it can never have a ground to quit the clear evidence of its reason, to give place to a proposition whose *revelation* has not a greater evidence than those principles have.

6. Thus far a man has use of reason and ought to hearken to it, even in immediate and original *revelation*, where it is supposed to be made to himself. But to all those who pretend not to immediate *revelation*, but are required to pay obedience and to receive the truths revealed to others which, by the tradition of writings or word of mouth, are conveyed down to them, reason has a great deal more to do, and is that only which can induce us to receive them. For matter of faith being only divine revelation and nothing else, *faith*, as we use the word (called commonly, *divine faith*) has to do with no propositions but those which are supposed to be divinely revealed. So that I do not see how those who make revelation alone the sole object of *faith* can say that it is a matter of *faith*, and not of *reason*, to believe that such or such a proposition, to be found in such or such a book, is of divine inspiration, unless it be revealed that that proposition, or all in that book, was communicated by divine inspiration. Without such a *revelation*, the believing or not believing that proposition or book to be of divine authority can never be matter of *faith*, but matter of reason, and such as I must come to an assent to only by the use of my reason, which can never require or enable me to believe that which is contrary to itself: it being impossible for reason ever to procure any assent to that which to itself appears unreasonable.

In all things, therefore, where we have clear evidence from our *ideas* and those principles of knowledge I have above mentioned, *reason* is the proper judge; and *revelation*, though it may, in consenting with it, confirm its dictates, yet cannot in such cases invalidate its decrees; *nor can we be obliged, where we have the clear and evident sentence of reason, to quit it for the contrary opinion, under a pretence that it is matter of faith*, which can have no authority against the plain and clear dictates of reason.

7. But, *thirdly*, there being many things wherein we have very imperfect notions, or none at all; and other things, of whose past, present, or future existence, by the natural use of our faculties, we can have no knowledge at all: these, as being beyond the discovery of our natural faculties and above *reason*, are, when revealed, *the proper matter of faith*. Thus, that part of the angels rebelled against God and thereby lost their first happy state, and that the dead shall rise and live again: these and the like, being beyond the discovery of *reason*, are purely matters of *faith*, with which *reason* has, directly, nothing to do.

8. But since God, in giving us the light of *reason*, has not thereby tied up his own hands from affording us, when he thinks fit, the light of *revelation* in any of those matters wherein our natural faculties are able

to give a probable determination: *revelation*, where God has been pleased to give it, *must carry it against the probable conjectures of reason.* Because the mind, not being certain of the truth of that it does not evidently know, but only yielding to the probability that appears in it, is bound to give up its assent to such a testimony which, it is satisfied, comes from one who cannot err and will not deceive. But yet, it still belongs to *reason* to judge of the truth of its being a revelation and of the signification of the words wherein it is delivered. Indeed, if anything shall be thought *revelation* which is contrary to the plain principles of reason and the evident knowledge the mind has of its own clear and distinct *ideas*, there *reason* must be hearkened to, as to a matter within its province: since a man can never have so certain a knowledge that a proposition which contradicts the clear principles and evidence of his own knowledge was divinely revealed, or that he understands the words rightly wherein it is delivered, as he has that the contrary is true; and so is bound to consider and judge of it as a matter of reason and not swallow it, without examination, as a matter of *faith*.

9. *First*, Whatever proposition is revealed of whose truth our mind, by its natural faculties and notions, cannot judge, that is purely *matter of faith*, and above reason.

Secondly, All propositions whereof the mind, by the use of its natural faculties, can come to determine and judge, from naturally acquired *ideas*, are *matter of reason*, with this difference still: that, in those concerning which it has but an uncertain evidence and so is persuaded of their truth only upon probable grounds, which still admit a possibility of the contrary to be true without doing violence to the certain evidence of its own knowledge and overturning the principles of all reason, in such probable propositions, I say, an evident *revelation* ought to determine our assent, even against probability. For where the principles of reason have not evidenced a proposition to be certainly true or false, there clear *revelation*, as another principle of truth and ground of assent, may determine; and so it may be matter of *faith* and be also above *reason*. Because *reason*, in that particular matter, being able to reach no higher than probability, *faith* gave the determination where *reason* came short, and *revelation* discovered on which side the truth lay.

10. Thus far the dominion of *faith* reaches, and that without any violence or hindrance to *reason*, which is not injured or disturbed, but assisted and improved by new discoveries of truth coming from the eternal fountain of all knowledge. Whatever God hath revealed is certainly true: no doubt can be made of it. This is the proper object of *faith*; but whether it be a divine revelation or no, *reason* must judge, which can never permit the mind to reject a greater evidence to

embrace what is less evident, nor allow it to entertain probability in opposition to knowledge and certainty. There can be no evidence that any traditional revelation is of divine original, in the words we receive it and in the sense we understand it, so clear and so certain as that of the principles of reason; and therefore *nothing that is contrary to, and inconsistent with, the clear and self-evident dictates of reason has a right to be urged or assented to as a matter of faith, wherein reason hath nothing to do.* Whatsoever is divine *revelation*, ought to overrule all our opinions, prejudices, and interests, and hath a right to be received with full assent; such a submission as this, of our *reason* to *faith*, takes not away the landmarks of knowledge: this shakes not the foundations of reason, but leaves us that use of our faculties for which they were given us.

11. *If the provinces of faith and reason are not kept distinct by these boundaries,* there will, in matter of religion, be no room for *reason* at all, and those extravagant opinions and ceremonies that are to be found in the several religions of the world will not deserve to be blamed. For, to this crying up of *faith* in opposition to *reason*, we may, I think, in good measure ascribe those absurdities that fill almost all the religions which possess and divide mankind. For men, having been principled with an opinion that they must not consult *reason* in the things of religion, however apparently contradictory to common sense and the very principles of all their knowledge, have let loose their fancies and natural superstition, and have been by them led into so strange opinions and extravagant practices in religion that a considerate man cannot but stand amazed at their follies and judge them so far from being acceptable to the great and wise God, that he cannot avoid thinking them ridiculous and offensive to a sober, good man. So that in effect religion, which should most distinguish us from beasts and ought most peculiarly to elevate us as rational creatures above brutes, is that wherein men often appear most irrational and more senseless than beasts themselves. *Credo, quia impossibile est: I believe, because it is impossible,* might, in a good man, pass for a sally of zeal, but would prove a very ill rule for men to choose their opinions or religion by.

Chapter XIX

Of enthusiasm

1. He that would seriously set upon the search of truth ought in the first place to prepare his mind with a love of it. For he that loves it not will not take much pains to get it, nor be much concerned when he misses it. There is nobody in the commonwealth of learning who does

not profess himself a lover of truth; and there is not a rational creature that would not take it amiss to be thought otherwise of. And yet, for all this, one may truly say there are very few lovers of truth for truth's sake, even amongst those who persuade themselves that they are so. How a man may know whether he be so in earnest, is worth inquiry; and I think there is this one unerring mark of it, viz. the not entertaining any proposition with greater assurance than the proofs it is built upon will warrant. Whoever goes beyond this measure of assent, it is plain, receives not truth in the love of it, loves not truth for truth's sake but for some other by-end. For the evidence that any proposition is true (except such as are self-evident) lying only in the proofs a man has of it, whatsoever degrees of assent he affords it beyond the degrees of that evidence, it is plain all that surplusage of assurance is owing to some other affection and not to the love of truth: it being as impossible that the love of truth should carry my assent above the evidence that there is to me that it is true, as that the love of truth should make me assent to any proposition for the sake of that evidence which it has not, that it is true; which is in effect to love it as a truth because it is possible or probable that it may not be true. In any truth that gets not possession of our minds by the irresistible light of self-evidence or by the force of demonstration, the arguments that gain it assent are the vouchers and gauge of its probability to us; and we can receive it for no other than such as they deliver it to our understandings. Whatsoever credit or authority we give to any proposition more than it receives from the principles and proofs it supports itself upon is owing to our inclinations that way, and is so far a derogation from the love of truth as such; which, as it can receive no evidence from our passions or interests, so it should receive no tincture from them.

2. The assuming an authority of dictating to others and a forwardness to prescribe to their opinions is a constant concomitant of this bias and corruption of our judgments. For how almost can it be otherwise but that he should be ready to impose on another's belief, who has already imposed on his own? Who can reasonably expect arguments and conviction from him in dealing with others whose understanding is not accustomed to them in his dealing with himself? Who does violence to his own faculties, tyrannizes over his own mind, and usurps the prerogative that belongs to truth alone, which is to command assent by only its own authority, i.e. by and in proportion to that evidence which it carries with it.

3. Upon this occasion I shall take the liberty to consider a third ground of assent, which with some men has the same authority and is as confidently relied on as either *faith* or *reason*, I mean *enthusiasm*. Which, laying by reason, would set up revelation without it. Whereby in effect it takes away both reason and revelation, and substitutes in

the room of them the ungrounded fancies of a man's own brain, and assumes them for a foundation both of opinion and conduct.

4. *Reason* is natural *revelation*, whereby the eternal Father of light and fountain of all knowledge communicates to mankind that portion of truth which he has laid within the reach of their natural faculties; *revelation* is natural *reason* enlarged by a new set of discoveries communicated by God immediately, which *reason* vouches the truth of, by the testimony and proofs it gives that they come from God. So that he that takes away *reason*, to make way for *revelation*, puts out the light of both, and does much what the same as if he would persuade a man to put out his eyes, the better to receive the remote light of an invisible star by a telescope.

5. Immediate *revelation* being a much easier way for men to establish their opinions and regulate their conduct than the tedious and not always successful labour of strict reasoning, it is no wonder that some have been very apt to pretend to revelation, and to persuade themselves that they are under the peculiar guidance of heaven in their actions and opinions, especially in those of them which they cannot account for by the ordinary methods of knowledge and principles of reason. Hence we see that, in all ages, men in whom melancholy has mixed with devotion, or whose conceit of themselves has raised them into an opinion of a greater familiarity with God and a nearer admittance to his favour than is afforded to others, have often flattered themselves with a persuasion of an immediate intercourse with the Deity and frequent communications from the Divine Spirit. God I own cannot be denied to be able to enlighten the understanding by a ray darted into the mind immediately from the fountain of light; this they understand he has promised to do; and who then has so good a title to expect it as those who are his peculiar people, chosen by him and depending on him?

6. Their minds being thus prepared, whatever groundless opinion comes to settle itself strongly upon their fancies is an illumination from the Spirit of God, and presently of divine authority; and whatsoever odd action they find in themselves a strong inclination to do, that impulse is concluded to be a call or direction from heaven and must be obeyed: it is a commission from above, and they cannot err in executing it.

7. This I take to be properly enthusiasm, which, though founded neither on reason nor divine revelation, but rising from the conceits of a warmed or overweening brain, works yet, where it once gets footing, more powerfully on the persuasions and actions of men than either of those two, or both together: men being most forwardly obedient to the impulses they receive from themselves, and the whole man is sure to act more vigorously where the whole man is carried by a natural

motion. For strong conceit, like a new principle, carries all easily with it when, got above common sense and freed from all restraint of reason and check of reflection, it is heightened into a divine authority, in concurrence with our own temper and inclination.

8. Though the odd opinions and extravagant actions *enthusiasm* has run men into were enough to warn them against this wrong principle, so apt to misguide them both in their belief and conduct: yet the love of something extraordinary, the ease and glory it is to be inspired and be above the common and natural ways of knowledge, so flatters many men's laziness, ignorance, and vanity that, when once they are got into this way of immediate revelation, of illumination without search, and of certainty without proof and without examination, it is a hard matter to get them out of it. Reason is lost upon them, they are above it; they see the light infused into their understandings, and cannot be mistaken: it is clear and visible there, like the light of bright sunshine, shows itself, and needs no other proof but its own evidence; they feel the hand of God moving them within and the impulses of the Spirit, and cannot be mistaken in what they feel. Thus they support themselves and are sure reason hath nothing to do with what they see and feel in themselves: what they have a sensible experience of admits no doubt, needs no probation. Would he not be ridiculous who should require to have it proved to him that the light shines and that he sees it? It is its own proof and can have no other. When the spirit brings light into our minds, it dispels darkness. We see it as we do that of the sun at noon, and need not the twilight of reason to show it us. This light from heaven is strong, clear, and pure, carries its own demonstration with it, and we may as rationally take a glow-worm to assist us to discover the sun as to examine the celestial ray by our dim candle, reason.

9. This is the way of talking of these men: they are sure because they are sure, and their persuasions are right only because they are strong in them. For, when what they say is stripped of the metaphor of seeing and feeling, this is all it amounts to; and yet these similes so impose on them that they serve them for certainty in themselves and demonstration to others.

10. But to examine a little soberly this internal light, and this feeling on which they build so much. These men have, they say, clear light, and they see; they have an awakened sense, and they feel: this cannot, they are sure, be disputed them. For when a man says he sees or he feels, nobody can deny it him that he does so. But here let me ask: This seeing, is it the perception of the truth of the proposition, or of this, that it is a revelation from God? This feeling, is it a perception of an inclination or fancy to do something, or of the Spirit of God moving that inclination? These are two very different perceptions, and must

be carefully distinguished, if we would not impose upon ourselves. I may perceive the truth of a proposition, and yet not perceive that it is an immediate revelation from God. I may perceive the truth of a proposition in *Euclid*, without its being, or my perceiving it to be, a revelation: nay, I may perceive I came not by this knowledge in a natural way, and so may conclude it revealed, without perceiving that it is a revelation from God. Because there be spirits which, without being divinely commissioned, may excite those *ideas* in me and lay them in such order before my mind, that I may perceive their connexion. So that the knowledge of any proposition coming into my mind, I know not how, is not a perception that it is from God. Much less is a strong persuasion that it is true, a perception that it is from God, or so much as true. But however it be called light and seeing, I suppose it is at most but belief and assurance: and the proposition taken for a revelation is not such as they know to be true, but take to be true. For where a proposition is known to be true, revelation is needless; and it is hard to conceive how there can be a revelation to anyone of what he knows already. If therefore it be a proposition which they are persuaded, but do not know, to be true, whatever they may call it, it is not seeing, but believing. For these are two ways whereby truth comes into the mind, wholly distinct, so that one is not the other. What I see, I know to be so, by the evidence of the thing itself; what I believe, I take to be so upon the testimony of another; but this testimony I must know to be given, or else what ground have I of believing? I must see that it is God that reveals this to me, or else I see nothing. The question then here is: How do I know that God is the revealer of this to me, that this impression is made upon my mind by his Holy Spirit, and that therefore I ought to obey it? If I know not this, how great soever the assurance is that I am possessed with, it is groundless: whatever light I pretend to, it is but *enthusiasm*. For, whether the proposition supposed to be revealed be in itself evidently true or visibly probable or, by the natural ways of knowledge, uncertain, the proposition that must be well grounded and manifested to be true is this, that God is the revealer of it, and that what I take to be a revelation is certainly put into my mind by him, and is not an illusion dropped in by some other spirit or raised by my own fancy. For, if I mistake not, these men receive it for true because they presume God revealed it. Does it not, then, stand them upon to examine upon what grounds they presume it to be a revelation from God? or else all their confidence is mere presumption, and this light they are so dazzled with is nothing but an *ignis fatuus* that leads them continually round in this circle: *it is a revelation, because they firmly believe it*; and *they believe it, because it is a revelation.*

11. In all that is of divine *revelation*, there is need of no other proof but

that it is an inspiration from God: for he can neither deceive nor be deceived. But how shall it be known that any proposition in our minds is a truth infused by God; a truth that is revealed to us by him, which he declares to us, and therefore we ought to believe? Here it is that *enthusiasm* fails of the evidence it pretends to. For men thus possessed boast of a light whereby they say they are enlightened and brought into the knowledge of this or that truth. But if they know it to be a truth, they must know it to be so either by its own self-evidence to natural reason, or by the rational proofs that make it out to be so. If they see and know it to be a truth either of these two ways, they in vain suppose it to be a revelation. For they know it to be true by the same way that any other man naturally may know that it is so, without the help of revelation. For thus all the truths, of what kind soever, that men uninspired are enlightened with came into their minds and are established there. If they say they know it to be true because it is a *revelation* from God, the reason is good; but then it will be demanded how they know it to be a revelation from God. If they say by the light it brings with it, which shines bright in their minds and they cannot resist, I beseech them to consider whether this be any more than what we have taken notice of already, viz. that it is a revelation because they strongly believe it to be true. For all the light they speak of is but a strong, though ungrounded, persuasion of their own minds that it is a truth. For rational grounds from proofs that it is a truth, they must acknowledge to have none: for then it is not received as a *revelation*, but upon the ordinary grounds that other truths are received; and if they believe it to be true because it is a *revelation*, and have no other reason for its being a *revelation* but because they are fully persuaded, without any other reason, that it is true, they believe it to be a revelation only because they strongly believe it to be a revelation; which is a very unsafe ground to proceed on, either in our tenets or actions; and what readier way can there be to run ourselves into the most extravagant errors and miscarriages than thus to set up fancy for our supreme and sole guide, and to believe any proposition to be true, any action to be right, only because we believe it to be so? The strength of our persuasions are no evidence at all of their own rectitude: crooked things may be as stiff and inflexible as straight, and men may be as positive and peremptory in error as in truth. How come else the intractable zealots in different and opposite parties? For if the light which everyone thinks he has in his mind, which in this case is nothing but the strength of his own persuasion, be an evidence that it is from God, contrary opinions may have the same title to be inspirations; and God will be not only the father of lights but of opposite and contradictory lights, leading men contrary ways; and contradictory propositions will be divine truths, if an ungrounded strength of

assurance be an evidence that any proposition is a divine revelation.
12. This cannot be otherwise, whilst firmness of persuasion is made
the cause of believing, and confidence of being in the right is made an
argument of truth: St *Paul* himself believed he did well and that he
had a call to it, when he persecuted the Christians, whom he confidently thought in the wrong; but yet it was he and not they who were
mistaken. Good men are men still, liable to mistakes, and are sometimes warmly engaged in errors, which they take for divine truths,
shining in their minds with the clearest light.
13. Light, true light, in the mind is, or can be, nothing else but the
evidence of the truth of any proposition; and if it be not a self-evident
proposition, all the light it has or can have is from the clearness and
validity of those proofs upon which it is received. To talk of any other
light in the understanding is to put ourselves in the dark, or in the
power of the Prince of Darkness, and, by our own consent, to give
ourselves up to delusion to believe a lie. For if strength of persuasion
be the light which must guide us, I ask how shall anyone distinguish
between the delusions of Satan and the inspirations of the Holy
Ghost? He can transform himself into an angel of light. And they who
are led by this son of the morning are as fully satisfied of the illumination, i.e. are as strongly persuaded, that they are enlightened by the
spirit of God as anyone who is so: they acquiesce and rejoice in it, are
acted by it, and nobody can be more sure nor more in the right (if their
own strong belief may be judge) than they.
14. He, therefore, that will not give himself up to all the extravagan-
cies of delusion and error must bring this guide of his *light within* to the
trial. God when he makes the prophet does not unmake the man. He
leaves all his faculties in their natural state, to enable him to judge of
his inspirations, whether they be of divine original or no. When he
illuminates the mind with supernatural light, he does not extinguish
that which is natural. If he would have us assent to the truth of any
proposition, he either evidences that truth by the usual methods of
natural reason, or else makes it known to be a truth which he would
have us assent to by his authority, and convinces us that it is from him
by some marks which reason cannot be mistaken in. *Reason* must be
our last judge and guide in everything. I do not mean that we must
consult reason and examine whether a proposition revealed from God
can be made out by natural principles, and if it cannot, that then we
may reject it; but consult it we must, and by it examine whether it be a
revelation from God or no; and if *reason* finds it to be revealed from
God, *reason* then declares for it as much as for any other truth, and
makes it one of her dictates. Every conceit that thoroughly warms our
fancies must pass for an inspiration, if there be nothing but the
strength of our persuasions whereby to judge of our persuasions; if

reason must not examine their truth by something extrinsical to the persuasions themselves, inspirations and delusions, truth and falsehood will have the same measure and will not be possible to be distinguished.

15. If this internal light, or any proposition which under that title we take for inspired, be conformable to the principles of reason or to the word of God, which is attested revelation, *reason* warrants it and we may safely receive it for true and be guided by it in our belief and actions; if it receive no testimony nor evidence from either of these rules, we cannot take it for a revelation or so much as for true, till we have some other mark that it is a *revelation*, besides our believing that it is so. Thus we see the holy men of old, who had *revelations* from God, had something else besides that internal light of assurance in their own minds to testify to them that it was from God. They were not left to their own persuasions alone that those persuasions were from God, but had outward signs to convince them of the author of those revelations. And when they were to convince others, they had a power given them to justify the truth of their commission from heaven, and by visible signs to assert the divine authority of a message they were sent with. *Moses* saw the bush burn without being consumed, and heard a voice out of it. This was something besides finding an impulse upon his mind to go to *Pharaoh*, that he might bring his brethren out of *Egypt*; and yet he thought not this enough to authorize him to go with that message, till God by another miracle, of his rod turned into a serpent, had assured him of a power to testify his mission by the same miracle repeated before them whom he was sent to. *Gideon* was sent by an angel to deliver *Israel* from the *Midianites*, and yet he desired a sign to convince him that this commission was from God. These and several the like instances to be found among the prophets of old are enough to show that they thought not an inward seeing or persuasion of their own minds, without any other proof, a sufficient evidence that it was from God, though the Scripture does not everywhere mention their demanding or having such proofs.

16. In what I have said I am far from denying that God can or doth sometimes enlighten men's minds in the apprehending of certain truths, or excite them to good actions by the immediate influence and assistance of the Holy Spirit, without any extraordinary signs accompanying it. But in such cases too we have reason and the Scripture, unerring rules to know whether it be from God or no. Where the truth embraced is consonant to the *revelation* in the written word of God, or the action conformable to the dictates of right *reason* or Holy Writ, we may be assured that we run no risk in entertaining it as such, because, though perhaps it be not an immediate revelation from God extraordinarily operating on our minds, yet we are sure it is warranted by that

revelation which he has given us of truth. But it is not the strength of our private persuasion within ourselves that can warrant it to be a light or motion from heaven: nothing can do that but the written word of God without us, or that standard of reason which is common to us with all men. Where reason or Scripture is express for any opinion or action, we may receive it as of divine authority; but it is not the strength of our own persuasions which can by itself give it that stamp. The bent of our own minds may favour it as much as we please: that may show it to be a fondling of our own, but will by no means prove it to be an offspring of heaven and of divine original.

- From *An Essay concerning Human Understanding*, Book IV, Chapters 18–19.

15

Leibniz
A Cosmological Argument

Gottfried Wilhelm Leibniz was born in Leipzig in 1646, and pursued a career of great intellectual variety. He excelled in philosophy, logic and mathematics, but also worked in theology, law and history. His correspondence with Samuel Clarke gives a fine critique of Sir Isaac Newton, whilst that with Bossuet discusses the possible reunion of the churches. He strongly influenced the development of modern mathematical logic. Unfortunately he never published a comprehensive exposition of his system: the longest work published in his life-time was the *Theodicy* (1710), later lampooned in Voltaire's *Candide*; his *New Essays on Human Understanding*, a substantial critique of Locke's *Essay*, was not published until 1765, long after his death in 1716. His thought is best approached through short works like the *Discourse on Metaphysics*, *Principles of Nature and Grace* and *Monadology* (named after 'monads', which are the fundamental simple substances in Leibniz's system).

One of Leibniz's basic principles is that there is a reason for everything, i.e. not just a cause but a rational, purposive explanation; from this it follows that the universe is a harmony. This principle plays a role in the following version of the Cosmological Argument, which Leibniz wrote in 1697.

On the Radical Origination of Things

Besides the world or aggregate of finite things, there is a certain One which is dominant, not only as the soul is dominant in me or rather, as the Ego itself is dominant in my body, but also by a much higher reason. For the dominant One of the universe not only rules the world but fabricates or makes it; it is superior to the world and, so to speak, extramundane, and hence is the ultimate reason for things. For a sufficient reason for existence cannot be found merely in any one individual thing or even in the whole aggregate and series of things. Let us imagine the book on the *Elements of Geometry* to have been eternal, one copy always being made from another; then it is clear that though we can give a reason for the present book based on the preceding book from which it was copied, we can never arrive at a complete reason, no matter how many books we may assume in the past, for one can always wonder why such books should have existed at all times; why there should be books at all, and why they should be written in this way. What is true of books is true also of the different states of the world; every subsequent state is somehow copied from the preceding one (although according to certain laws of change). No matter how far we may have gone back to earlier states, therefore, we will never discover in them a full reason why there should be a world at all, and why it should be such as it is.

Even if we should imagine the world to be eternal, therefore, the reason for it would clearly have to be sought elsewhere, since we would still be assuming nothing but a succession of states, in any one of which we can find no sufficient reason, nor can we advance the slightest toward establishing a reason, no matter how many of these states we assume. For even though there be no cause for eternal things, there must yet be understood to be a reason for them. For permanent things this reason is their necessity or essence itself; but in a series of changing things (if this is taken a priori[1] to be eternal) it is a prevailing of inclinations, as we shall see presently, for here reasons do not necessitate (in the sense of an absolute or metaphysical necessity, whose contrary implies a contradiction) but incline. These considerations show clearly that we cannot escape an ultimate extramundane reason for things, or God, even by assuming the eternity of the world.

The reasons for the world therefore lie in something extramundane, different from the chain of states or series of things whose aggregate constitutes the world. And so we must go from physical or hypothetical necessity, which determines later things in the world from earlier ones, to something which has absolute or metaphysical necessity, for which no reason can be given. The present world is necessary in a physical or hypothetical sense, not absolutely or metaphysically. That is, once it is established to be such as it is, it follows that things such as they are will come into being. Therefore, since there must be an ultimate root in something which has metaphysical necessity, and since there is no reason for an existing thing except in another existing thing, there must necessarily exist some one being of metaphysical necessity, or a being to whose essence belongs existence. So there must exist something which is distinct from the plurality of beings, or from the world, which, as we have admitted and shown, has no metaphysical necessity.

To explain a little more distinctly, however, how temporal, contingent, or physical truths arise out of truths that are eternal and essential, or if you like, metaphysical, we should first acknowledge that from the very fact that something exists rather than nothing, there is a certain urgency [*exigentia*] toward existence in possible things or in possibility or essence itself—a pre-tension to exist, so to speak—and in a word, that essence in itself tends to exist. From this it follows further that all possible things, or things expressing an essence or possible reality, tend toward existence with equal right in proportion to the quantity of essence or reality, or to the degree of perfection which they involve; for perfection is nothing but quantity of essence.

Hence it is very clearly understood that out of the infinite combinations and series of possible things, one exists through which the greatest amount of essence or possibility is brought into existence. There is always a principle of determination in nature which must be sought by maxima and minima; namely, that a maximum effect should be achieved with a minimum outlay, so to speak. And at this point time and place, or in a word, the receptivity or capacity to the world, can be taken for the outlay, or the terrain on which a building is to be erected as commodiously as possible, the variety of forms corresponding to the spaciousness of the building and the number and elegance of its chambers. The case is like that of certain games in which all the spaces on a board are to be filled according to definite rules, but unless we use a certain device, we find ourself at the end blocked from the difficult spaces and compelled to leave more spaces vacant than we needed or wished to. Yet there is a definite rule by which a maximum number of spaces can be filled in the easiest way. Therefore, assuming that it is ordered that there shall be a triangle with no other further determining principle, the result is that an equilateral triangle is produced. And assuming that there is to be motion from one point to another without anything more determining the route, that path will be chosen which is easiest or shortest. Similarly, once having assumed that being involves more perfection than nonbeing, or that there is a reason why something should come to exist rather than nothing, or that a transition from possibility to actuality must take place, it follows that even if there is no further determining principle, there does exist the greatest amount possible in proportion to the given capacity of time and space (or the possible order of existence), in much the same way as tiles are laid so that as many as possible are contained in a given space.

We can now understand in a wonderful way how a kind of divine mathematics or metaphysical mechanism is used in the origin of things and how the determination of the maximum takes place. So the right angle is the determined one of all angles in geometry, and so liquids placed in a different medium compose themselves in the most spacious figure, a sphere. But best of all is the example in ordinary mechanics itself; when many heavy bodies pull upon each other, the resulting motion is such that the maximum possible total descent is secured.[2] For just as all possibilities tend with equal right to existence in proportion to their reality, so all heavy objects tend to descend with equal right in proportion to their weight. And just as, in the latter case, that motion is produced which involves the greatest possible descent of these weights, so in the former a world is produced in which a maximum production of possible things takes place.

Thus we now have a physical necessity derived from a metaphysical necessity. For even if the world is not necessary metaphysically, in the sense that its contrary would imply a contradiction or logical absurdity, it is nonetheless necessary physically, or determined in such a way that its contrary would imply imperfection or moral absurdity. And just as possibility is the principle of essence, so perfection or degree of essence is the principle of existence (since the degree of perfection determines the largest number of things that are compossible). This shows at once how there may be freedom in the Author of the world, even though he does all things determinately because he acts on the principle of wisdom or perfection. Indifference arises from ignorance, and the wiser a man is, the more determined he is toward the most perfect.

But, you will say, however elegant this comparison of a kind of determining metaphysical mechanism with the physical mechanism of heavy bodies may seem, it is faulty in this respect—heavy bodies which act against each other truly exist, whereas possibilities or essences, whether prior to or abstracted from existence, are imaginary or fictitious, and therefore we cannot look for a reason for existence in them. I answer that neither these essences nor the so-called eternal truths about them are fictitious but exist in a certain region of ideas, if I may so call it, namely, in God himself, who is the source of all essence and of the existence of the rest. The very existence of the actual series of things shows that this is not merely a gratuitous assertion of mine. For since no reason can be found for this series within itself, as I have shown above, but this reason is to be sought in metaphysical necessity or in eternal truth, and since, furthermore, existing things can come into being only from existing things, as I have also explained, it is necessary for eternal truths to have their existence in an absolutely or metaphysically necessary subject, that is, in God, through whom those possibilities which would otherwise be imaginary are (to use an outlandish but expressive word) realized.

And we do in fact observe that everything in the world takes place in accordance with the laws of the eternal truths and not merely geometric but also metaphysical laws; that is, not merely according to material necessities but also according to formal reasons. And not only is this true in general, on the principle which we have just explained—that there should exist a world rather than none and that this world should exist rather than another. (This may be learned in any case from the tendency of possibles toward existence.) But it is true also when we descend to special cases and see the wonderful way in which metaphysical laws of cause, power, and action are present throughout all nature, and how they predominate over the purely geometric laws of matter themselves, as I found to my great admiration when I was explaining the laws of motion. As I have fully explained elsewhere, I was at length compelled to give up the law of the geometric composition of conatuses which I had formerly defended when, as a youth, I was more materialistic.[3]

We therefore have the ultimate reason for the reality of essences as well as existences in one being, which must necessarily be greater, higher, and prior to the world itself, since not only the existing things which compose the world but also all possibilities have their reality through it. But because of the interconnection of all these things, this ultimate reason can be found only in a single source. It is evident, however, that existing things are continuously issuing from this source and are being produced and have been produced by it, since no reason appears why one state of the world should issue from it rather than another, that of yesterday rather than today's. It is clear, too, how God acts not merely physically but freely as well, and how there is in him not only the efficient but the final cause of the world. Thus we have in him the reason not merely for the greatness and power in the world mechanism as already established, but also for the goodness and wisdom exerted in establishing it.

In case anyone may think that this confuses moral perfection or goodness with metaphysical perfection or greatness, and may deny the former while granting the latter, it must be recognized that it follows from what has been said that the world is not only the most perfect naturally or if you prefer, metaphysically—in other words, that that series of things has been produced which actually presents the greatest amount of reality—but also that it is the most perfect morally, because moral perfection is truly natural[4] in minds themselves. Hence the world not only is the most wonderful mechanism but is also, insofar as it consists of minds, the best commonwealth, through which there is conferred on minds as much felicity or joy as possible; it is in this that their natural perfection consists.

You may object, however, that we experience the very opposite of this in the world, for often the very worst things happen to the best; innocent beings, not only beasts but men, are struck down and killed, even tortured. In fact, especially if we consider the government of mankind, the world seems rather a kind of confused chaos than something ordained by a supreme wisdom. So it seems at first sight, I admit, but when we look more deeply, the opposite can be established. A priori it is obvious from the principles which I have already given that the highest perfection possible is obtained for all things and therefore also for minds.

And as the jurisconsults say, it is truly unjust to render a judgment without having studied the whole law. We know but a very small part of an eternity stretching out beyond all measure. How tiny is the memory of the few thousand years which history imparts to us! Yet from such slight experience we venture to judge about the immeasurable and the eternal; as if men born and reared in prison or in the underground salt mines of Sarmatia should think that there is no other light in the world but the wretched torch which is scarcely sufficient to guide their steps. If we look at a very beautiful picture but cover up all of it but a tiny spot, what more will appear in it, no matter how closely we study it, indeed, all the more, the more closely we examine it, than a confused mixture of colors without beauty and without art. Yet when the covering is removed and the whole painting is viewed from a position that suits it, we come to understand that what seemed to be a thoughtless smear on the canvas has really been done with the highest artistry by the creator of the work. And what the eyes experience in painting is experienced by the ears in music. Great composers very often mix dissonances with harmonious chords to stimulate the hearer and to sting him, as it were, so that he becomes concerned about the outcome and is all the more pleased when everything is restored to order. Similarly we may enjoy trivial dangers or the experience of evils from the very sense they give us of our own power or our happiness or our fondness for display. Or again, in witnessing performances of rope-dancing or sword-dancing [*sauts périlleux*], we are delighted by the very fears they arouse, and we playfully half-drop children, pretending to be about to throw them away for much the same reason that the ape carried King Christian of Denmark, when he was still a baby dressed in long clothes, to a rooftop and then, while everyone waited in terror, returned him, as if in play, to his cradle. By the same principle it is insipid always to eat sweets; sharp, sour, and even bitter things should be mixed with them to excite the taste. He who has not tasted the bitter does not deserve the sweet; indeed, he will not appreciate it. This is the very law of enjoyment, that pleasure does not run an even course, for this produces aversion and makes us dull, not joyful.

But what I have said about a part being disordered without destroying the harmony in the whole must not be interpreted as if there is no reason for the parts or as if it were enough for the world to be perfect as a whole, even though the human race should be wretched and there should be no concern in the universe for justice and no account taken of us, as is held by some people who have not made sound judgments about the totality of things. For we must recognize that just as care is taken in the best-ordered republic that individuals shall fare as well as possible, so the universe would not be perfect enough unless as much care is shown for individuals as is consistent with the universal harmony. No better measure for this matter can be set up than the law of justice itself, which dictates that each one shall take part in the perfection of the universe and his own happiness according to the measure of his own virtue and the degree to which his will is moved toward the common good. And in this very thing is fulfilled what we call the charity and the love of God, in which alone the force and power of the Christian religion also consist, according to the opinion of wise theologians. Nor should it seem remarkable that so much respect should be shown to minds in the universe, since they resemble most closely the image of the supreme Author and are related to him not merely as machines to their maker—as are other beings—but also as citizens to their prince. Moreover, they are to endure as long as the universe itself and in some way to express the whole and concentrate it in themselves, so that it can be said that minds are total-parts.

As for the afflictions, especially of good men, however, we must take it as certain that these lead to their greater good and that this is true not only theologically but also naturally. So a seed sown in the earth suffers before it bears fruit. In general, one may say that though afflictions are temporary evils, they are good in effect, for they are short cuts to greater perfection. So in physics the liquids which ferment slowly also are slower to settle, while those in which there is a stronger disturbance settle more promptly, throwing off impurities with greater force. We may well call this stepping back in order to spring forward with greater force [*qu'on recule pour mieux sauter*]. These views must therefore be affirmed not merely as gratifying and comforting but also as most true. And in general, I hold that there is nothing truer than happiness and nothing happier and sweeter than truth.

As the crown of the universal beauty and perfection of the works of God, we must also recognize that the entire universe is involved in a perpetual and most free progress, so that it is always advancing toward greater culture. Thus a great part of our earth has now received cultivation and will receive it more and more. And though it is true that some sections occasionally revert into wilderness or are destroyed and sink back again, this must be understood in the same sense in which I have just explained the nature of afflictions, namely, that this very destruction and decline lead to a better result, so that we somehow gain through our very loss.

To the objection which could be offered, moreover, that if this were so, the world should long since have become a paradise, there is an answer near at hand. Although many substances have already attained great perfection, yet because of the infinite divisibility of the continuum, there always remain in the abyss of things parts which are still asleep. These are to be aroused and developed into something greater and better and in a word, to a better culture. And hence progress never comes to an end.

1 Reading '*a priori*' with the Hanover manuscript. Others read '*a priore*'— 'from an earlier state'.
2 The example apparently alluded to is the catenary, discovered by John and James Bernoulli, and solved by Leibniz, Huygens and others in 1696.
3 The allusion is to the *Theory of Abstract Motion* (1671).
4 *physica*. The extrusion of nature to include human purposes and actions is characteristic of much of Leibniz's writing.

● From G. W. F. Leibniz, *Philosophical Papers and Letters*, trans. Leroy Loemker (2nd ed., Dordrecht, 1969), pp. 486–491.

16

Hume
Miracles

David Hume was born in Edinburgh in 1711, and became a leading figure of
the Scottish Enlightenment. He also spent some years at the Embassy in
Paris, where he encountered the French *philosophes*, and in London as an
Under Secretary of State. In his own lifetime he was perhaps more famous as a
historian than as a philosopher, through his *History of England*. His philosophical works are *A Treatise of Human Nature, An Inquiry concerning Human
Understanding* and *An Inquiry concerning the Principles of Morals*. In them
Hume took the empiricism of Locke and Berkeley a stage further, reaching
sceptical conclusions about, for instance, the existence of a substantial self
and of a necessary causal nexus in nature. He died in 1776.

The essay 'Of Miracles' was originally written while Hume was in his early
twenties, but not published until 1748 as section 10 of the first *Inquiry*. In it
Hume attacks one strand of the conventional eighteenth-century Christian
apologetic, the appeal to prophecy and miracles as vouching for claimed
revelations.

Section X: Of Miracles

Part I

There is, in Dr Tillotson's writings, an argument against the *real
presence*, which is as concise, and elegant, and strong as any argument
can possibly be supposed against a doctrine, so little worthy of a
serious refutation. It is acknowledged on all hands, says that learned
prelate, that the authority, either of the scripture or of tradition, is
founded merely in the testimony of the apostles, who were eye-
witnesses to those miracles of our Saviour, by which he proved his
divine mission. Our evidence, then, for the truth of the *Christian*
religion is less than the evidence for the truth of our senses; because,
even in the first authors of our religion, it was no greater; and it is
evident it must diminish in passing from them to their disciples; nor
can any one rest such confidence in their testimony, as in the immedi-

ate object of his senses. But a weaker evidence can never destroy a stronger; and therefore, were the doctrine of the real presence ever so clearly revealed in scripture, it were directly contrary to the rules of just reasoning to give our assent to it. It contradicts sense, though both the scripture and tradition, on which it is supposed to be built, carry not such evidence with them as sense; when they are considered merely as external evidences, and are not brought home to every one's breast, by the immediate operation of the Holy Spirit.

Nothing is so convenient as a decisive argument of this kind, which must at least *silence* the most arrogant bigotry and superstition, and free us from their impertinent solicitations. I flatter myself, that I have discovered an argument of a like nature, which, if just, will, with the wise and learned, be an everlasting check to all kinds of superstitious delusion, and consequently, will be useful as long as the world endures. For so long, I presume, will the accounts of miracles and prodigies be found in all history, sacred and profane.

Though experience be our only guide in reasoning concerning matters of fact; it must be acknowledged, that this guide is not altogether infallible, but in some cases is apt to lead us into errors. One, who in our climate, should expect better weather in any week of June than in one of December, would reason justly, and conformably to experience; but it is certain, that he may happen, in the event, to find himself mistaken. However, we may observe, that, in such a case, he would have no cause to complain of experience; because it commonly informs us beforehand of the uncertainty, by that contrariety of events, which we may learn from a diligent observation. All effects follow not with like certainty from their supposed causes. Some events are found, in all countries and all ages, to have been constantly conjoined together: Others are found to have been more variable, and sometimes to disappoint our expectations; so that, in our reasonings concerning matter of fact, there are all imaginable degrees of assurance, from the highest certainty to the lowest species of moral evidence.

A wise man, therefore, proportions his belief to the evidence. In such conclusions as are founded on an infallible experience, he expects the event with the last degree of assurance, and regards his past experience as a full *proof* of the future existence of that event. In other cases, he proceeds with more caution: He weighs the opposite experiments: He considers which side is supported by the greater number of experiments: to that side he inclines, with doubt and hesitation; and when at last he fixes his judgement, the evidence exceeds not what we properly call *probability*. All probability, then, supposes an opposition of experiments and observations, where the one side is found to overbalance the other, and to produce a degree of evidence, proportioned to the superiority. A hundred instances or experiments on one side, and fifty on another, afford a doubtful expectation of any event; though a hundred uniform experiments, with only one that is contradictory, reasonably beget a pretty strong degree of assurance. In all cases, we must balance the opposite experiments, where they are opposite, and deduct the smaller number from the greater, in order to know the exact force of the superior evidence.

To apply these principles to a particular instance; we may observe, that there is no species of reasoning more common, more useful, and even necessary to human life, than that which is derived from the testimony of men, and the reports of eye-witnesses and spectators. This species of reasoning, perhaps, one may deny to be founded on the relation of cause and effect. I shall not dispute about a word. It will be sufficient to observe that our assurance in any argument of this kind is derived from no other principle than our observation of the veracity of human testimony, and of the usual conformity of facts to the reports of witnesses. It being a general maxim, that no objects have any discoverable connexion together, and that all the inferences, which we can draw from one to another, are founded merely on our experience of their constant and regular conjunction; it is evident, that we ought not to make an exception to this maxim in favour of human testimony, whose connexion with any event seems, in itself, as little necessary as any other. Were not the memory tenacious to a certain degree, had not men commonly an inclination to truth and a principle of probity; were they not sensible to shame, when detected in a falsehood: Were not these, I say, discovered by *experience* to be qualities, inherent in human nature, we should never repose the least confidence in human testimony. A man delirious, or noted for false-hood and villainy, has no manner of authority with us.

And as the evidence, derived from witnesses and human testimony, is founded on past experience, so it varies with the experience, and is regarded either as a *proof* or a *probability*, according as the conjunction between any particular kind of report and any kind of object has been found to be constant or variable. There are a number of circumstances to be taken into consideration in all judgements of this kind; and the ultimate standard, by which we determine all disputes, that may arise concerning them, is always derived from experience and observation. Where this experience is not entirely uniform on any side, it is attended with an unavoidable contrariety in our judgements, and with the same opposition and mutual destruction of argument as in every other kind of evidence. We frequently hesitate concerning the reports of others. We balance the opposite circumstances, which cause any doubt or uncertainty; and when we discover a superiority on any side, we incline to it; but still with a diminution of assurance, in proportion to the force of its antagonist.

This contrariety of evidence, in the present case, may be derived from several different causes; from the opposition of contrary testimony; from the character or number of the witnesses; from the manner of their delivering their testimony; or from the union of all these circumstances. We entertain a suspicion concerning any matter of fact, when the witnesses contradict each other; when they are but few, or of a doubtful character; when they have an interest in what they affirm; when they deliver their testimony with hesitation, or on the contrary, with too violent asseverations. There are many other particulars of the same kind, which may diminish or destroy the force of any argument, derived from human testimony.

Suppose, for instance, that the fact, which the testimony endeavours to establish, partakes of the extraordinary and the marvellous; in that case, the evidence, resulting from the testimony, admits of a diminution, greater or less, in proportion as the fact is more or less unusual. The reason why we place any credit in witnesses and historians, is not derived from any *connexion*, which we perceive *a priori*, between testimony and reality, but because we are accustomed to find a conformity between them. But when the fact attested is such a one as has seldom fallen under our observation, here is a contest of two opposite experiences; of which the one destroys the other, as far as its force goes, and the superior can only operate on the mind by the force, which remains. The very same principle of experience, which gives us a certain degree of assurance in the testimony of witnesses, gives us also, in this case, another degree of assurance against the fact, which they endeavour to establish; from which contradiction there necessarily arises a counterpoize, and mutual destruction of belief and authority.

I should not believe such a story were it told me by Cato, was a proverbial saying in Rome, even during the lifetime of that philosophical patriot.[1] The incredibility of a fact, it was allowed, might invalidate so great an authority.

The Indian prince, who refused to believe the first relations concerning the effects of frost, reasoned justly; and it naturally required very strong testimony to engage his assent to facts, that arose from a state of nature, with which he was unacquainted, and which bore so little analogy to those events, of which he had had constant and uniform experience. Though they were not contrary to his experience, they were not conformable to it.[2]

But in order to encrease the probability against the testimony of witnesses, let us suppose, that the fact, which they affirm, instead of being only marvellous, is really miraculous; and suppose also, that the testimony considered apart and in itself, amounts to an entire proof;

in that case, there is proof against proof, of which the strongest must prevail, but still with a diminution of its force, in proportion to that of its antagonist.

A miracle is a violation of the laws of nature; and as a firm and unalterable experience has established these laws, the proof against a miracle, from the very nature of the fact, is as entire as any argument from experience can possibly be imagined. Why is it more than probable, that all men must die; that lead cannot, of itself, remain suspended in the air; that fire consumes wood, and is extinguished by water; unless it be, that these events are found agreeable to the laws of nature, and there is required a violation of these laws, or in other words, a miracle to prevent them? Nothing is esteemed a miracle, if it ever happen in the common course of nature. It is no miracle that a man, seemingly in good health, should die on a sudden: because such a kind of death, though more unusual than any other, has yet been frequently observed to happen. But it is a miracle, that a dead man should come to life; because that has never been observed in any age or country. There must, therefore, be a uniform experience against every miraculous event, otherwise the event would not merit that appellation. And as a uniform experience amounts to a proof, there is here a direct and full *proof*, from the nature of the fact, against the existence of any miracle; nor can such a proof be destroyed, or the miracle rendered credible, but by an opposite proof, which is superior.[3]

The plain consequence is (and it is a general maxim worthy of our attention), 'That no testimony is sufficient to establish a miracle, unless the testimony be of such a kind, that its falsehood would be more miraculous, than the fact, which it endeavours to establish; and even in that case there is a mutual destruction of arguments, and the superior only gives us an assurance suitable to that degree of force, which remains, after deducting the inferior'. When anyone tells me, that he saw a dead man restored to life, I immediately consider with myself, whether it be more probable, that this person should either deceive or be deceived, or that the fact, which he relates, should really have happened. I weigh the one miracle against the other; and according to the superiority, which I discover, I pronounce my decision, and always reject the greater miracle. If the falsehood of his testimony would be more miraculous, than the event which he relates; then, and not till then, can he pretend to command my belief or opinion.

Part II

In the foregoing reasoning we have supposed, that the testimony, upon which a miracle is founded, may possibly amount to an entire proof, and that the falsehood of that testimony would be a real prodigy: But it is easy to shew, that we have been a great deal too liberal in our concession, and that there never was a miraculous event established on so full an evidence.

For *first*, there is not to be found, in all history, any miracle attested by a sufficient number of men, of such unquestioned good-sense, education, and learning, as to secure us against all delusion in themselves; of such undoubted integrity, as to place them beyond all suspicion of any design to deceive others; of such credit and reputation in the eyes of mankind, as to have a great deal to lose in case of their being detected in any falsehood; and at the same time, attesting facts performed in such a public manner and in so celebrated a part of the world, as to render the detection unavoidable: All which circumstances are requisite to give us a full assurance in the testimony of men.

Secondly. We may observe in human nature a principle which, if strictly examined, will be found to diminish extremely the assurance, which we might, from human testimony, have, in any kind of prodigy. The maxim, by which we commonly conduct ourselves in our reasonings, is, that the objects, of which we have no experience, resemble those, of which we have; that what we have found to be most usual is always most probable; and that where there is an opposition of arguments, we ought to give the preference to such as are founded on the greatest number of past observations. But though, in proceeding by this rule, we readily reject any fact which is unusual and incredible in an ordinary degree; yet in advancing farther, the mind observes not always the same rule; but when anything is affirmed utterly absurd and miraculous, it rather the more readily admits of such a fact, upon account of that very circumstance, which ought to destroy all its authority. The passion of *surprise* and *wonder*, arising from miracles, being an agreeable emotion, gives a sensible tendency towards the belief of those events, from which it is derived. And this goes so far, that even those who cannot enjoy this pleasure immediately, nor can believe those miraculous events, of which they are informed, yet love to partake of the satisfaction at second-hand or by rebound, and place a pride and delight in exciting the admiration of others.

With what greediness are the miraculous accounts of travellers received, their descriptions of sea and land monsters, their relations of wonderful adventures, strange men, and uncouth manners? But if the spirit of religion join itself to the love of wonder, there is an end of common sense; and human testimony, in these circumstances, loses all pretensions to authority. A religionist may be an enthusiast, and imagine he sees what has no reality: he may know his narrative to be false, and yet persevere in it, with the best intentions in the world, for the sake of promoting so holy a cause: or even where this delusion has not place, vanity, excited by so strong a temptation, operates on him more powerfully than on the rest of mankind in any other circumstances; and self-interest with equal force. His auditors may not have, and commonly have not, sufficient judgement to canvass his evidence: what judgement they have, they renounce by principle, in these sublime and mysterious subjects: or if they were ever so willing to employ it, passion and a heated imagination disturb the regularity of its operations. Their credulity increases his impudence: and his impudence overpowers their credulity.

Eloquence, when at its highest pitch, leaves little room for reason or reflection; but addressing itself entirely to the fancy or the affections, captivates the willing hearers, and subdues their understanding. Happily, this pitch it seldom attains. But what a Tully or a Demosthenes could scarcely effect over a Roman or Athenian audience, every *Capuchin*, every itinerant or stationary teacher can perform over the generality of mankind, and in a higher degree, by touching such gross and vulgar passions.

The many instances of forged miracles, and prophecies, and supernatural events, which, in all ages, have either been detected by contrary evidence, or which detect themselves by their absurdity, prove sufficiently the strong propensity of mankind to the extraordinary and the marvellous, and ought reasonably to beget a suspicion against all relations of this kind. This is our natural way of thinking, even with regard to the most common and most credible events. For instance: There is no kind of report which rises so easily, and spreads so quickly, especially in country places and provincial towns, as those concerning marriages; insomuch that two young persons of equal condition never see each other twice, but the whole neighbourhood immediately join them together. The pleasure of telling a piece of news so interesting, of propagating it, and of being the first reporters of it, spreads the intelligence. And this is so well known, that no man of sense gives attention to these reports, till he finds them confirmed by some greater evidence. Do not the same passions, and others still stronger, incline the generality of mankind to believe and report, with the greatest vehemence and assurance, all religious miracles?

Thirdly. It forms a strong presumption against all supernatural and miraculous relations, that they are observed chiefly to abound among ignorant and barbarous nations; or if a civilized people has ever given admission to any of them, that people will be found to have received them from ignorant and barbarous ancestors, who transmitted them with that inviolable sanction and authority, which always attend received opinions. When we peruse the first histories of all nations, we are apt to imagine ourselves transported into some new world; where the whole frame of nature is disjointed, and every element performs its operations in a different manner, from what it does at present. Battles, revolutions, pestilence, famine and death, are never the effect of those natural causes, which we experience. Prodigies, omens, oracles, judgements, quite obscure the few natural events, that are intermingled with them. But as the former grow thinner every page, in proportion as we advance nearer the enlightened ages, we soon learn, that there is nothing mysterious or supernatural in the case, but that all proceeds from the usual propensity of mankind towards the marvellous, and that, though this inclination may at intervals receive a check from sense and learning, it can never be thoroughly extirpated from human nature.

It is strange, a judicious reader is apt to say, upon the perusal of these wonderful historians, *that such prodigious events never happen in our days.* But it is nothing strange, I hope, that men should lie in all ages. You must surely have seen instances enough of that frailty. You have yourself heard many such marvellous relations started, which, being treated with scorn by all the wise and judicious, have at last been abandoned even by the vulgar. Be assured, that those renowned lies, which have spread and flourished to such a monstrous height, arose from like beginnings; but being sown in a more proper soil, shot up at last into prodigies almost equal to those which they relate.

It was a wise policy in that false prophet, Alexander, who though now forgotten, was once so famous, to lay the first scene of his impostures in Paphlagonia, where, as Lucian tells us, the people were extremely ignorant and stupid, and ready to swallow even the grossest delusion. People at a distance, who are weak enough to think the matter at all worth enquiry, have no opportunity of receiving better information. The stories come magnified to them by a hundred circumstances. Fools are industrious in propagating the imposture; while the wise and learned are contented, in general, to deride its absurdity, without informing themselves of the particular facts, by which it may be distinctly refuted. And thus the impostor above mentioned was enabled to proceed, from his ignorant Paphlagonians, to the enlisting of votaries, even among the Grecian philosophers, and men of the most eminent rank and distinction in Rome: nay, could engage the attention of that sage emperor Marcus Aurelius; so far as to make him trust the success of a military expedition to his delusive prophecies.

The advantages are so great, of starting an imposture among an ignorant people, that, even though the delusion should be too gross to impose on the generality of them (*which, though seldom, is sometimes the case*) it has a much better chance for succeeding in remote countries, than if the first scene had been laid in a city renowned for arts and knowledge. The most ignorant and barbarous of these barbarians carry the report abroad. None of their countrymen have a large correspondence, or sufficient credit and authority to contradict and beat down the delusion. Men's inclination to the marvellous has full opportunity to display itself. And thus a story, which is universally exploded in the place where it was first started, shall pass for certain at a thousand miles distance. But had Alexander fixed his residence at Athens, the philosophers of that renowned mart of learning had immediately spread, throughout the whole Roman empire, their sense of the matter; which, being supported by so great authority, and displayed by all the force of reason and eloquence, had entirely opened the eyes of mankind. It is true; Lucian, passing by chance through Paphlagonia, had an opportunity of performing this good office. But, though much to be wished, it does not always happen, that every Alexander meets with a Lucian, ready to expose and detect his impostures.

I may add as a *fourth* reason, which diminishes the authority of prodigies, that there is no testimony for any, even those which have not been expressly detected, that is not opposed by an infinite number of witnesses; so that not only the miracle destroys the credit of testimony, but the testimony destroys itself. To make this the better understood, let us consider, that, in matters of religion, whatever is different is contrary; and that it is impossible the religions of ancient Rome, of Turkey, of Siam, and of China should, all of them, be established on any solid foundation. Every miracle, therefore, pretended to have been wrought in any of these religions (and all of them abound in miracles), as its direct scope is to establish the particular system to which it is attributed; so has it the same force, though more indirectly, to overthrow every other system. In destroying a rival system, it likewise destroys the credit of those miracles, on which that system was established; so that all the prodigies of different religions are to be regarded as contrary facts, and the evidences of these prodigies, whether weak or strong, as opposite to each other. According to this method of reasoning, when we believe any miracle of Mahomet or his successors, we have for our warrant the testimony of a few barbarous Arabians: And on the other hand, we are to regard the authority of Titus Livius, Plutarch, Tacitus, and, in short, of all the authors and witnesses, Grecian, Chinese, and Roman Catholic, who have related any miracle in their particular religion; I say, we are to regard their testimony in the same light as if they had mentioned that Mahometan miracle, and had in express terms contradicted it, with the same certainty as they have for the miracle they relate. This argument may appear over subtile and refined; but is not in reality different from the reasoning of a judge, who supposes, that the credit of two witnesses, maintaining a crime against any one, is destroyed by the testimony of two others, who affirm him to have been two hundred leagues distant, at the same instant when the crime is said to have been committed.

One of the best attested miracles in all profane history, is that which Tacitus reports of Vespasian, who cured a blind man in Alexandria, by means of his spittle, and a lame man by the mere touch of his foot; in obedience to a vision of the god Serapis, who had enjoined them to have recourse to the Emperor, for these miraculous cures. The story may be seen in that fine historian;[4] where every circumstance seems to add weight to the testimony, and might be displayed at large with all the force of argument and eloquence, if any one were now concerned to enforce the evidence of that exploded and idolatrous superstition. The gravity, solidity, age, and probity of so great an emperor, who, through the whole course of his life, conversed in a familiar manner with his friends and courtiers, and never affected those extraordinary airs of divinity assumed by Alexander and Demetrius. The historian, a contemporary writer, noted for candour and veracity, and withal, the greatest and most penetrating genius, perhaps, of all antiquity; and so free from any tendency to credulity, that he even lies under the contrary imputation, of atheism and profaneness: The persons, from whose authority he related the miracle, of established character for judgement and veracity, as we may well presume; eye-witnesses of the fact, and confirming their testimony, after the Flavian family was despoiled of the empire, and could no longer give any reward, as the price of a lie. *Utrumque, qui interfuere, nunc quoque memorant, postquam nullum mendacio pretium.* To which if we add the public nature of the facts, as related, it will appear, that no evidence can well be supposed stronger for so gross and so palpable a falsehood.

There is also a memorable story related by Cardinal de Retz, which may well deserve our consideration. When that intriguing politician fled into Spain, to avoid the persecution of his enemies, he passed through Saragossa, the capital of Arragon, where he was shewn, in the cathedral, a man, who had served seven years as a door-keeper, and was well known to every body in town, that had ever paid his devotions at that church. He had been seen, for so long a time, wanting a leg; but recovered that limb by the rubbing of holy oil upon the stump; and the cardinal assures us that he saw him with two legs. This miracle was vouched by all the canons of the church; and the whole company in town were appealed to for a confirmation of the fact; whom the cardinal found, by their zealous devotion, to be thorough believers of the miracle. Here the relater was also contemporary to the supposed prodigy, of an incredulous and libertine character, as well as of great genius; the miracle of so *singular* a nature as could scarcely admit of a counterfeit, and the witnesses very numerous, and all of them, in a manner, spectators of the fact, to which they gave their testimony. And what adds mightily to the force of the evidence, and may double our surprise on this occasion, is, that the cardinal himself, who relates the story, seems not to give any credit to it, and consequently cannot be suspected of any concurrence in the holy fraud. He considered justly, that it was not requisite, in order to reject a fact of this nature, to be able accurately to disprove the testimony, and to trace its falsehood, through all the circumstances of knavery and credulity which produced it. He knew, that, as this was commonly altogether impossible at any small distance of time and place; so was it extremely difficult, even where one was immediately present, by reason of the bigotry, ignorance, cunning, and roguery of a great part of mankind. He therefore concluded, like a just reasoner, that such an evidence carried falsehood upon the very face of it, and that a miracle, supported by any human testimony, was more properly a subject of derision than of argument.

There surely never was a greater number of miracles ascribed to one person, than those, which were lately said to have been wrought in France upon the tomb of Abbé Paris, the famous Jansenist, with whose sanctity the people were so long deluded. The curing of the sick, giving hearing to the deaf, and sight to the blind, were every where talked of as the usual effects of that holy sepulchre. But what is more extraordinary; many of the miracles were immediately proved upon the spot, before judges of unquestioned integrity, attested by witnesses of credit and distinction, in a learned age, and on the most eminent theatre that is now in the world. Nor is this all: a relation of them was published and dispersed every where; nor were the *Jesuits*, though a learned body, supported by the civil magistrate, and determined enemies to those opinions, in whose favour the miracles were said to have been wrought, ever able distinctly to refute or detect them. Where shall we find such a number of circumstances, agreeing to the corroboration of one fact? And what have we to oppose to such a cloud of witnesses, but the absolute impossibility or miraculous nature of the events, which they relate? And this surely, in the eyes of all reasonable people, will alone be regarded as a sufficient refutation.

Is the consequence just, because some human testimony has the utmost force and authority in some cases, when it relates the battle of Philippi or Pharsalia for instance; that therefore all kinds of testimony must, in all cases, have equal force and authority? Suppose that the Caesarean and Pompeian factions had, each of them, claimed the victory in these battles, and that the historians of each party had uniformly ascribed the advantage to their own side; how could mankind, at this distance, have been able to determine between them? The contrariety is equally strong between the miracles related by Herodotus or Plutarch, and those delivered by Mariana, Bede, or any monkish historian.

The wise lend a very academic faith to every report which favours the passion of the reporter; whether it magnifies his country, his family, or himself, or in any other way strikes in with his natural inclinations and propensities. But what greater temptation than to appear a missionary, a prophet, an ambassador from heaven? Who would not encounter many dangers and difficulties, in order to attain so sublime a character? Or if, by the help of vanity and a heated imagination, a man has first made a convert of himself, and entered seriously into the delusion; who ever scruples to make use of pious frauds, in support of so holy and meritorious a cause?

The smallest spark may here kindle into the greatest flame; because the materials are always prepared for it. The *avidum genus auricularum*, the gazing populace, receive greedily, without examination, whatever sooths superstition, and promotes wonder.

How many stories of this nature have, in all ages, been detected and exploded in their infancy? How many more have been celebrated for a time, and have afterwards sunk into neglect and oblivion? Where such reports, therefore, fly about, the solution of the phenomenon is obvious; and we judge in conformity to regular experience and observation, when we account for it by the known and natural principles of credulity and delusion. And shall we, rather than have a recourse to so natural a solution, allow of a miraculous violation of the most established laws of nature?

I need not mention the difficulty of detecting a falsehood in any private or even public history, at the place, where it is said to happen; much more when the scene is removed to ever so small a distance. Even a court of judicature, with all the authority, accuracy, and judgement, which they can employ, find themselves often at a loss to distinguish between truth and falsehood in the most recent actions. But the matter never comes to any issue, if trusted to the common method of altercations and debate and flying rumours; especially when men's passions have taken part on either side.

In the infancy of new religions, the wise and learned commonly esteem the matter too inconsiderable to deserve their attention or regard. And when afterwards they would willingly detect the cheat, in order to undeceive the deluded multitude, the season is now past, and the records and witnesses, which might clear up the matter, have perished beyond recovery.

No means of detection remain, but those which must be drawn from the very testimony itself of the reporters: and these, though always sufficient with the judicious and knowing, are commonly too fine to fall under the comprehension of the vulgar.

Upon the whole, then, it appears, that no testimony for any kind of miracle has ever amounted to a probability, much less to a proof; and that, even supposing it amounted to a proof, it would be opposed by another proof; derived from the very nature of the fact, which it would endeavour to establish. It is experience only, which gives authority to human testimony; and it is the same experience, which assures us of the laws of nature. When, therefore, these two kinds of experience are contrary, we have nothing to do but substract the one from the other, and embrace an opinion, either on one side or the other, with that assurance which arises from the remainder. But according to the principle here explained, this substraction, with regard to all popular religions, amounts to an entire annihilation; and therefore we may establish it as a maxim, that no human testimony can have such force as to prove a miracle, and make it a just foundation for any such system of religion.

I beg the limitations here made may be remarked, when I say, that a miracle can never be proved, so as to be the foundation of a system of religion. For I own, that otherwise, there may possibly be miracles, or violations of the usual course of nature, of such a kind as to admit of proof from human testimony; though, perhaps, it will be impossible to find any such in all the records of history. Thus, suppose, all authors, in all languages, agree, that, from the first of January 1600, there was a total darkness over the whole earth for eight days: suppose that the tradition of this extraordinary event is still strong and lively among the people: that all travellers, who return from foreign countries, bring us accounts of the same tradition, without the least variation or contradiction: it is evident, that our present philosophers, instead of doubting the fact, ought to receive it as certain, and ought to search for the causes whence it might be derived. The decay, corruption, and dissolution of nature, is an event rendered probable by so many analogies, that any phenomenon, which seems to have a tendency towards that catastrophe, comes within the reach of human testimony, if that testimony be very extensive and uniform.

But suppose, that all the historians who treat of England, should agree, that, on the first of January 1600, Queen Elizabeth died; that both before and after her death she was seen by her physicians and the whole court, as is usual with persons of her rank; that her successor was acknowledged and proclaimed by the parliament; and that, after being interred a month, she again appeared, resumed the throne, and governed England for three years: I must confess that I should be surprised at the concurrence of so many odd circumstances, but should not have the least inclination to believe so miraculous an event. I should not doubt of her pretended death, and of those other public circumstances that followed it: I should only assert it to have been pretended, and that it neither was, nor possibly could be real. You would in vain object to me the difficulty, and almost impossibility of deceiving the world in an affair of such consequence; the wisdom and solid judgement of that renowned queen; with the little or no advantage which she could reap from so poor an artifice: All this might astonish me; but I would still reply, that the knavery and folly of men are such common phenomena, that I should rather believe the most extraordinary events to arise from their concurrence, than admit of so signal a violation of the laws of nature.

But should this miracle be ascribed to any new system of religion; men, in all ages, have been so much imposed on by ridiculous stories of that kind, that this very circumstance would be a full proof of a cheat, and sufficient, with all men of sense, not only to make them reject the fact, but even reject it without farther examination. Though the Being to whom the miracle is ascribed, be, in this case, Almighty, it does not, upon that account, become a whit more probable; since it is impossible for us to know the attributes or actions of such a Being, otherwise than from the experience which we have of his productions, in the usual course of nature. This still reduces us to past observation, and obliges us to compare the instances of the violation of truth in the testimony of men, with those of the violation of the laws of nature by miracles, in order to judge which of them is most likely and probable. As the violations of truth are more common in the testimony concerning religious miracles, than in that concerning any other matter of fact; this must diminish very much the authority of the former testimony, and make us form a general resolution, never to lend any attention to it, with whatever specious pretence it may be covered.

Lord Bacon seems to have embraced the same principles of reasoning. 'We ought', says he, 'to make a collection or particular history of all monsters and prodigious births or productions, and in a word of every thing new, rare, and extraordinary in nature. But this must be done with the most severe scrutiny, lest we depart from truth. Above all, every relation must be considered as suspicious, which depends in any degree upon religion, as the prodigies of Livy: And no less so, every thing that is to be found in the writers of natural magic or alchimy, or such authors, who seem, all of them, to have an unconquerable appetite for falsehood and fable.'[5]

I am the better pleased with the method of reasoning here delivered, as I think it may serve to confound those dangerous friends or disguised enemies to the *Christian Religion*, who have undertaken to defend it by the principles of human reason. Our most holy religion is founded on *Faith*, not on reason; and it is a sure method of exposing it to put it to such a trial as it is, by no means, fitted to endure. To make this more evident, let us examine those miracles, related in scripture; and not to lose ourselves in too wide a field, let us confine ourselves to such as we find in the *Pentateuch*, which we shall examine, according to the principles of these pretended Christians, not as the word or testimony of God himself, but as the production of a mere human writer and historian. Here then we are first to consider a book, presented to us by a barbarous and ignorant people, written in an age when they were still more barbarous, and in all probability long after the facts which it relates, corroborated by no concurring testimony, and resembling those fabulous accounts, which every nation gives of its origin. Upon reading this book, we find it full of prodigies and miracles. It gives an account of a state of the world and of human nature entirely different from the present: Of our fall from that state: Of the age of man, extended to near a thousand years; of the destruction of the world by a deluge: Of the arbitrary choice of one people, as the favourites of heaven; and that people the countrymen of the author: Of their deliverance from bondage by prodigies the most astonishing imaginable: I desire any one to lay his hand upon his heart, and after a serious consideration declare, whether he thinks that the falsehood of such a book, supported by such a testimony, would be more extraordinary and miraculous than all the miracles it relates; which is, however, necessary to make it be received, according to the measures of probability above established.

What we have said of miracles may be applied, without any variation, to prophecies; and indeed, all prophecies are real miracles, and as such only, can be admitted as proofs of any revelation. If it did not exceed the capacity of human nature to foretell future events, it would be absurd to employ any prophecy as an argument for a divine mission or authority from heaven. So that, upon the whole, we may conclude, that the *Christian Religion* not only was at first attended with miracles, but even at this day cannot be believed by any reasonable person without one. Mere reason is insufficient to convince us of its veracity: And whoever is moved by *Faith* to assent to it, is conscious of a continued miracle in his own person, which subverts all the principles of his understanding, and gives him a determination to believe what is most contrary to custom and experience.

1 Plutarch, in vita Catonis.
2 No Indian, it is evident, could have experience that water did not freeze in cold climates. This is placing nature in a situation quite unknown to him; and it is impossible for him to tell *a priori* what will result from it. It is making a new experiment, the consequence of which is always uncertain. One may sometimes conjecture from analogy what will follow; but still this is but conjecture. And it must be confessed, that, in the present case of freezing, the event follows contrary to the rules of analogy, and is such as a rational Indian would not look for. The operations of cold upon water are not gradual, according to the degrees of cold; but whenever it comes to the freezing point, the water passes in a moment, from the utmost liquidity to perfect hardness. Such an event, therefore, may be denominated *extraordinary*, and requires a pretty strong testimony, to render it credible to people in a warm climate: But still it is not *miraculous*, nor contrary to uniform experience of the course of nature in cases where all the circumstances are the same. The inhabitants of Sumatra have always seen water fluid in their own climate, and the freezing of their rivers ought to be deemed a prodigy: But they never saw water in Muscovy during the winter; and therefore they cannot reasonably be positive what would there be the consequence.
3 Sometimes an event may not, *in itself*, seem to be contrary to the laws of nature, and yet, if it were real, it might, by reason of some circumstances, be denominated a miracle; because, in *fact*, it is contrary to these laws. Thus if a person, claiming a divine authority, should command a sick person to be well, a healthful man to fall down dead, the clouds to pour rain, the winds to blow, in short, should order many natural events, which immediately follow upon his command; these might justly be esteemed miracles, because they are really, in this case, contrary to the laws of nature. For if any suspicion remain, that the event and command concurred by accident, there is no miracle and no transgression of the laws of nature. If this suspicion be removed, there is evidently a miracle, and a transgression of these laws; because nothing can be more contrary to nature than that the voice or command of a man should have such an influence. A miracle may be accurately defined, *a transgression of a law of nature by a particular volition of the Deity, or by the interposition of some invisible agent.* A miracle may either be discoverable by men or not. This alters not its nature and essence. The raising of a house or ship into the air is a visible miracle. The raising of a feather, when the wind wants ever so little of a force requisite for that purpose, is as real a miracle, though not so sensible with regard to us.
4 Hist. lib. iv. cap. 81. Suetonius gives nearly the same account *in vita* Vesp.
5 Nov. Org. lib. ii. aph. 29.

• From *An Inquiry concerning Human Understanding.* The long note which Hume appends about the accounts of the miracles at the tomb of the Abbé Paris is omitted here.

17

Hume
The Problem of Evil

The *Dialogues concerning Natural Religion* were written about 1751, revised
shortly before Hume's death in 1776 and published posthumously in 1779.
Much of them consists of an attack on arguments for God's existence from
design in the world, the favourite kind of theistic argument in the eighteenth
century. Hume's discussion of evil in *Dialogues* X–XI should be regarded
primarily as part of this attack, for he considers that the evil in the world
obstructs any inference to the existence of an almighty and perfectly good
god.

There are three disputants in the *Dialogues*, besides the narrator, Pamphi-
lus: Philo, whose sceptical position seems closest to that of Hume himself;
Cleanthes, who represents the standpoint of those who seek to establish the
existence of God *a posteriori* from evidence of design in the world; and Demea,
the spokesman for an *a priori* approach to theology, who is introduced as
expounding 'rigid, inflexible orthodoxy'.

Part 10

It is my opinion, I own, replied Demea, that each man feels, in a
manner, the truth of religion within his own breast; and, from a
consciousness of his imbecility and misery rather than from any
reasoning, is led to seek protection from that Being on whom he and
all nature are dependent. So anxious or so tedious are even the best
scenes of life that futurity is still the object of all our hopes and fears.
We incessantly look forward and endeavour, by prayers, adoration.
and sacrifice, to appease those unknown powers whom we find, by
experience, so able to afflict and oppress us. Wretched creatures that
we are! What resource for us amidst the innumerable ills of life did not
religion suggest some methods of atonement, and appease those terrors with which we are incessantly agitated and tormented?

I am indeed persuaded, said Philo, that the best and indeed the only
method of bringing everyone to a due sense of religion is by just
representations of the misery and wickedness of men. And for that
purpose a talent of eloquence and strong imagery is more requisite

than that of reasoning and argument. For is it necessary to prove what everyone feels within himself? It is only necessary to make us feel it, if possible, more intimately and sensibly.

The people, indeed, replied Demea, are sufficiently convinced of this great and melancholy truth. The miseries of life, the unhappiness of man, the general corruptions of our nature, the unsatisfactory enjoyment of pleasures, riches, honours—these phrases have become almost proverbial in all languages. And who can doubt of what all men declare from their own immediate feeling and experience?

In this point, said Philo, the learned are perfectly agreed with the vulgar; and in all letters, *sacred* and *profane*, the topic of human misery has been insisted on with the most pathetic eloquence that sorrow and melancholy could inspire. The poets, who speak from sentiment, without a system, and whose testimony has therefore the more authority, abound in images of this nature. From Homer down to Dr Young, the whole inspired tribe have ever been sensible that no other representation of things would suit the feeling and observation of each individual.

As to authorities, replied Demea, you need not seek them. Look round this library of Cleanthes. I shall venture to affirm that, except authors of particular sciences, such as chemistry or botany, who have no occasion to treat of human life, there is scarce one of those innumerable writers from whom the sense of human misery has not, in some passage or other, extorted a complaint and confession of it. At least, the chance is entirely on that side; and no one author has ever, so far as I can recollect, been so extravagant as to deny it.

There you must excuse me, said Philo: Leibniz has denied it; and is perhaps the first[1] who ventured upon so bold and paradoxical an opinion; at least, the first who made it essential to his philosophical system.

And by being the first, replied Demea, might he not have been sensible of his error? For is this a subject in which philosophers can propose to make discoveries especially in so late an age? And can any man hope by a simple denial (for the subject scarcely admits of reasoning) to bear down the united testimony of mankind, founded on sense and consciousness?

And why should man, added he, pretend to an exemption from the lot of all other animals? The whole earth, believe me, Philo, is cursed and polluted. A perpetual war is kindled amongst all living creatures. Necessity, hunger, want stimulate the strong and courageous; fear, anxiety, terror agitate the weak and infirm. The first entrance into life gives anguish to the new-born infant and to its wretched parent; weakness, impotence, distress attend each stage of that life, and it is, at last, finished in agony and horror.

Observe, too, says Philo, the curious artifices of nature in order to embitter the life of every living being. The stronger prey upon the weaker and keep them in perpetual terror and anxiety. The weaker, too, in their turn, often prey upon the stronger, and vex and molest them without relaxation. Consider that innumerable race of insects, which either are bred on the body of each animal or, flying about, infix their stings in him. These insects have others still less than themselves which torment them. And thus on each hand, before and behind, above and below, every animal is surrounded with enemies which incessantly seek his misery and destruction.

Man alone, said Demea, seems to be, in part, an exception to this rule. For by combination in society he can easily master lions, tigers, and bears, whose greater strength and agility naturally enable them to prey upon him.

On the contrary, it is here chiefly, cried Philo, that the uniform and equal maxims of nature are most apparent. Man, it is true, can, by combination, surmount all his *real* enemies and become master of the whole animal creation; but does he not immediately raise up to himself *imaginary* enemies, the demons of his fancy, who haunt him with superstitious terrors and blast every enjoyment of life? His pleasure, as he imagines, becomes in their eyes a crime; his food and repose give them umbrage and offence; his very sleep and dreams furnish new materials to anxious fear; and even death, his refuge from every other ill, presents only the dread of endless and innumerable woes. Nor does the wolf molest more the timid flock than superstition does the anxious breast of wretched mortals.

Besides, consider, Demea: This very society by which we surmount those wild beasts, our natural enemies, what new enemies does it not raise to us? What woe and misery does it not occasion? Man is the greatest enemy of man. Oppression, injustice, contempt, contumely, violence, sedition, war, calumny, treachery, fraud—by these they mutually torment each other, and they would soon dissolve that society which they had formed were it not for the dread of still greater ills which must attend their separation.

But though these external insults, said Demea, from animals, from men, from all the elements, which assault us form a frightful catalogue of woes, they are nothing in comparison of those which arise within ourselves, from the distempered condition of our mind and body. How many lie under the lingering torment of diseases? Hear the pathetic enumeration of the great poet.

> Intestine stone and ulcer, colic-pangs,
> Demoniac frenzy, moping melancholy,
> And moon-struck madness, pining atrophy,

> Marasmus, and wide-wasting pestilence.
> Dire was the tossing, deep the groans: *Despair*
> Tended the sick, busiest from couch to couch.
> And over them triumphant *Death* his dart
> Shook: but delay'd to strike, thought oft invok'd
> With vows, as their chief good and final hope.[2]

The disorders of the mind, continued Demea, though more secret, are not perhaps less dismal and vexatious. Remorse, shame, anguish, rage, disappointment, anxiety, fear, dejection, despair—who has ever passed through life without cruel inroads from these tormentors? How many have scarcely ever felt any better sensations? Labour and poverty, so abhorred by everyone, are the certain lot of the far greater number; and those few privileged persons who enjoy ease and opulence never reach contentment or true felicity. All the goods of life united would not make a very happy man, but all the ills united would make a wretch indeed; and any one of them almost (and who can be free from every one), nay, often the absence of one good (and who can possess all) is sufficient to render life ineligible.

Were a stranger to drop on a sudden into this world, I would show him, as a specimen of its ills, a hospital full of diseases, a prison crowded with malefactors and debtors, a field of battle strewed with carcasses, a fleet foundering in the ocean, a nation languishing under tyranny, famine, or pestilence. To turn the gay side of life to him and give him a notion of its pleasures—whither should I conduct him? To a ball, to an opera, to court? He might justly think that I was only showing him a diversity of distress and sorrow.

There is no evading such striking instances, said Philo, but by apologies which still further aggravate the charge. Why have all men, I ask, in all ages, complained incessantly of the miseries of life? ... They have no just reason, says one: These complaints proceed only from their discontented, repining, anxious disposition. ... And can there possibly, I reply, be a more certain foundation of misery than such a wretched temper?

But if they were really as unhappy as they pretend, says my antagonist, why do they remain in life? ...

> Not satisfied with life, afraid of death.

This is the secret chain, say I, that holds us. We are terrified, not bribed to the continuance of our existence.

It is only a false delicacy, he may insist, which a few refined spirits indulge, and which has spread these complaints among the whole race of mankind. ... And what is this delicacy, I ask, which you blame? Is it anything but a greater sensibility to all the pleasures and pains of life? And if the man of a delicate, refined temper, by being so much more alive than the rest of the world, is only so much more unhappy, what judgement must we form in general of human life?

Let men remain at rest, says our adversary, and they will be easy. They are willing artificers of their own misery. ... No! reply I: An anxious languor follows their repose; disappointment, vexation, trouble, their activity and ambition.

I can observe something like what you mention in some others, replied Cleanthes; but I confess I feel little or nothing of it in myself, and hope that it is not so common as you represent it.

If you feel not human misery yourself, cried Demea, I congratulate you on so happy a singularity. Others, seemingly the most prosperous, have not been ashamed to vent their complaints in the most melancholy strains. Let us attend to the great, the fortunate emperor, Charles V, when, tired with human grandeur, he resigned all his extensive dominions into the hands of his son. In the last harangue which he made on that memorable occasion, he publicly avowed *that the greatest prosperities which he had ever enjoyed had been mixed with so many adversities that he might truly say he had never enjoyed any satisfaction or contentment.* But did the retired life in which he sought for shelter afford him any greater happiness? If we may credit his son's account, his repentance commenced the very day of his resignation.

Cicero's fortune, from small beginnings, rose to the greatest lustre and renown; yet what pathetic complaints of the ills of life do his familiar letters, as well as philosophical discourses, contain? And suitably to his own experience, he introduces Cato, the great, the fortunate Cato protesting in his old age that had he a new life in his offer he would reject the present.

Ask yourself, ask any of your acquaintance, whether they would live over again the last ten or twenty years of their life. No! but the next twenty, they say, will be better:

> And from the dregs of life, hope to receive
> What the first sprightly running could not give.[3]

Thus, at last, they find (such is the greatness of human misery, it reconciles even contradictions) that they complain at once of the shortness of life and of its vanity and sorrow.

And it is possible, Cleanthes, said Philo, that after all these reflections, and infinitely more which might be suggested, you can still persevere in your anthropomorphism, and assert the moral attributes of the Deity, his justice, benevolence, mercy, and rectitude, to be of the same nature with these virtues in human creatures? His power, we allow, is infinite; whatever he wills is executed; but neither man nor any other animal is happy; therefore, he does not will their happiness.

His wisdom is infinite; he is never mistaken in choosing the means to any end; but the course of nature tends not to human or animal felicity; therefore, it is not established for that purpose. Through the whole compass of human knowledge there are no inferences more certain and infallible than these. In what respect, then, do his benevolence and mercy resemble the benevolence and mercy of men? Epicurus' old questions are yet unanswered. Is he willing to prevent evil, but not able? then is he impotent. Is he able, but not willing? then is he malevolent. Is he both able and willing? whence then is evil?

You ascribe, Cleanthes (and I believe justly), a purpose and intention to nature. But what, I beseech you, is the object of that curious artifice and machinery which she has displayed in all animals—the preservation alone of individuals, and propagation of the species? It seems enough for her purpose, if such a rank be barely upheld in the universe, without any care or concern for the happiness of the members that compose it. No resource for this purpose: no machinery in order merely to give pleasure or ease: no fund of pure joy and contentment: no indulgence without some want or necessity accompanying it. At least, the few phenomena of this nature are overbalanced by opposite phenomena of still greater importance.

Our sense of music, harmony, and indeed beauty of all kinds, gives satisfaction, without being absolutely necessary to the preservation and propagation of the species. But what racking pains, on the other hand, arise from gouts, gravels, megrims, toothaches, rheumatisms, where the injury to the animal machinery is either small or incurable? Mirth, laughter, play, frolic seem gratuitous satisfactions which have no further tendency; spleen, melancholy, discontent, superstition are pains of the same nature. How then does the divine benevolence display itself, in the sense of you anthropomorphites? None but we mystics, as you were pleased to call us, can account for this strange mixture of phenomena, by deriving it from attributes infinitely perfect but incomprehensible.

And have you, at last, said Cleanthes smiling, betrayed your intentions, Philo? Your long agreement with Demea did indeed a little surprise me, but I find you were all the while erecting a concealed battery against me. And I must confess that you have now fallen upon a subject worthy of your noble spirit of opposition and controversy. If you can make out the present point, and prove mankind to be unhappy or corrupted, there is an end at once of all religion. For to what purpose establish the natural attributes of the Deity, while the moral are still doubtful and uncertain?

You take umbrage very easily, replied Demea, at opinions the most innocent and the most generally received, even amongst the religious and devout themselves; and nothing can be more surprising than to find a topic like this—concerning the wickedness and misery of man—charged with no less than atheism and profaneness. Have not all pious divines and preachers who have indulged their rhetoric on so fertile a subject; have they not easily, I say, given a solution of any difficulties which may attend it? This world is but a point in comparison of the universe; this life but a moment in comparison of eternity. The present evil phenomena, therefore, are rectified in other regions, and in some future period of existence. And the eyes of men, being then opened to larger views of things, see the whole connection of general laws, and trace, with adoration, the benevolence and rectitude of the Deity through all the mazes and intricacies of his providence.

No! replied Cleanthes, no! These arbitrary suppositions can never be admitted, contrary to matter of fact, visible and uncontroverted. Whence can any cause be known but from its known effects? Whence can any hypothesis be proved but from the apparent phenomena? To establish one hypothesis upon another is building entirely in the air; and the utmost we ever attain by these conjectures and fictions is to ascertain the bare possibility of our opinion, but never can we, upon such terms, establish its reality.

The only method of supporting divine benevolence—and it is what I willingly embrace—is to deny absolutely the misery and wickedness of man. Your representations are exaggerated; your melancholy views mostly fictitious; your inferences contrary to fact and experience. Health is more common than sickness; pleasure than pain; happiness than misery. And for one vexation which we meet with, we attain, upon computation, a hundred enjoyments.

Admitting your position, replied Philo, which yet is extremely doubtful, you must at the same time allow that, if pain be less frequent than pleasure, it is infinitely more violent and durable. One hour of it is often able to outweigh a day, a week, a month of our common insipid enjoyments; and how many days, weeks, and months are passed by several in the most acute torments? Pleasure, scarcely in one instance, is ever able to reach ecstasy and rapture; and in no one instance can it continue for any time at its highest pitch and altitude. The spirits evaporate, the nerves relax, the fabric is disordered, and the enjoyment quickly degenerates into fatigue and uneasiness. But pain often, good God, how often! rises to torture and agony; and the longer it continues, it becomes still more genuine agony and torture. Patience is exhausted, courage languishes, melancholy seizes us, and nothing terminates our misery but the removal of its cause or another event which is the sole cure of all evil, but which, from our natural folly, we regard with still greater horror and consternation.

But not to insist upon these topics, continued Philo, though most obvious, certain, and important, I must use the freedom to admonish you, Cleanthes, that you have put the controversy upon a most dangerous issue, and are unawares introducing a total scepticism into the most essential articles of natural and revealed theology. What! no method of fixing a just foundation for religion unless we allow the happiness of human life, and maintain a continued existence even in this world, with all our present pains, infirmities, vexations, and follies, to be eligible and desirable! But this is contrary to everyone's feeling and experience; it is contrary to an authority so established as nothing can subvert. No decisive proofs can ever be produced against this authority; nor is it possible for you to compute, estimate, and compare all the pains and all the pleasures in the lives of all men and of all animals; and thus, by your resting the whole system of religion on a point which, from its very nature, must forever be uncertain, you tacitly confess that that system is equally uncertain.

But allowing you what never will be believed, at least, what you never possibly can prove, that animal or, at least, human happiness in this life exceeds its misery, you have yet done nothing; for this is not, by any means, what we expect from infinite power, infinite wisdom, and infinite goodness. Why is there any misery at all in the world? Not by chance, surely. From some cause then. Is it from the intention of the Deity? But he is perfectly benevolent. Is it contrary to his intention? But he is almighty. Nothing can shake the solidity of this reasoning, so short, so clear, so decisive, except we assert that these subjects exceed all human capacity, and that our common measures of truth and falsehood are not applicable to them—a topic which I have all along insisted on, but which you have, from the beginning, rejected with scorn and indignation.

But I will be contented to retire still from this intrenchment, for I deny that you can ever force me in it. I will allow that pain or misery in man is *compatible* with infinite power and goodness in the Deity, even in your sense of these attributes: what are you advanced by all these concessions? A mere possible compatibility is not sufficient. You must *prove* these pure, unmixed and uncontrollable attributes from the present mixed and confused phenomena, and from these alone. A hopeful undertaking! Were the phenomena ever so pure and unmixed, yet, being finite, they would be insufficient for that purpose. How much more, where they are also so jarring and discordant!

Here, Cleanthes, I find myself at ease in my argument. Here I triumph. Formerly, when we argued concerning the natural attributes of intelligence and design, I needed all my sceptical and metaphysical subtilty to elude your grasp. In many views of the universe and of its parts, particularly the latter, the beauty and fitness of final causes strike us with such irresistible force that all objections appear (what I believe they really are) mere cavils and sophisms; nor can we then imagine how it was ever possible for us to repose any weight on them. But there is no view of human life or of the condition of mankind from which, without the greatest violence, we can infer the moral attributes or learn that infinite benevolence, conjoined with infinite power and infinite wisdom, which we must discover by the eyes of faith alone. It is your turn now to tug the labouring oar, and to support your philosophical subtilties against the dictates of plain reason and experience.

Part 11

I scruple not to allow, said Cleanthes, that I have been apt to suspect the frequent repetition of the word *infinite*, which we meet with in all theological writers, to savour more of panegyric than of philosophy, and that any purposes of reasoning, and even of religion, would be better served were we to rest contented with more accurate and more moderate expressions. The terms *admirable, excellent, superlatively great, wise,* and *holy*—these sufficiently fill the imaginations of men, and anything beyond, besides that it leads into absurdities, has no influence on the affections or sentiments. Thus, in the present subject, if we abandon all human analogy, as seems your intention, Demea, I am afraid we abandon all religion and retain no conception of the great object of our adoration. If we preserve human analogy, we must forever find it impossible to reconcile any mixture of evil in the universe with infinite attributes; much less can we ever prove the latter from the former. But supposing the Author of Nature to be finitely perfect, though far exceeding mankind, a satisfactory account may then be given of natural and moral evil, and every untoward phenomenon be explained and adjusted. A less evil may then be chosen in order to avoid a greater; inconveniences be submitted to in order to reach a desirable end; and, in a word, benevolence, regulated by wisdom and limited by necessity, may produce just such a world as the present. You, Philo, who are so prompt at starting views and reflections and analogies, I would gladly hear, at length, without interruption, your opinion of this new theory; and if it deserve our attention, we may afterwards, at more leisure, reduce it into form.

My sentiments, replied Philo, are not worth being made a mystery of; and, therefore, without any ceremony, I shall deliver what occurs to me with regard to the present subject. It must, I think, be allowed that, if a very limited intelligence whom we shall suppose utterly unacquainted with the universe were assured that it were the production of a very good, wise, and powerful being, however finite, he would, from his conjectures, form *beforehand* a different notion of it from what we find it to be by experience; nor would he ever imagine, merely from these attributes of the cause of which he is informed, that the effect could be so full of vice and misery and disorder, as it appears in this life. Supposing now that this person were brought into the world, still assured that it was the workmanship of such a sublime and benevolent being, he might, perhaps, be surprised at the disappointment, but would never retract his former belief if founded on any very solid argument, since such a limited intelligence must be sensible of his own blindness and ignorance, and must allow that there may be many solutions of those phenomena which will forever escape his comprehension. But supposing, which is the real case with regard to man, that this creature is not antecedently convinced of a supreme intelligence, benevolent, and powerful, but is left to gather such a belief from the appearances of things—this entirely alters the case, nor will he ever find any reason for such a conclusion. He may be fully convinced of the narrow limits of his understanding, but this will not help him in forming an inference concerning the goodness of superior powers, since he must form that inference from what he knows, not from what he is ignorant of. The more you exaggerate his weakness and ignorance, the more diffident you render him, and give him the greater suspicion that such subjects are beyond the reach of his faculties. You are obliged, therefore, to reason with him merely from the known phenomena, and to drop every arbitrary supposition or conjecture.

Did I show you a house or palace where there was not one apartment convenient or agreeable; where the windows, doors, fires, passages, stairs, and the whole economy of the building were the source of noise, confusion, fatigue, darkness, and the extremes of heat and cold, you would certainly blame the contrivance, without any further examination. The architect would in vain display his subtilty, and prove to you that, if this door or that window were altered, greater ills would ensue. What he says may be strictly true: The alteration of one particular, while the other parts of the building remain, may only augment the inconveniences. But still you would assert in general that, if the architect had had skill and good intentions, he might have formed such a plan of the whole, and might have adjusted the parts in such a manner as would have remedied all or most of these inconveniences. His ignorance, or even your own ignorance of such a plan, will never convince you of the impossibility of it. If you find any inconveniences and deformities in the building, you will always, without entering into any detail, condemn the architect.

In short, I repeat the question: Is the world, considered in general and as it appears to us in this life, different from what a man or such a limited being would, *beforehand*, expect from a very powerful, wise, and benevolent Deity? It must be strange prejudice to assert the contrary. And from thence I conclude that, however consistent the world may be, allowing certain suppositions and conjectures with the idea of such a Deity, it can never afford us an inference concerning his existence. The consistency is not absolutely denied, only the inference. Conjectures, especially where infinity is excluded from the divine attributes, may perhaps be sufficient to prove a consistency, but can never be foundations for any inference.

There seem to be *four* circumstances on which depend all or the greatest part of the ills that molest sensible creatures; and it is not impossible but all these circumstances may be necessary and unavoidable. We know so little beyond common life, or even of common life, that, with regard to the economy of a universe, there is no conjecture, however wild, which may not be just; nor any one, however plausible, which may not be erroneous. All that belongs to human understanding, in this deep ignorance and obscurity, is to be sceptical or at least cautious, and not to admit of any hypothesis whatever, much less of any which is supported by no appearance of probability. Now this I assert to be the case with regard to all the causes of evil and the circumstances on which it depends. None of them appear to human reason in the least degree necessary or unavoidable, nor can we suppose them such, without the utmost licence of imagination.

The *first* circumstance which introduces evil is that contrivance or economy of the animal creation by which pains, as well as pleasures, are employed to excite all creatures to action, and make them vigilant in the great work of self-preservation. Now pleasure alone, in its various degrees, seems to human understanding sufficient for this purpose. All animals might be constantly in a state of enjoyment; but when urged by any of the necessities of nature, such as thirst, hunger, weariness; instead of pain, they might feel a diminution of pleasure by which they might be prompted to seek that object which is necessary to their subsistence. Men pursue pleasure as eagerly as they avoid pain; at least, they might have been so constituted. It seems, therefore, plainly possible to carry on the business of life without any pain. Why then is any animal ever rendered susceptible of such a sensation? If animals can be free from it an hour, they might enjoy a perpetual exemption from it, and it required as particular a contrivance of their organs to produce that feeling as to endow them with sight, hearing, or any of the senses. Shall we conjecture that such a contrivance was necessary, without any appearance of reason; and shall we build on that conjecture as on the most certain truth?

But a capacity of pain would not alone produce pain were it not for the *second* circumstance, viz., the conducting of the world by general laws; and this seems nowise necessary to a very perfect being. It is true, if everything were conducted by particular volitions, the course of nature would be perpetually broken, and no man could employ his reason in the conduct of life. But might not other particular volitions remedy this inconvenience? In short, might not the Deity exterminate all ill, wherever it were to be found, and produce all good, without any preparation or long progress of causes and effects?

Besides, we must consider that, according to the present economy of the world, the course of nature, though supposed exactly regular, yet to us appears not so, and many events are uncertain, and many disappoint our expectations. Health and sickness, calm and tempest, with an infinite number of other accidents whose causes are unknown and variable, have a great influence both on the fortunes of particular persons and on the prosperity of public societies; and indeed all human life, in a manner, depends on such accidents. A being, therefore, who knows the secret springs of the universe might easily, by particular volitions, turn all these accidents to the good of mankind and render the whole world happy, without discovering himself in any operation. A fleet whose purposes were salutary to society might always meet with a fair wind; good princes enjoy sound health and long life; persons born to power and authority be framed with good tempers and virtuous dispositions. A few such events as these, regularly and wisely conducted, would change the face of the world; and yet would no more seem to disturb the course of nature or confound human conduct than the present economy of things where the causes are secret and variable and compounded. Some small touches given to Caligula's brain in his infancy might have converted him into a Trajan. One wave, a little higher than the rest, by burying Caesar and his fortune in the bottom of the ocean, might have restored liberty to a considerable part of mankind. There may, for aught we know, be good reasons why Providence interposes not in this manner, but they are unknown to us; and, though the mere supposition that such reasons exist may be sufficient to *save* the conclusion concerning the divine attributes, yet surely it can never be sufficient to *establish* that conclusion.

If everything in the universe be conducted by general laws, and if animals be rendered susceptible of pain, it scarcely seems possible but some ill must arise in the various shocks of matter and the various concurrence and opposition of general laws; but this ill would be very rare were it not for the *third* circumstance which I proposed to mention, viz., the great frugality with which all powers and faculties are distributed to every particular being. So well adjusted are the organs and capacities of all animals, and so well fitted to their preservation, that, as far as history or tradition reaches, there appears not to be any single species which has yet been extinguished in the universe. Every animal has the requisite endowments, but these endowments are bestowed with so scrupulous an economy that any considerable diminution must entirely destroy the creature. Wherever one power is increased, there is a proportional abatement in the others. Animals which excel in swiftness are commonly defective in force. Those which possess both are either imperfect in some of their senses or are oppressed with the most craving wants. The human species, whose chief excellence is reason and sagacity, is of all others the most necessitous, and the most deficient in bodily advantages, without clothes, without arms, without food, without lodging, without any convenience of life, except what they owe to their own skill and industry. In short, nature seems to have formed an exact calculation of the necessities of her creatures; and, like a *rigid master*, has afforded them little more powers or endowments than what are strictly sufficient to supply those necessities. An *indulgent parent* would have bestowed a large stock in order to guard against accidents, and secure the happiness and welfare of the creature in the most unfortunate concurrence of circumstances. Every course of life would not have been so surrounded with precipices that the least departure from the true path, by mistake or necessity, must involve us in misery and ruin. Some reserve, some fund, would have been provided to ensure happiness, nor would the powers and the necessities have been adjusted with so rigid an economy. The Author of Nature is inconceivably powerful; his force is supposed great, if not altogether inexhaustible; nor is there any reason, as far as we can judge, to make him observe this strict frugality in his dealings with his creatures. It would have been better, were his power extremely limited, to have created fewer animals, and to have endowed these with more faculties for their happiness and preservation. A builder is never esteemed prudent who undertakes a plan beyond what his stock will enable him to finish.

In order to cure most of the ills of human life, I require not that man should have the wings of the eagle, the swiftness of the stag, the force of the ox, the arms of the lion, the scales of the crocodile or rhinoceros; much less do I demand the sagacity of an angel or cherubim. I am contented to take an increase in one single power or faculty of his soul. Let him be endowed with a greater propensity to industry and labour, a more vigorous spring and activity of mind, a more constant bent to business and application. Let the whole species possess naturally an equal diligence with that which many individuals are able to attain by habit and reflection, and the most beneficial consequences, without any allay of ill, is the immediate and necessary result of this endowment. Almost all the moral as well as natural evils of human life arise from idleness; and were our species, by the original constitution of their frame, exempt from this vice or infirmity, the perfect cultivation of land, the improvement of arts and manufactures, the exact execution of every office and duty, immediately follow; and men at once may fully reach that state of society which is so imperfectly attained by the best regulated government. But as industry is a power, and the most valuable of any, nature seems determined, suitably to her usual maxims, to bestow it on men with a very sparing hand; and rather to punish him severely for his deficiency in it than to reward him for his attainments. She has so contrived his frame that nothing but the most violent necessity can oblige him to labour; and she employs all his other wants to overcome, at least in part, the want of diligence, and to endow him with some share of a faculty of which she has thought fit naturally to bereave him. Here our demands may be allowed very humble, and therefore the more reasonable. If we required the endowments of superior penetration and judgement, of a more delicate taste of beauty, of a nicer sensibility to benevolence and friendship, we might be told that we impiously pretend to break the order of nature, that we want to exalt ourselves into a higher rank of being, that the presents which we require, not being suitable to our state and condition, would only be pernicious to us. But it is hard, I dare to repeat it, it is hard that, being placed in a world so full of wants and necessities, where almost every being and element is either our foe or refuses its assistance ... we should also have our own temper to struggle with, and should be deprived of that faculty which can alone fence against these multiplied evils.

The *fourth* circumstance whence arises the misery and ill of the universe is the inaccurate workmanship of all the springs and principles of the great machine of nature. It must be acknowledged that there are few parts of the universe which seem not to serve some purpose, and whose removal would not produce a visible defect and disorder in the whole. The parts hang all together, nor can one be touched without affecting the rest, in a greater or less degree. But at the same time, it must be observed that none of these parts or principles, however useful, are so accurately adjusted as to keep precisely within those bounds in which their utility consists; but they are, all of them, apt, on every occasion, to run into the one extreme or the other. One would imagine that this grand production had not received the last hand of the maker—so little finished is every part, and so coarse are the strokes with which it is executed. Thus the winds are requisite to convey the vapours along the surface of the globe, and to assist men in navigation; but how often, rising up to tempests and hurricanes, do they become pernicious? Rains are necessary to nourish all the plants and animals of the earth; but how often are they defective? how often excessive? Heat is requisite to all life and vegetation, but is not always found in the due proportion. On the mixture and secretion of the humours and juices of the body depend the health and prosperity of the animal; but the parts perform not regularly their proper function. What more useful than all the passions of the mind, ambition, vanity, love, anger? But how often do they break their bounds and cause the greatest convulsions in society? There is nothing so advantageous in the universe but what frequently becomes pernicious, by its excess or defect; nor has nature guarded, with the requisite accuracy, against all disorder or confusion. The irregularity is never perhaps so great as to destroy any species, but is often sufficient to involve the individuals in ruin and misery.

On the concurrence, then, of these *four* circumstances does all or the greatest part of natural evil depend. Were all living creatures incapable of pain, or were the world administered by particular volitions, evil never could have found access into the universe; and were animals endowed with a large stock of powers and faculties, beyond what strict necessity requires, or were the several springs and principles of the universe so accurately framed as to preserve always the just temperament and medium, there must have been very little ill in comparison of what we feel at present. What then shall we pronounce on this occasion? Shall we say that these circumstances are not necessary, and that they might easily have been altered in the contrivance of the universe? This decision seems too presumptuous for creatures so blind and ignorant. Let us be more modest in our conclusions. Let us allow that, if the goodness of the Deity (I mean a goodness like the human) could be established on any tolerable reasons *a priori*, these phenomena, however untoward, would not be sufficient to subvert that principle, but might easily, in some unknown manner, be reconcilable to it. But let us still assert that, as this goodness is not antecedently established but must be inferred from the phenomena, there can be no grounds for such an inference while there are so many ills in the universe, and while these ills might so easily have been remedied, as far as human understanding can be allowed to judge on such a subject. I am sceptic enough to allow that the bad appearances, notwithstanding all my reasonings, may be compatible with such attributes as you suppose, but surely they can never prove these attributes. Such a conclusion cannot result from scepticism, but must arise from the phenomena, and from our confidence in the reasonings which we deduce from these phenomena.

Look round this universe. What an immense profusion of beings, animated and organized, sensible and active! You admire this prodigious variety and fecundity. But inspect a little more narrowly these living existences, the only beings worth regarding. How hostile and destructive to each other! How insufficient all of them for their own happiness! How contemptible or odious to the spectator! The whole presents nothing but the idea of a blind nature, impregnated by a great vivifying principle, and pouring forth from her lap, without discernment or parental care, her maimed and abortive children!

Here the Manichaean system occurs as a proper hypothesis to solve the difficulty; and, no doubt, in some respects it is very specious and has more probability than the common hypothesis, by giving a plausible account of the strange mixture of good and ill which appears in life. But if we consider, on the other hand, the perfect uniformity and agreement of the parts of the universe, we shall not discover in it any marks of the combat of a malevolent with a benevolent being. There is indeed an opposition of pains and pleasures in the feelings of sensible creatures; but are not all the operations of nature carried on by an opposition of principles, of hot and cold, moist and dry, light and heavy? The true conclusion is that the original source of all things is entirely indifferent to all these principles, and has no more regard to good above ill than to heat above cold, or to drought above moisture, or to light above heavy.

There may *four* hypotheses be framed concerning the first causes of the universe: that they are endowed with perfect goodness; that they have perfect malice; that they are opposite and have both goodness and malice; that they have neither goodness nor malice. Mixed phenomena can never prove the two former unmixed principles; and the uniformity and steadiness of general laws seem to oppose the third. The fourth, therefore, seems by far the most probable.

What I have said concerning natural evil will apply to moral with little or no variation; and we have no more reason to infer that the rectitude of the Supreme Being resembles human rectitude than that his benevolence resembles the human. Nay, it will be thought that we have still greater cause to exclude from him moral sentiments, such as we feel them, since moral evil, in the opinion of many, is much more predominant above moral good than natural evil above natural good.

But even though this should not be allowed, and though the virtue which is in mankind should be acknowledged much superior to the vice; yet, so long as there is any vice at all in the universe, it will very much puzzle you anthropomorphites how to account for it. You must assign a cause for it, without having recourse to the first cause. But as every effect must have a cause, and that cause another, you must either carry on the progression *in infinitum* or rest on that original principle, who is the ultimate cause of all things....

Hold! hold! cried Demea: Whither does your imagination hurry you? I joined in alliance with you in order to prove the incomprehensible nature of the Divine Being, and refute the principles of Cleanthes, who would measure everything by human rule and standard. But I now find you running into all the topics of the greatest libertines and infidels, and betraying that holy cause which you seemingly espoused. Are you secretly, then, a more dangerous enemy than Cleanthes himself?

And are you so late in perceiving it? replied Cleanthes. Believe me, Demea, your friend Philo, from the beginning, has been amusing himself at both our expense; and it must be confessed that the injudicious reasoning of our vulgar theology has given him but too just a handle of ridicule. The total infirmity of human reason, the absolute incomprehensibility of the Divine Nature, the great and universal misery, and still greater wickedness of men—these are strange topics, surely, to be so fondly cherished by orthodox divines and doctors. In ages of stupidity and ignorance, indeed, these principles may safely be espoused; and perhaps no views of things are more proper to promote superstition than such as encourage the blind amazement, the diffidence, and melancholy of mankind. But at present . . .

Blame not so much, interposed Philo, the ignorance of these reverend gentlemen. They know how to change their style with the times. Formerly, it was a most popular theological topic to maintain that human life was vanity and misery, and to exaggerate all the ills and pains which are incident to men. But of late years, divines, we find, begin to retract this position and maintain, though still with some hesitation, that there are more goods than evils, more pleasures than pains, even in this life. When religion stood entirely upon temper and education, it was thought proper to encourage melancholy; as, indeed, mankind never have recourse to superior powers so readily as in that disposition. But as men have now learned to form principles and to draw consequences, it is necessary to change the batteries, and to make use of such arguments as will endure at least some scrutiny and examination. This variation is the same (and from the same causes) with that which I formerly remarked with regard to scepticism.

Thus Philo continued to the last his spirit of opposition and his censure of established opinions. But I could observe that Demea did not at all relish the latter part of the discourse; and he took occasion soon after, on some pretence or other, to leave the company.

1 That sentiment had been maintained by Dr King and some few others before Leibniz, though by none of so great fame as that German philosopher.
2 [Milton, *Paradise Lost*, Book XI.]
3 [Dryden, *Areng-Zebe*, Act IV, Scene 1.]

• From *Dialogues concerning Natural Religion*.

18

Kant
A Critique of Natural Theology

Immanuel Kant, perhaps the greatest of modern philosophers, was born in Königsberg in 1724, and spent his professional life teaching at the university there. He produced his most significant work late in life after reading some of Hume's work which, as he put it, 'interrupted my dogmatic slumber'. It was then that he became concerned with transcendental philosophy, i.e. with investigating the ways in which our sensibility and understanding give form to our experience of the world. His later works include the three *Critiques*, the *Groundwork of the Metaphysic of Morals, Prolegomena to any Future Metaphysic* and *Religion within the Bounds of Reason Alone*. He died in 1804.

Kant's critique of natural theology comes towards the end of the *Critique of Pure Reason* (1781). It is to be regarded as part of a wider critique of traditional metaphysics: Kant argues that the human mind errs if it attempts to speculate about matters which go beyond our experience, for instance by trying to establish the reality of transcendent entities.

There are only three possible ways of proving the existence of God by means of speculative reason.
All the paths leading to this goal begin either from determinate experience and the specific constitution of the world of sense as thereby known, and ascend from it, in accordance with laws of causality, to the supreme cause outside the world; or they start from experience which is purely indeterminate, that is, from experience of existence in general, or finally they abstract from all experience, and argue completely *a priori*, from mere concepts, to the existence of a supreme cause. The first proof is the *physico-theological*, the second the *cosmological*, the third the *ontological*. There are, and there can be, no others.

I propose to show that reason is as little able to make progress on the one path, the empirical, as on the other path, the transcendental, and that it stretches its wings in vain in thus attempting to soar above the world of sense by the mere power of speculation. As regards the order in which these arguments should be dealt with, it will be exactly the reverse of that which reason takes in the progress of its own development, and therefore of that which we have ourselves followed in the above account. For it will be shown that, although experience is what first gives occasion to this enquiry, it is the *transcendental concept* which in all such endeavours marks out the goal that reason has set itself to attain, and which is indeed its sole guide in its efforts to achieve that goal. I shall therefore begin with the examination of the transcendental proof, and afterwards enquire what effect the addition of the empirical factor can have in enhancing the force of the argument.

Chapter III

Section 4

The Impossibility of an Ontological Proof of the Existence of God

It is evident, from what has been said, that the concept of an absolutely necessary being is a concept of pure reason, that is, a mere idea the objective reality of which is very far from being proved by the fact that reason requires it. For the idea instructs us only in regard to a certain unattainable completeness, and so serves rather to limit the understanding than to extend it to new objects. But we are here faced by what is indeed strange and perplexing, namely, that while the inference from a given existence in general to some absolutely necessary being seems to be both imperative and legitimate, all those conditions under which alone the understanding can form a concept of such a necessity are so many obstacles in the way of our doing so.

In all ages men have spoken of an *absolutely necessary* being, and in so doing have endeavoured, not so much to understand whether and how a thing of this kind allows even of being thought, but rather to prove its existence. There is, of course, no difficulty in giving a verbal definition of the concept, namely, that it is something the non-existence of which is impossible. But this yields no insight into the conditions which make it necessary to regard the non-existence of a thing as absolutely unthinkable. It is precisely these conditions that we desire to know, in order that we may determine whether or not, in resorting to this concept, we are thinking anything at all. The expedient of removing all those conditions which the understanding indispensably requires in order to regard something as necessary, simply through the introduction of the word *unconditioned*, is very far from sufficing to show whether I am still thinking anything in the concept of the unconditionally necessary, or perhaps rather nothing at all.

Nay more, this concept, at first ventured upon blindly, and now become so completely familiar, has been supposed to have its meaning exhibited in a number of examples; and on this account all further enquiry into its intelligibility has seemed to be quite needless. Thus the fact that every geometrical proposition, as, for instance, that a triangle has three angles, is absolutely necessary, has been taken as justifying us in speaking of an object which lies entirely outside the sphere of our understanding as if we understood perfectly what it is that we intend to convey by the concept of that object.

All the alleged examples are, without exception, taken from *judgments*, not from *things* and their existence. But the unconditioned necessity of judgments is not the same as an absolute necessity of things. The absolute necessity of the judgment is only a conditioned necessity of the thing, or of the predicate in the judgment. The above proposition does not declare that three angles are absolutely necessary, but that, under the condition that there is a triangle (that is, that a triangle is given), three angles will necessarily be found in it. So great, indeed, is the deluding influence exercised by this logical necessity that, by the simple device of forming an *a priori* concept of a thing in such a manner as to include existence within the scope of its meaning, we have supposed ourselves to have justified the conclusion that because existence necessarily belongs to the object of this concept—always under the condition that we posit the thing as given (as existing)—we are also of necessity, in accordance with the law of identity, required to posit the existence of its object, and that this being is therefore itself absolutely necessary—and this, to repeat, for the reason that the existence of this being has already been thought in a concept which is assumed arbitrarily and on condition that we posit its object.

If, in an identical proposition, I reject the predicate while retaining the subject, contradiction results; and I therefore say that the former belongs necessarily to the latter. But if we reject subject and predicate alike, there is no contradiction; for nothing is then left that can be contradicted. To posit a triangle, and yet to reject its three angles, is self-contradictory; but there is no contradiction in rejecting the triangle together with its three angles. The same holds true of the concept of an absolutely necessary being. If its existence is rejected, we reject the thing itself with all its predicates; and no question of contradiction can then arise. There is nothing outside it that would then be contradicted, since the necessity of the thing is not supposed to be derived from anything external; nor is there anything internal that would be contradicted, since in rejecting the thing itself we have at the same time rejected all its internal properties. 'God is omnipotent' is a necessary judgment. The omnipotence cannot be rejected if we posit a Deity, that is, an infinite being; for the two concepts are identical. But if we say, 'There is no God', neither the omnipotence nor any other of its predicates is given; they are one and all rejected together with the subject, and there is therefore not the least contradiction in such a judgment.

We have thus seen that if the predicate of a judgment is rejected together with the subject, no internal contradiction can result, and that this holds no matter what the predicate may be. The only way of evading this conclusion is to argue that there are subjects which cannot be removed, and must always remain. That, however, would only be another way of saying that there are absolutely necessary subjects; and that is the very assumption which I have called in question, and the possibility of which the above argument professes to establish. For I cannot form the least concept of a thing which, should it be rejected with all its predicates, leaves behind a contradiction; and in the absence of contradiction I have, through pure *a priori* concepts alone, no criterion of impossibility.

Notwithstanding all these general considerations, in which every one must concur, we may be challenged with a case which is brought forward as proof that in actual fact the contrary holds, namely, that there is one concept, and indeed only one, in reference to which the not-being or rejection of its object is in itself contradictory, namely, the concept of the *ens realissimum*. It is declared that it possesses all reality, and that we are justified in assuming that such a being is possible (the fact that a concept does not contradict itself by no means proves the possibility of its object: but the contrary assertion I am for the moment willing to allow).[1] Now [the argument proceeds] 'all reality' includes existence; existence is therefore contained in the concept of a thing that is possible. If, then, this thing is rejected, the internal possibility of the thing is rejected—which is self-contradictory.

My answer is as follows. There is already a contradiction in introducing the concept of existence—no matter under what title it may be disguised—into the concept of a thing which we profess to be thinking solely in reference to its possibility. If that be allowed as legitimate, a seeming victory has been won; but in actual fact nothing at all is said: the assertion is a mere tautology. We must ask: Is the proposition that *this or that thing* (which, whatever it may be, is allowed as possible) *exists*, an analytic or a synthetic proposition? If it is analytic, the assertion of the existence of the thing adds nothing to the thought of the thing; but in that case either the thought, which is in us, is the thing itself, or we have presupposed an existence as belonging to the realm of the possible, and have then, on that pretext, inferred its existence from its internal possibility—which is nothing but a miserable tautology. The word 'reality', which in the concept of the thing sounds other than the word 'existence' in the concept of the predicate, is of no avail in meeting this objection. For if all positing (no matter what it may be that is posited) is entitled reality, the thing with all its predicates is already posited in the concept of the subject, and is assumed as actual; and in the predicate this is merely repeated. But if, on the other hand, we admit, as every reasonable person must, that all existential propositions are synthetic, how can we profess to maintain that the predicate of existence cannot be rejected without contradiction? This is a feature which is found only in analytic propositions, and is indeed precisely what constitutes their analytic character.

I should have hoped to put an end to these idle and fruitless disputations in a direct manner, by an accurate determination of the concept of existence, had I not found that the illusion which is caused by the confusion of a logical with a real predicate (that is, with a predicate which determines a thing) is almost beyond correction. Anything we please can be made to serve as a logical predicate; the subject can even be predicated of itself; for logic abstracts from all content. But a *determining* predicate is a predicate which is added to the concept of the subject and enlarges it. Consequently, it must not be already contained in the concept.

'*Being*' is obviously not a real predicate; that is, it is not a concept of something which could be added to the concept of a thing. It is merely the positing of a thing, or of certain determinations, as existing in themselves. Logically, it is merely the copula of a judgment. The proposition, 'God is omnipotent', contains two concepts, each of which has its object—God and omnipotence. The small word 'is' adds no new predicate, but only serves to posit the predicate *in its relation* to the subject. If, now, we take the subject (God) with all its predicates (among which is omnipotence), and say 'God is', or 'There is a God', we attach no new predicate to the concept of God, but only posit the subject in itself with all its predicates, and indeed posit it as being an *object* that stands in relation to my *concept*. The content of both must be one and the same; nothing can have been added to the concept, which expresses merely what is possible, by my thinking its object (through the expression 'it is') as given absolutely. Otherwise stated, the real contains no more than the merely possible. A hundred real thalers do not contain the least coin more than a hundred possible thalers. For as the latter signify the concept, and the former the object and the positing of the object, should the former contain more than the latter, my concept would not, in that case, express the whole object, and would not therefore be an adequate concept of it. My financial position is, however, affected very differently by a hundred real thalers than it is by the mere concept of them (that is, of their possibility). For the object, as it actually exists, is not analytically contained in my concept, but is added to my concept (which is a determination of my state) synthetically; and yet the conceived hundred thalers are not themselves in the least increased through thus acquiring existence outside my concept.

By whatever and by however many predicates we may think a thing—even if we completely determine it—we do not make the least addition to the thing when we further declare that this thing *is*. Otherwise, it would not be exactly the same thing that exists, but something more than we had thought in the concept; and we could not, therefore, say that the exact object of my concept exists. If we think in a thing every feature of reality except one, the missing reality is not added by my saying that this defective thing exists. On the contrary, it exists with the same defect with which I have thought it, since otherwise what exists would be something different from what I thought. When, therefore, I think a being as the supreme reality, without any defect, the question still remains whether it exists or not. For though, in my concept, nothing may be lacking of the possible real content of a thing in general, something is still lacking in its relation to my whole state of thought, namely, [in so far as I am unable to assert] that knowledge of this object is also possible *a posteriori*. And here we find the source of our present difficulty. Were we dealing with an object of the senses, we could not confound the existence of the thing with the mere concept of it. For through the concept the object is thought only as conforming to the *universal conditions* of possible empirical knowledge in general, whereas through its existence it is thought as belonging to the context of experience as a whole. In being thus connected with the *content* of experience as a whole, the concept of the object is not, however, in the least enlarged; all that has happened is that our thought has thereby obtained an additional possible perception. It is not, therefore, surprising that, if we attempt to think existence through the pure category alone, we cannot specify a single mark distinguishing it from mere possibility.

Whatever, therefore, and however much, our concept of an object may contain, we must go outside it, if we are to ascribe existence to the object. In the case of objects of the senses, this takes place through their connection with some one of our perceptions, in accordance with empirical laws. But in dealing with objects of pure thought, we have no means whatsoever of knowing their existence, since it would have to be known in a completely *a priori* manner. Our consciousness of all existence (whether immediately through perception, or mediately through inferences which connect something with perception) belongs exclusively to the unity of experience; any [alleged] existence outside this field, while not indeed such as we can declare to be absolutely impossible, is of the nature of an assumption which we can never be in a position to justify.

The concept of a supreme being is in many respects a very useful idea; but just because it is a mere idea, it is altogether incapable, by itself alone, of enlarging our knowledge in regard to what exists. It is not even competent to enlighten us as to the *possibility* of any existence beyond that which is known in and through experience. The analytic criterion of possibility, as consisting in the principle that bare positives (realities) give rise to no contradiction, cannot be denied to it. But since the realities are not given to us in their specific characters; since even if they were, we should still not be in a position to pass judgment; since the criterion of the possibility of synthetic knowledge is never to be looked for save in experience, to which the object of an idea cannot belong, the connection of all real properties in a thing is a synthesis, the possibility of which we are unable to determine *a priori*. And thus the celebrated Leibniz is far from having succeeded in what he plumed himself on achieving—the comprehension *a priori* of the possibility of this sublime ideal being.

The attempt to establish the existence of a supreme being by means of the famous ontological argument of Descartes is therefore merely so much labour and effort lost; we can no more extend our stock of [theoretical] insight by mere ideas, than a merchant can better his position by adding a few noughts to his cash account.

Chapter III

Section 5

The impossibility of a cosmological proof of the existence of God

To attempt to extract from a purely arbitrary idea the existence of an object corresponding to it is a quite unnatural procedure and a mere innovation of scholastic subtlety. Such an attempt would never have been made if there had not been antecedently, on the part of our reason, the need to assume as a basis of existence in general something necessary (in which our regress may terminate); and if, since this necessity must be unconditioned and certain *a priori*, reason had not, in consequence, been forced to seek a concept which would satisfy, if possible, such a demand, and enable us to know an existence in a completely *a priori* manner. Such a concept was supposed to have been found in the idea of an *ens realissimum*; and that idea was therefore used only for the more definite knowledge of that necessary being, of the necessary existence of which we were already convinced, or persuaded, on other grounds. This natural procedure of reason was, however, concealed from view, and instead of ending with this concept, the attempt was made to begin with it, and so to deduce from it that necessity of existence which it was only fitted to supplement. Thus arose the unfortunate ontological proof, which yields satisfaction neither to the natural and healthy understanding nor to the more academic demands of strict proof.

The *cosmological proof*, which we are now about to examine, retains the connection of absolute necessity with the highest reality, but instead of reasoning, like the former proof, from the highest reality to necessity of existence, it reasons from the previously given unconditioned necessity of some being to the unlimited reality of that being. It thus enters upon a course of reasoning which, whether rational or only pseudo-rational, is at any rate natural, and the most convincing not only for common sense but even for speculative understanding. It also sketches the first outline of all the proofs in natural theology, an outline which has always been and always will be followed, however much embellished and disguised by superfluous additions. This proof, termed by Leibniz the proof *a contingentia mundi*, we shall now proceed to expound and examine.

It runs thus: If anything exists, an absolutely necessary being must also exist. Now I, at least, exist. Therefore an absolutely necessary being exists. The minor premiss contains an experience, the major premiss the inference from there being any experience at all to the existence of the necessary.[2] The proof therefore really begins with experience, and is not wholly *a priori* or ontological. For this reason, and because the object of all possible experience is called the world, it is entitled the *cosmological* proof. Since, in dealing with the objects of experience, the proof abstracts from all special properties through which this world may differ from any other possible world, the title also serves to distinguish it from the physico-theological proof, which is based upon observations of the particular properties of the world disclosed to us by our senses.

The proof then proceeds as follows: The necessary being can be determined in one way only, that is, by one out of each possible pair of opposed predicates. It must therefore be *completely* determined through its own concept. Now there is only one possible concept which determines a thing completely *a priori*, namely, the concept of the *ens realissimum*. The concept of the *ens realissimum* is therefore the only concept through which a necessary being can be thought. In other words, a supreme being necessarily exists.

In this cosmological argument there are combined so many pseudorational principles that speculative reason seems in this case to have brought to bear all the resources of its dialectical skill to produce the greatest possible transcendental illusion. The testing of the argument may meantime be postponed while we detail in order the various devices whereby an old argument is disguised as a new one, and by which appeal is made to the agreement of two witnesses, the one with credentials of pure reason and the other with those of experience. In reality the only witness is that which speaks in the name of pure reason; in the endeavour to pass as a second witness it merely changes its dress and voice. In order to lay a secure foundation for itself, this proof takes its stand on experience, and thereby makes profession of being distinct from the ontological proof, which puts its entire trust in pure *a priori* concepts. But the cosmological proof uses this experience only for a single step in the argument, namely, to conclude the existence of a necessary being. What properties this being may have, the empirical premiss cannot tell us. Reason therefore abandons experience altogether, and endeavours to discover from mere concepts what properties an absolutely necessary being must have, that is, which among all possible things contains in itself the conditions (*requisita*) essential to absolute necessity. Now these, it is supposed, are nowhere to be found save in the concept of an *ens realissimum*; and the conclusion is therefore drawn, that the *ens realissimum* is the absolutely necessary being. But it is evident that we are here presupposing that the concept of the highest reality is completely adequate to the concept of absolute necessity of existence; that is, that the latter can be inferred from the former. Now this is the proposition maintained by the ontological proof; it is here being assumed in the cosmological proof, and indeed made the basis of the proof; and yet it is an assumption with which this latter proof has professed to dispense. For absolute necessity is an existence determined from mere concepts. If I say, the concept of the *ens realissimum* is a concept, and indeed the only concept, which is appropriate and adequate to necessary existence, I must also admit that necessary existence can be inferred from this concept. Thus the so-called cosmological proof really owes any cogency which it may have to the ontological proof from mere concepts. The appeal to experience is quite superfluous; experience may perhaps lead us to the concept of absolute necessity, but is unable to demonstrate this necessity as belonging to any determinate thing. For immediately we endeavour to do so, we must abandon all experience and search among pure concepts to discover whether any one of them contains the conditions of the possibility of an absolutely necessary being. If in this way we can determine the possibility of a necessary being, we likewise establish its existence. For what we are then saying is this: that of all possible beings there is one which carries with it absolute necessity, that is, that this being exists with absolute necessity.

Fallacious and misleading arguments are most easily detected if set out in correct syllogistic form. This we now proceed to do in the instance under discussion.

If the proposition, that every absolutely necessary being is likewise the most real of all beings, is correct (and this is the *nervus probandi* of the cosmological proof), it must, like all affirmative judgments, be convertible, at least *per accidens*. It therefore follows that some *entia realissima* are likewise absolutely necessary beings. But one *ens realissimum* is in no respect different from another, and what is true of *some* under this concept is true also of *all*. In this case, therefore, I can convert the proposition *simpliciter*, not only *per accidens*, and say that every *ens realissimum* is a necessary being. But since this proposition is determined from its *a priori* concepts alone, the mere concept of the *ens realissimum* must carry with it the absolute necessity of that being; and this is precisely what the ontological proof has asserted and what the cosmological proof has refused to admit, although the conclusions of the latter are indeed covertly based on it.

Thus the second path upon which speculative reason enters in its attempt to prove the existence of a supreme being is not only as deceptive as the first, but has this additional defect, that it is guilty of an *ignoratio elenchi*. It professes to lead us by a new path, but after a short circuit brings us back to the very path which we had deserted at its bidding.

I have stated that in this cosmological argument there lies hidden a whole nest of dialectical assumptions, which the transcendental critique can easily detect and destroy. These deceptive principles I shall merely enumerate, leaving to the reader, who by this time will be sufficiently expert in these matters, the task of investigating them further, and of refuting them.

We find, for instance, (1) the transcendental principle whereby from the contingent we infer a cause. This principle is applicable only in the sensible world; outside that world it has no meaning whatsoever. For the mere intellectual concept of the contingent cannot give rise to any synthetic proposition, such as that of causality. The principle of causality has no meaning and no criterion for its application save only in the sensible world. But in the cosmological proof it is precisely in order to enable us to advance beyond the sensible world that it is employed. (2) The inference to a first cause, from the impossibility of an infinite series of causes, given one after the other, in the sensible world. The principles of the employment of reason do not justify this conclusion even within the world of experience, still less beyond this world in a realm into which this series can never be extended. (3) The unjustified self-satisfaction of reason in respect of the completion of this series. The removal of all the conditions without which no concept of necessity is possible is taken by reason to be a completion of the concept of the series, on the ground that we can then conceive nothing further. (4) The confusion between the logical possibility of a concept of all reality united into one (without inner contradiction) and the transcendental possibility of such a reality. In the case of the latter there is needed a principle to establish the practicability of such a synthesis, a principle which itself, however, can apply only to the field of possible experiences—etc.

The procedure of the cosmological proof is artfully designed to enable us to escape having to prove the existence of a necessary being *a priori* through mere concepts. Such proof would require to be carried out in the ontological manner, and that is an enterprise for which we feel ourselves to be altogether incompetent. Accordingly, we take as the starting-point of our inference an actual existence (an experience in general), and advance, in such manner as we can, to some absolutely necessary condition of this existence. We have then no need to show the possibility of this condition. For if it has been proved to exist, the question as to its possibility is entirely superfluous. If now we want to determine more fully the nature of this necessary being, we do not endeavour to do so in the manner that would be really adequate, namely, by discovering from its concept the necessity of its existence. For could we do that, we should be in no need of an empirical starting-point. No, all we seek is the negative condition (*conditio sine qua non*), without which a being would not be absolutely necessary. And in all other kinds of reasoning from a given consequence to its ground this would be legitimate; but in the present case it unfortunately happens that the condition which is needed for absolute necessity is only to be found in one single being. This being must therefore contain in its concept all that is required for absolute necessity, and consequently it enables me to infer this absolute necessity *a priori*. I must therefore be able also to reverse the inference, and to say: Anything to which this concept (of supreme reality) applies is absolutely necessary. If I cannot make this inference (as I must concede, if I am to avoid admitting the ontological proof), I have come to grief in the new way that I have been following, and am back again at my starting-point. The concept of the supreme being satisfies all questions *a priori* which can be raised regarding the inner determinations of a thing, and is therefore an ideal that is quite unique, in that the concept, while universal, also at the same time designates an individual as being among the things that are possible. But it does not give satisfaction concerning the question of its own existence— though this is the real purpose of our enquiries—and if anyone admitted the existence of a necessary being but wanted to know which among all [existing] things is to be identified with that being, we could not answer: 'This, not that, is the necessary being'.

We may indeed be allowed to *postulate* the existence of an all-sufficient being, as the cause of all possible effects, with a view to lightening the task of reason in its search for the unity of the grounds of explanation. But in presuming so far as to say that such a being *necessarily exists*, we are no longer giving modest expression to an admissible hypothesis, but are confidently laying claim to apodeictic certainty. For the knowledge of what we profess to know as absolutely necessary must itself carry with it absolute necessity.

The whole problem of the transcendental ideal amounts to this: either, given absolute necessity, to find a concept which possesses it, or, given the concept of something, to find that something to be absolutely necessary. If either task be possible, so must the other; for reason recognises that only as absolutely necessary which follows of necessity from its concept. But both tasks are quite beyond our utmost efforts to *satisfy* our understanding in this matter; and equally unavailing are all attempts to induce it to acquiesce in its incapacity.

Unconditioned necessity, which we so indispensably require as the last bearer of all things, is for human reason the veritable abyss. Eternity itself, in all its terrible sublimity, as depicted by a Haller,[3] is far from making the same overwhelming impression on the mind; for it only *measures* the duration of things, it does not *support* them. We cannot put aside, and yet also cannot endure the thought, that a being, which we represent to ourselves as supreme amongst all possible beings, should, as it were, say to itself: 'I am from eternity to eternity, and outside me there is nothing save what is through my will, *but whence then am I?*' All support here fails us; and the *greatest* perfection, no less than the *least* perfection, is unsubstantial and baseless for the merely speculative reason, which makes not the least effort to retain either the one or the other, and feels indeed no loss in allowing them to vanish entirely.

Many forces in nature, which manifest their existence through certain effects, remain for us inscrutable; for we cannot track them sufficiently far by observation. Also, the transcendental object lying at the basis of appearances (and with it the reason why our sensibility is subject to certain supreme conditions rather than to others) is and remains for us inscrutable. The thing itself is indeed given, but we can have no insight into its nature. But it is quite otherwise with an ideal of pure reason; it can never be said to be inscrutable. For since it is not required to give any credentials of its reality save only the need on the part of reason to complete all synthetic unity by means of it; and since, therefore, it is in no wise given as thinkable *object*, it cannot be inscrutable in the manner in which an object is. On the contrary it must, as a mere idea, find its place and its solution in the nature of reason, and must therefore allow of investigation. For it is of the very essence of reason that we should be able to give an account of all our concepts, opinions, and assertions, either upon objective or, in the case of mere illusion, upon subjective grounds.

Discovery and Explanation

of the dialectical illusion in all transcendental proofs of the existence of a necessary being

Both the above proofs were transcendental, that is, were attempted independently of empirical principles. For although the cosmological proof presupposes an experience in general, it is not based on any particular property of this experience but on pure principles of reason, as applied to an existence given through empirical consciousness in general. Further, it soon abandons this guidance and relies on pure concepts alone. What, then, in these transcendental proofs is the cause of the dialectical but natural illusion which connects the concepts of necessity and supreme reality, and which realises and hypostatises what can be an idea only? Why are we constrained to assume that some one among existing things is in itself necessary, and yet at the same time to shrink back from the existence of such a being as from an abyss? And how are we to secure that reason may come to an agreement with itself in this matter, and that from the wavering condition of a diffident approval, ever again withdrawn, it may arrive at settled insight?

There is something very strange in the fact, that once we assume something to exist we cannot avoid inferring that something exists necessarily. The cosmological argument rests on this quite natural (although not therefore certain) inference. On the other hand, if I take the concept of anything, no matter what, I find that the existence of this thing can never be represented by me as absolutely necessary, and that, whatever it may be that exists, nothing prevents me from thinking its non-existence. Thus while I may indeed be obliged to assume something necessary as a condition of the existent in general, I cannot think any particular thing as in itself necessary. In other words, I can never *complete* the regress to the conditions of existence save by assuming a necessary being, and yet am never in a position to *begin* with such a being.

If I am constrained to think something necessary as a condition of existing things, but am unable to think any particular thing as in itself necessary, it inevitably follows that necessity and contingency do not concern the things themselves; otherwise there would be a contradiction. Consequently, neither of these two principles can be objective. They may, however, be regarded as subjective principles of reason. The one calls upon us to seek something necessary as a condition of all that is given as existent, that is, to stop nowhere until we have arrived at an explanation which is complete *a priori*; the other forbids us ever to hope for this completion, that is, forbids us to treat anything empirical as unconditioned and to exempt ourselves thereby from the toil of its further derivation. Viewed in this manner, the two principles, as merely heuristic and *regulative*, and as concerning only the formal interest of reason, can very well stand side by side. The one prescribes that we are to philosophise about nature as if there were a necessary first ground for all that belongs to existence—solely, however, for the purpose of bringing systematic unity into our knowledge, by always pursuing such an idea, as an imagined ultimate ground. The other warns us not to regard any determination whatsoever of existing things as such an ultimate ground, that is, as absolutely necessary, but to keep the way always open for further derivation, and so to treat each and every determination as always conditioned by something else. But if everything which is perceived in things must necessarily be treated by us as conditioned, nothing that allows of being empirically given can be regarded as absolutely necessary.

Since, therefore, the absolutely necessary is only intended to serve as a principle for obtaining the greatest possible unity among appearances, as being their ultimate ground; and since—inasmuch as the second rule commands us always to regard all empirical causes of unity as themselves derived—we can never reach this unity within the world, it follows that we must regard the absolutely necessary as being *outside* the world.

While the philosophers of antiquity regard all form in nature as contingent, they follow the judgment of the common man in their view of matter as original and necessary. But if, instead of regarding matter relatively, as *substratum* of appearances, they had considered it *in itself*, and as regards its existence, the idea of absolute necessity would at once have disappeared. For there is nothing which absolutely binds reason to accept such an existence; on the contrary it can always annihilate it in thought, without contradiction; absolute necessity is a necessity that is to be found in thought alone. This belief must therefore have been due to a certain regulative principle. In fact extension and impenetrability (which between them make up the concept of matter) constitute the supreme empirical principle of the unity of appearances; and this principle, so far as it is empirically unconditioned, has the character of a regulative principle. Nevertheless, since every determination of the matter which constitutes what is real in appearances, including impenetrability, is an effect (action) which must have its cause and which is therefore always derivative in character, matter is not compatible with the idea of a necessary being as a principle of all derived unity. (For its real properties, being derivative, are one and all only conditionally necessary, and so allow of being removed—wherewith the whole existence of matter would be removed.) If this were not the case, we should have reached the ultimate ground of unity by empirical means—which is forbidden by the second regulative principle. It therefore follows that matter, and in general whatever belongs to the world, is not compatible with the idea of a necessary original being, even when the latter is regarded simply as a principle of the greatest empirical unity. That being or principle must be set outside the world, leaving us free to derive the appearances of the world and their existence from other appearances, with unfailing confidence, just as if there were no necessary being, while yet we are also free to strive unceasingly towards the completeness of that derivation, just as if such a being were presupposed as an ultimate ground.

As follows from these considerations, the ideal of the supreme being is nothing but a *regulative principle* of reason, which directs us to look upon all connection in the world *as if* it originated from an all-sufficient necessary cause. We can base upon the ideal the rule of a systematic and, in accordance with universal laws, necessary unity in the explanation of that connection; but the ideal is not an assertion of an existence necessary in itself. At the same time we cannot avoid the transcendental subreption, by which this formal principle is represented as constitutive, and by which this unity is hypostatised. We proceed here just as we do in the case of space. Space is only a principle of sensibility, but since it is the primary source and condition of all shapes, which are only so many limitations of itself, it is taken as something absolutely necessary, existing in its own right, and as an object given *a priori* in itself. In the same way, since the systematic unity of nature cannot be prescribed as a principle for the empirical employment of our reason, except in so far as we presuppose the idea of an *ens realissimum* as the supreme cause, it is quite natural that this latter idea should be represented as an actual object, which, in its character of supreme condition, is also necessary—thus changing a *regulative* into a *constitutive* principle. That such a substitution has been made becomes evident, when we consider this supreme being, which relatively to the world is absolutely (unconditionally) necessary, as a thing in and by itself. For we are then unable to conceive what can be meant by its necessity. The concept of necessity is only to be found in our reason, as a formal condition of thought; it does not allow of being hypostatised as a material condition of existence.

Chapter III

Section 6

The impossibility of the physico-theological proof

If, then, neither the concept of things in general nor the experience of any *existence in general* can supply what is required, it remains only to try whether a *determinate experience*, the experience of the things of the present world, and the constitution and order of these, does not provide the basis of a proof which may help us to attain to an assured conviction of a supreme being. Such proof we propose to entitle the *physico-theological*. Should this attempt also fail, it must follow that no satisfactory proof of the existence of a being corresponding to our transcendental idea can be possible by pure speculative reason.

In view of what has already been said, it is evident that we can count upon a quite easy and conclusive answer to this enquiry. For how can any experience ever be adequate to an idea? The peculiar nature of the latter consists just in the fact that no experience can ever be equal to it. The transcendental idea of a necessary and all-sufficient original being is so overwhelmingly great, so high above everything empirical, the latter being always conditioned, that it leaves us at a loss, partly because we can never find in experience material sufficient to satisfy such a concept, and partly because it is always in the sphere of the conditioned that we carry out our search, seeking there ever vainly for the unconditioned—no law of any empirical synthesis giving us an example of any such unconditioned or providing the least guidance in its pursuit.

If the supreme being should itself stand in this chain of conditions, it would be a member of the series, and like the lower members which it precedes, would call for further enquiry as to the still higher ground from which it follows. If, on the other hand, we propose to separate it from the chain, and to conceive it as a purely intelligible being, existing apart from the series of natural causes, by what bridge can reason contrive to pass over to it? For all laws governing the transition from effects to causes, all synthesis and extension of our knowledge, refer to nothing but possible experience, and therefore solely to objects of the sensible world, and apart from them can have no meaning whatsoever.

This world presents to us so immeasurable a stage of variety, order, purposiveness, and beauty, as displayed alike in its infinite extent and in the unlimited divisibility of its parts, that even with such knowledge as our weak understanding can acquire of it, we are brought face to face with so many marvels immeasurably great, that all speech loses its force, all numbers their power to measure, our thoughts themselves all definiteness, and that our judgment of the whole resolves itself into an amazement which is speechless, and only the more eloquent on that account. Everywhere we see a chain of effects and causes, of ends and means, a regularity in origination and dissolution. Nothing has of itself come into the condition in which we find it to exist, but always points to something else as its cause, while this in turn commits us to repetition of the same enquiry. The whole universe must thus sink into the abyss of nothingness, unless, over and above this infinite chain of contingencies, we assume something to support it—something which is original and independently self-subsistent, and which as the cause of the origin of the universe secures also at the same time its continuance. What magnitude are we to ascribe to this supreme cause—admitting that it is supreme in respect of all things in the world? We are not acquainted with the whole content of the world, still less do we know how to estimate its magnitude by comparison with all that is possible. But since we cannot, as regards causality, dispense with an ultimate and supreme being, what is there to prevent us ascribing to it a degree of perfection that sets it *above everything else that is possible*? This we can easily do—though only through the slender outline of an abstract concept—by representing this being to ourselves as combining in itself all possible perfection, as in a single substance. This concept is in conformity with the demand of our reason for parsimony of principles; it is free from self-contradiction, and is never decisively contradicted by any experience; and it is likewise of such a character that it contributes to the extension of the employment of reason within experience, through the guidance which it yields in the discovery of order and purposiveness.

This proof always deserves to be mentioned with respect. It is the oldest, the clearest, and the most accordant with the common proof of mankind. It enlivens the study of nature, just as it itself derives its existence and gains ever new vigour from that source. It suggests ends and purposes, where our observation would not have detected them by itself, and extends our knowledge of nature by means of the guiding-concept of a special unity, the principle of which is outside nature. This knowledge again reacts on its cause, namely, upon the idea which has led to it, and so strengthens the belief in a supreme Author [of nature] that the belief acquires the force of an irresistible conviction.

It would therefore not only be uncomforting but utterly vain to attempt to diminish in any way the authority of this argument. Reason, constantly upheld by this ever-increasing evidence, which, though empirical, is yet so powerful, cannot be so depressed through doubts suggested by subtle and abstruse speculation, that it is not at once aroused from the indecision of all melancholy reflection, as from a dream, by one glance at the wonders of nature and the majesty of the universe—ascending from height to height up to the all-highest, from the conditioned to its conditions, up to the supreme and unconditioned Author [of all conditioned being].

But although we have nothing to bring against the rationality and utility of this procedure, but have rather to commend and to further it, we still cannot approve the claims, which this mode of argument would fain advance, to apodeictic certainty and to an assent founded on no special favour or support from other quarters. It cannot hurt the good cause, if the dogmatic language of the overweening sophist be toned down to the more moderate and humble requirements of a belief adequate to quieten our doubts, though not to command unconditional submission. I therefore maintain that the physico-theological proof can never by itself establish the existence of a supreme being, but must always fall back upon the ontological argument to make good its deficiency. It only serves as an introduction to the ontological argument; and the latter therefore contains (in so far as a speculative proof is possible at all) *the one possible ground of proof* with which human reason can never dispense.

The chief points of the physico-theological proof are as follows: (1) In the world we everywhere find clear signs of an order in accordance with a determinate purpose, carried out with great wisdom; and this in a universe which is indescribably varied in content and unlimited in extent. (2) This purposive order is quite alien to the things of the world, and only belongs to them contingently; that is to say, the diverse things could not of themselves have co-operated, by so great a combination of diverse means, to the fulfilment of determinate final purposes, had they not been chosen and designed for these purposes by an ordering rational principle in conformity with underlying ideas. (3) There exists, therefore, a sublime and wise cause (or more than one), which must be the cause of the world not merely as a blindly working all-powerful nature, by *fecundity*, but as intelligence, through *freedom*. (4) The unity of this cause may be inferred from the unity of the reciprocal relations existing between the parts of the world, as members of an artfully arranged structure—inferred with certainty in so far as our observation suffices for its verification, and beyond these limits with probability, in accordance with the principles of analogy.

We need not here criticise natural reason too strictly in regard to its conclusion from the analogy between certain natural products and what our human art produces when we do violence to nature, and constrain it to proceed not according to its own ends but in conformity with ours—appealing to the similarity of these particular natural products with houses, ships, watches. Nor need we here question its conclusion that there lies at the basis of nature a causality similar to that responsible for artificial products, namely, an understanding and a will; and that the inner possibility of a self-acting nature (which is what makes all art, and even, it may be, reason itself, possible) is therefore derived from another, though superhuman, art—a mode of reasoning which could not perhaps withstand a searching transcendental criticism. But at any rate we must admit that, if we are to specify a cause at all, we cannot here proceed more securely than by analogy with those purposive productions of which alone the cause and mode of action are fully known to us. Reason could never be justified in abandoning the causality which it knows for grounds of explanation which are obscure, of which it does not have any knowledge, and which are incapable of proof.

On this method of argument, the purposiveness and harmonious adaptation of so much in nature can suffice to prove the contingency of the form merely, not of the matter, that is, not of the substance in the world. To prove the latter we should have to demonstrate that the things in the world would not of themselves be capable of such order and harmony, in accordance with universal laws, if they were not *in their substance* the product of supreme wisdom. But to prove this we should require quite other grounds of proof than those which are derived from the analogy with human art. The utmost, therefore, that the argument can prove is an *architect* of the world who is always very much hampered by the adaptability of the material in which he works, not a *creator* of the world to whose idea everything is subject. This, however, is altogether inadequate to the lofty purpose which we have before our eyes, namely, the proof of an all-sufficient primordial being. To prove the contingency of matter itself, we should have to resort to a transcendental argument, and this is precisely what we have here set out to avoid.

The inference, therefore, is that the order and purposiveness everywhere observable throughout the world may be regarded as a completely contingent arrangement, and that we may argue to the existence of a cause *proportioned* to it. But the concept of this cause must enable us to know something quite *determinate* about it, and can therefore be no other than the concept of a being who possesses all might, wisdom, etc., in a word, all the perfection which is proper to an all-sufficient being. For the predicates—'very great', 'astounding', 'immeasurable' in power and excellence—give no determinate concept at all, and do not really tell us what the thing is in itself. They are only relative representations of the magnitude of the object, which the observer, in contemplating the world, compares with himself and with his capacity of comprehension, and which are equally terms of eulogy whether we be magnifying the object or be depreciating the observing subject in relation to that object. Where we are concerned with the magnitude (of the perfection) of a thing, there is no determinate concept except that which comprehends all possible perfection; and in that concept only the allness (*omnitudo*) of the reality is completely determined.

Now no one, I trust, will be so bold as to profess that he comprehends the relation of the magnitude of the world as he has observed it (alike as regards both extent and content) to omnipotence, of the world order to supreme wisdom, of the world unity to the absolute unity of its Author, etc. Physico-theology is therefore unable to give any determinate concept of the supreme cause of the world, and cannot therefore serve as the foundation of a theology which is itself in turn to form the basis of religion.

To advance to absolute totality by the empirical road is utterly impossible. None the less this is what is attempted in the physico-theological proof. What, then, are the means which have been adopted to bridge this wide abyss?

The physico-theological argument can indeed lead us to the point of admiring the greatness, wisdom, power, etc., of the Author of the world, but can take us no further. Accordingly, we then abandon the argument from empirical grounds of proof, and fall back upon the contingency which, in the first steps of the argument, we had inferred from the order and purposiveness of the world. With this contingency as our sole premiss, we then advance, by means of transcendental concepts alone, to the existence of an absolutely necessary being, and [as a final step] from the concept of the absolute necessity of the first cause to the completely determinate or determinable concept of that necessary being, namely, to the concept of an all-embracing reality. Thus the physico-theological proof, failing in its undertaking, has in face of this difficulty suddenly fallen back upon the cosmological proof; and since the latter is only a disguised ontological proof, it has really achieved its purpose by pure reason alone—although at the start it disclaimed all kinship with pure reason and professed to establish its conclusions on convincing evidence derived from experience.

Those who propound the physico-theological argument have therefore no ground for being so contemptuous in their attitude to the transcendental mode of proof, posing as clear-sighted students of nature, and complacently looking down upon that proof as the artificial product of obscure speculative refinements. For were they willing to scrutinise their own procedure, they would find that, after advancing some considerable way on the solid ground of nature and experience, and finding themselves just as far distant as ever from the object which discloses itself to their reason, they suddenly leave this ground, and pass over into the realm of mere possibilities, where they hope upon the wings of ideas to draw near to the object—the object that has refused itself to all their *empirical* enquiries. For after this tremendous leap, when they have, as they think, found firm ground, they extend their concept—the *determinate* concept, into the possession of which they have now come, they know not how—over the whole sphere of creation. And the ideal, [which this reasoning thus involves, and] which is entirely a product of pure reason, they then elucidate by reference to experience, though inadequately enough, and in a manner far below the dignity of its object; and throughout they persist in refusing to admit that they have arrived at this knowledge or hypothesis by a road quite other than that of experience.

Thus the physico-theological proof of the existence of an original or supreme being rests upon the cosmological proof, and the cosmological upon the ontological. And since, besides these three, there is no other path open to speculative reason, the ontological proof from pure concepts of reason is the only possible one, if indeed any proof of a proposition so far exalted above all empirical employment of the understanding is possible at all.

1 A concept is always possible if it is not self-contradictory. This is the logical criterion of possibility, and by it the object of the concept is distinguishable from the *nihil negativum*. But it may none the less be an empty concept, unless the objective reality of the synthesis through which the concept is generated has been specifically proved; and such proof, as we have shown above, rests on principles of possible experience, and not on the principle of analysis (the law of contradiction). This is a warning against arguing directly from the logical possibility of concepts to the real possibility of things.

2 This inference is too well known to require detailed statement. It depends on the supposedly transcendental law of natural causality: that everything contingent has a cause, which, if itself contingent, must likewise have a cause, till the series of subordinate causes ends with an absolutely necessary cause, without which it would have no completeness.

3 [Albrecht von Haller (1708–77), a writer on medical and kindred subjects, author of *Die Alpen* and other poems.]

- From *Critique of Pure Reason* A (= 1st ed.) 590–630, B (= 2nd ed.) 618–658, trans. Norman Kemp Smith (London, 1933), pp. 499–524.

19

Kant
God and Morality

A more positive conclusion about theology is reached by Kant in his *Critique of Practical Reason* (1788). In his first *Critique* he had denied that theoretical reason can speculate about God. But in his second *Critique* he allows that beliefs in God, freedom and immortality are necessarily presupposed in the operation of practical or moral reason.

V. The Existence of God as a Postulate of Pure Practical Reason

The moral law led, in the foregoing analysis, to a practical problem which is assigned solely by pure reason and without any concurrence of sensuous incentives. It is the problem of the completeness of the first and principal part of the highest good, viz., morality; since this problem can be solved only in eternity, it led to the postulate of immortality. The same law must also lead us to affirm the possibility of the second element of the highest good, i.e., happiness proportional to that morality; it must do so just as disinterestedly as heretofore, by a purely impartial reason. This it can do on the supposition of the existence of a cause adequate to this effect, i.e., it must postulate the existence of God as necessarily belonging to the possibility of the highest good (the object of our will which is necessarily connected with the moral legislation of pure reason). We proceed to exhibit this connection in a convincing manner.

Happiness is the condition of a rational being in the world, in whose whole existence everything goes according to wish and will. It thus rests on the harmony of nature with his entire end and with the essential determining ground of his will. But the moral law commands as a law of freedom through motives wholly independent of nature and of its harmony with our faculty of desire (as incentives). Still, the acting rational being in the world is not at the same time the cause of the world and of nature itself. Hence there is not the slightest ground in the moral law for a necessary connection between the morality and proportionate happiness of a being which belongs to the world as one of its parts and as thus dependent oñ it. Not being nature's cause, his will cannot by its own strength bring nature, as it touches on his happiness, into complete harmony with his practical principles. Nevertheless, in the practical task of pure reason, i.e., in the necessary endeavor after the highest good, such a connection is postulated as necessary: we *should* seek to further the highest good (which therefore must be at least possible). Therefore also the existence is postulated of a cause of the whole of nature, itself distinct from nature, which contains the ground of the exact coincidence of happiness with morality. This supreme cause, however, must contain the ground of the agreement of nature not merely with a law of the will of rational beings but with the idea of this law so far as they make it the supreme ground of determination of the will. Thus it contains the ground of the agreement of nature not merely with actions moral in their form but also with their morality as the motives to such actions, i.e., with their moral intention. Therefore, the highest good is possible in the world only on the supposition of a supreme cause of nature which has a causality corresponding to the moral intention. Now a being which is capable of actions by the idea of laws is an intelligence (a rational being), and the causality of such a being according to this idea of laws is his will. Therefore, the supreme cause of nature, in so far as it must be presupposed for the highest good, is a being which is the cause (and consequently the author) of nature through understanding and will, i.e., God. As a consequence, the postulate of the possibility of a highest derived good (the best world) is at the same time the postulate of the reality of a highest original good, namely, the existence of God. Now it was our duty to promote the highest good; and it is not merely our privilege but a necessity connected with duty as a requisite to presuppose the possibility of this highest good. This presupposition is made only under the condition of the existence of God, and this condition inseparably connects this supposition with duty. Therefore, it is morally necessary to assume the existence of God.

It is well to notice here that this moral necessity is subjective, i.e., a need, and not objective, i.e., duty itself. For there cannot be any duty to assume the existence of a thing, because such a supposition concerns only the theoretical use of reason. It is also not to be understood that the assumption of the existence of God is necessary as a ground of all obligation in general (for this rests, as has been fully shown, solely on the autonomy of reason itself). All that here belongs to duty is the endeavor to produce and to further the highest good in the world, the possibility of which may thus be postulated though our reason cannot conceive it except by presupposing a highest intelligence. To assume its existence is thus connected with the consciousness of our duty, though this assumption itself belongs to the realm of theoretical reason. Considered only in reference to the latter, it is a hypothesis, i.e., a ground of explanation. But in reference to the comprehensibility of an object (the highest good) placed before us by the moral law, and thus as a practical need, it can be called *faith* and even pure *rational faith*, because pure reason alone (by its theoretical as well as practical employment) is the source from which it springs.

From this deduction it now becomes clear why the Greek schools could never succeed in solving their problem of the practical possibility of the highest good. It was because they made the rule of the use which the human will makes of its freedom the sole and self-sufficient ground of its possibility, thinking that they had no need of the existence of God for this purpose. They were certainly correct in establishing the principle of morals by itself, independently of this postulate and merely from the relation of reason to the will, thus making the principle of morality the *supreme* practical condition of the highest good; but this principle was not the *entire* condition of possibility. The Epicureans had indeed raised a wholly false principle of morality, i.e., that of happiness, into the supreme one, and for law had substituted a maxim of arbitrary choice of each according to his inclination. But they proceeded consistently enough, in that they degraded their highest good in proportion to the baseness of their principle and expected no greater happiness than that which could be attained through human prudence (wherein both temperance and the moderation of inclinations belong), though everyone knows prudence to be scarce enough and to produce diverse results according to circumstances, not to mention the exceptions which their maxims continually had to admit and which made them worthless as laws. The Stoics, on the other hand, had chosen their supreme practical principle, virtue, quite correctly as the condition of the highest good. But as they imagined the degree of virtue which is required for its pure law as completely attainable in this life, they not only exaggerated the moral capacity of man, under the name of 'sage', beyond all the limits of his nature, making it into something which is contradicted by all our knowledge of men; they also refused to accept the second component of the highest good, i.e., happiness, as a special object of human desire. Rather, they made their sage, like a god in the consciousness of the excellence of his person, wholly independent of nature (as regards his own contentment), exposing him to the evils of life but not subjecting him to them. (They also represented him as free from everything morally evil.) Thus they really left out of the highest good the second element (personal happiness), since they placed the highest good only in acting and in contentment with one's own personal worth, including it in the consciousness of moral character. But the voice of their own nature could have sufficiently refuted this.

The doctrine of Christianity,[1] even when not regarded as a religious doctrine, gives at this point a concept of the highest good (the Kingdom of God) which is alone sufficient to the strictest demand of practical reason. The moral law is holy (unyielding) and demands holiness of morals, although all moral perfection to which man can attain is only virtue, i.e., a law-abiding disposition resulting from respect for the law and thus implying consciousness of a continuous propensity to transgress it or at least to a defilement, i.e., to an admixture of many spurious (not moral) motives to obedience to the law; consequently, man can achieve only a self-esteem combined with humility. And thus with respect to the holiness required by the Christian law, nothing remains to the creature but endless progress, though for the same reason hope of endless duration is justified. The worth of a character completely accordant with the moral law is infinite, because all possible happiness in the judgment of a wise and omnipotent dispenser of happiness has no other limitation than the lack of fitness of rational beings to their duty. But the moral law does not of itself promise happiness, for the latter is not, according to concepts of any order of nature, necessarily connected with obedience to the law. Christian ethics supplies this defect of the second indispensable component of the highest good by presenting a world wherein reasonable beings single-mindedly devote themselves to the moral law; this is the Kingdom of God, in which nature and morality come into a harmony, which is foreign to each as such, through a holy Author of the world, who makes possible the derived highest good. The holiness of morals is prescribed to them even in this life as a guide to conduct, but the well-being proportionate to this, which is bliss, is thought of as attainable only in eternity. This is due to the fact that the former must always be the pattern of their conduct in every state, and progressing toward it is even in this life possible and necessary, whereas the latter, under the name of happiness, cannot (as far as our own capacity is concerned) be reached in this life and therefore is made only an object of hope. Nevertheless, the Christian principle of morality is not theological and thus heteronomous, being rather the autonomy of pure practical reason itself, because it does not make the knowledge of God and His will the basis of these laws but makes such knowledge the basis only of succeeding to the highest good on condition of obedience to these laws; it places the real incentive for obedience to the law not in the desired consequences of obedience but in the conception of duty alone, in true observance of which the worthiness to attain the latter alone consists.

In this manner, through the concept of the highest good as the object and final end of pure practical reason, the moral law leads to religion. Religion is the recognition of all duties as divine commands, not as sanctions, i.e., arbitrary and contingent ordinances of a foreign will, but as essential laws of any free will as such. Even as such, they must be regarded as commands of the Supreme Being because we can hope for the highest good (to strive for which is our duty under the moral law) only from a morally perfect (holy and beneficent) and omnipotent will; and, therefore, we can hope to attain it only through harmony with this will. But here again everything remains disinterested and based only on duty, without being based on fear or hope as incentives, which, if they became principles, would destroy the entire moral worth of the actions. The moral law commands us to make the highest possible good in a world the final object of all our conduct. This I cannot hope to effect except through the agreement of my will with that of a holy and beneficent Author of the world. And although my own happiness is included in the concept of the highest good as a whole wherein the greatest happiness is thought of as connected in exact proportion to the greatest degree of moral perfection possible to creatures, still it is not happiness but the moral law (which, in fact, sternly places restricting conditions upon my boundless longing for happiness) which is proved to be the ground determining the will to further the highest good.

Therefore, morals is not really the doctrine of how to make ourselves happy but of how we are to be *worthy* of happiness. Only if religion is added to it can the hope arise of someday participating in happiness in proportion as we endeavored not to be unworthy of it.

One is worthy of possessing a thing or a state when his possession is harmonious with the highest good. We can easily see now that all worthiness is a matter of moral conduct, because this constitutes the condition of everything else (which belongs to one's state) in the concept of the highest good, i.e., participation in happiness. From this there follows that one must never consider morals itself as a doctrine of happiness, i.e., as an instruction in how to acquire happiness. For morals has to do only with the rational condition (*conditio sine qua non*) of happiness and not with means of achieving it. But when morals (which imposes only duties instead of providing rules for selfish wishes) is completely expounded, and a moral wish has been awakened to promote the highest good (to bring the Kingdom of God to us), which is a wish based on law and one to which no selfish mind could have aspired, and when for the sake of this wish the step to religion has been taken—then only can ethics be called a doctrine of happiness, because the *hope* for it first arises with religion.

From this it can also be seen that, if we inquire into God's final end in creating the world, we must name not the happiness of rational beings in the world but the highest good, which adds a further condition to the wish of rational beings to be happy, viz., the condition of being worthy of happiness, which is the morality of these beings, for this alone contains the standard by which they can hope to participate in happiness at the hand of a *wise* creator. For since wisdom, theoretically regarded, means the knowledge of the highest good and, practically, the suitability of the will to the highest good, one cannot ascribe to a supreme independent wisdom an end based merely on benevolence. For we cannot conceive the action of this benevolence (with respect to the happiness of rational beings) except as conformable to the restrictive conditions of harmony with the holiness[2] of His will as the highest original good. Then perhaps those who have placed the end of creation in the glory of God, provided this is not thought of anthropomorphically as an inclination to be esteemed, have found the best term. For nothing glorifies God more than what is the most estimable thing in the world, namely, respect for His command, the observance of sacred duty which His law imposes on us, when there is added to this His glorious plan of crowning such an excellent order with corresponding happiness. If the latter, to speak in human terms, makes Him worthy of love, by the former He is an object of adoration. Human beings can win love by doing good, but by this alone even they never win respect; the greatest well-doing does them honor only by being exercised according to worthiness.

It follows of itself that, in the order of ends, man (and every rational being) is an end-in-himself, i.e., he is never to be used merely as a means for someone (even for God) without at the same time being himself an end, and that thus the humanity in our person must itself be holy to us, because man is subject to the moral law and therefore subject to that which is of itself holy, and it is only on account of this and in agreement with this that anything can be called holy. For this moral law is founded on the autonomy of his will as a free will, which by its universal laws must necessarily be able to agree with that to which it subjects itself.

---

1 The view is commonly held that the Christian precept of morals has no advantage over the moral concept of the Stoics in respect to its purity; but the difference between them is nevertheless obvious. The Stoic system makes the consciousness of strength of mind the pivot around which all moral intentions should turn; and, if the followers of this system spoke of duties and even defined them accurately, they nevertheless placed the incentives and the real determining ground of the will in an elevation of character above the base incentives of the senses which have their power

only through weakness of the mind. Virtue was, therefore, for them a certain heroism of the sage who, raising himself above the animal nature of man, was sufficient to himself, subject to no temptation to transgress the moral law, and elevated above duties though he propounded duties to others. But all this they could not have done had they conceived this law in the same purity and rigor as does the precept of the Gospel. If I understand by 'idea' a perfection to which the senses can give nothing adequate, the moral ideas are not transcendent, i.e., of such a kind that we cannot even sufficiently define the concept or of which we are uncertain whether there is a corresponding object (as are the ideas of speculative reason); rather, they serve as models of practical perfection, as an indispensable rule of moral conduct, and as a standard for comparison. If I now regard Christian morals from their philosophical side, it appears in comparison with the ideas of the Greek schools as follows: the ideas of the Cynics, Epicureans, Stoics, and Christians are, respectively, the simplicity of nature, prudence, wisdom, and holiness. In respect to the way they achieve them, the Greek schools differ in that the Cynics found common sense sufficient, while the others found it in the path of science, and thus all held it to lie in the mere use of man's natural powers. Christian ethics, because it formulated its precept as pure and uncompromising (as befits a moral precept), destroyed man's confidence of being wholly adequate to it, at least in this life; but it re-established it by enabling us to hope that, if we act as well as lies in our power, what is not in our power will come to our aid from another source, whether we know in what way or not. Aristotle and Plato differed only as to the origin of our moral concepts.

2 Incidentally, and in order to make the peculiarity of this concept clear, I make the following remark. Since we ascribe various attributes to God, whose quality we find suitable also to creatures (e.g., power, knowledge, presence, goodness, etc.), though in God they are present in a higher degree under such names as omnipotence, omniscience, omnipresence, and perfect goodness, etc., there are three which exclusively and without qualification of magnitude are ascribed to God, and they are all moral. He is the only holy, the only blessed, and the only wise being, because these concepts of themselves imply unlimitedness. By the arrangement of these He is thus the holy lawgiver (and creator), the beneficent ruler (and sustainer), and the just judge. These three attributes contain everything whereby God is the object of religion, and in conformity to them the metaphysical perfections of themselves arise in reason.

• From *Critique of Practical Reason*, Book II, Chapter ii, § 5, trans. Lewis White Beck (Indianapolis, 1956), pp. 128–136.

20

Feuerbach
God as a Projection

Ludwig Feuerbach was born in Bavaria in 1804. He studied under both Hegel and Schleiermacher in Berlin, and held an academic post briefly at the University of Erlangen, but resigned it under pressure because of his unorthodox theological views. He spent the rest of his life in private scholarship, and died in 1872. His most important work is *The Essence of Christianity* (1841), which deeply influenced Marx and Engels in their view of religion, and also many later writers (e.g. Freud) who regarded religion as a 'projection'. Feuerbach continued his programme of translating theology into anthropology in his *Lectures on the Essence of Religion* (1851).

In the first section of Chapter 1 of *The Essence of Christianity* Feuerbach defines religion in terms of our consciousness of the infinite, which he regards as our consciousness of our own infinite nature. When we imagine higher beings, the predicates we ascribe to them are qualities we project from ourselves.

Ch. I, § 2. The Essence of Religion Considered Generally

What we have hitherto been maintaining generally, even with regard to sensational impressions, of the relation between subject and object, applies especially to the relation between the subject and the religious object.

In the perceptions of the senses consciousness of the object is distinguishable from consciousness of self; but in religion, consciousness of the object and self-consciousness coincide. The object of the senses is out of man, the religious object is within him, and therefore as little forsakes him as his self-consciousness or his conscience; it is the intimate, the closest object. 'God', says Augustine, for example, 'is nearer, more related to us, and therefore more easily known by us, than sensible, corporeal things.'[1] The object of the senses is in itself indifferent—independent of the disposition or of the judgment; but the object of religion is a selected object; the most excellent, the first, the supreme being; it essentially presupposes a critical judgment, a

156

discrimination between the divine and the non-divine, between that which is worthy of adoration and that which is not worthy. And here may be applied, without any limitation, the proposition: the object of any subject is nothing else than the subject's own nature taken objectively. Such as are a man's thoughts and dispositions, such is his God; so much worth as a man has, so much and no more has his God. Consciousness of God is self-consciousness, knowledge of God is self-knowledge. By his God thou knowest the man, and by the man his God; the two are identical. Whatever is God to a man, that is his heart and soul; and conversely, God is the manifested inward nature, the expressed self of a man,—religion the solemn unveiling of a man's hidden treasures, the revelation of his intimate thoughts, the open confession of his love-secrets.

But when religion—consciousness of God—is designated as the self-consciousness of man, this is not to be understood as affirming that the religious man is directly aware of this identity; for, on the contrary, ignorance of it is fundamental to the peculiar nature of religion. To preclude this misconception, it is better to say, religion is man's earliest and also indirect form of self-knowledge. Hence, religion everywhere precedes philosophy, as in the history of the race, so also in that of the individual. Man first of all sees his nature as if *out of* himself, before he finds it in himself. His own nature is in the first instance contemplated by him as that of another being. Religion is the childlike condition of humanity; but the child sees his nature— man—out of himself; in childhood a man is an object to himself, under the form of another man. Hence the historical progress of religion consists in this: that what by an earlier religion was regarded as objective, is now recognised as subjective; that is, what was formerly contemplated and worshipped as God is now perceived to be something *human*. What was at first religion becomes at a later period idolatry; man is seen to have adored his own nature. Man has given objectivity to himself, but has not recognised the object as his own nature: a later religion takes this forward step; every advance in religion is therefore a deeper self-knowledge. But every particular religion, while it pronounces its predecessors idolatrous, excepts itself—and necessarily so, otherwise it would no longer be religion— from the fate, the common nature of all religions: it imputes only to other religions what is the fault, if fault it be, of religion in general. Because it has a different object, a different tenor, because it has transcended the ideas of preceding religions, it erroneously supposes itself exalted above the necessary eternal laws which constitute the essence of religion—it fancies its object, its ideas, to be superhuman. But the essence of religion, thus hidden from the religious, is evident to the thinker, by whom religion is viewed objectively, which it cannot be by its votaries. And it is our task to show that the antithesis of divine and human is altogether illusory, that it is nothing else than the antithesis between the human nature in general and the human individual; that, consequently, the object and contents of the Christian religion are altogether human.

Religion, at least the Christian, is the relation of man to himself, or more correctly to his own nature (*i.e.*, his subjective nature); but a relation to it, viewed as a nature apart from his own. The divine being is nothing else than the human being, or, rather, the human nature purified, freed from the limits of the individual man, made objective—*i.e.*, contemplated and revered as another, a distinct being. All the attributes of the divine nature are, therefore, attributes of the human nature.

In relation to the attributes, the predicates, of the Divine Being, this is admitted without hesitation, but by no means in relation to the subject of these predicates. The negation of the subject is held to be irreligion, nay, atheism; though not so the negation of the predicates. But that which has no predicates or qualities, has no effect upon me; that which has no effect upon me has no existence for me. To deny all the qualities of a being is equivalent to denying the being himself. A being without qualities is one which cannot become an object to the mind, and such a being is virtually non-existent. Where man deprives God of all qualities, God is no longer anything more to him than a negative being. To the truly religious man, God is not a being without qualities, because to him he is a positive, real being. The theory that God cannot be defined, and consequently cannot be known by man, is therefore the offspring of recent times, a product of modern unbelief.

As reason is and can be pronounced finite only where man regards sensual enjoyment, or religious emotion, or aesthetic contemplation, or moral sentiment, as the absolute, the true; so the proposition that God is unknowable or undefinable, can only be enunciated and become fixed as a dogma, where this object has no longer any interest for the intellect; where the real, the positive, alone has any hold on man, where the real alone has for him the significance of the essential, of the absolute, divine object, but where at the same time, in contradiction with this purely worldly tendency, there yet exist some old remains of religiousness. On the ground that God is unknowable, man excuses himself to what is yet remaining of his religious conscience for his forgetfulness of God, his absorption in the world: he denies God practically by his conduct,—the world has possession of all his thoughts and inclinations,—but he does not deny him theoretically, he does not attack his existence; he lets that rest. But this existence does not affect or incommode him; it is a merely negative existence, an existence without existence, a self-contradictory existence,—a state of being which, as to its effects, is not distinguishable from non-being. The denial of determinate, positive predicates concerning the divine nature is nothing else than a denial of religion, with, however, an appearance of religion in its favour, so that it is not recognised as a denial; it is simply a subtle, disguised atheism. The alleged religious horror of limiting God by positive predicates is only the irreligious wish to know nothing more of God, to banish God from the mind. Dread of limitation is dread of existence. All real existence, *i.e.*, all existence which is truly such, is qualitative, determinative existence. He who earnestly believes in the Divine existence is not shocked at the attributing even of gross sensuous qualities of God. He who dreads an existence that may give offence, who shrinks from the grossness of a positive predicate, may as well renounce existence altogether. A God who is injured by determinate qualities has not the courage and the strength to exist. Qualities are the fire, the vital breath, the oxygen, the salt of existence. An existence in general, an existence without qualities, is an insipidity, an absurdity. But there can be no more in God than is supplied by religion. Only where man loses his taste for religion, and thus religion itself becomes insipid, does the existence of God become an insipid existence—an existence without qualities.

There is, however, a still milder way of denying the divine predicates than the direct one just described. It is admitted that the predicates of the divine nature are finite, and, more particularly, human qualities, but their rejection is rejected; they are even taken under protection, because it is necessary to man to have a definite conception of God, and since he is man he can form no other than a human conception of him. In relation to God, it is said, these predicates are certainly without any objective validity; but to me, if he is to exist for me, he cannot appear otherwise than as he does appear to me, namely, as a being with attributes analogous to the human. But this distinction between what God is in himself, and what he is for me destroys the peace of religion, and is besides in itself an unfounded and untenable distinction. I cannot know whether God is something else in himself or for himself than he is for me; what he is to me is to me all that he is. For me, there lies in these predicates under which he exists for me, what he is in himself, his very nature; he is for me what he can alone ever be for me. The religious man finds perfect satisfaction in that which God is in relation to himself; of any other relation he knows nothing, for God is to him what he can alone be to man. In the distinction above stated, man takes a point of view above himself, *i.e.*, above his nature, the absolute measure of his being; but this transcendentalism is only an illusion; for I can make the distinction between the object as it is in itself, and the object as it is for me, only where an object can really appear otherwise to me, not where it appears to me

such as the absolute measure of my nature determines it to appear—
such as it must appear to me. It is true that I may have a merely
subjective conception, *i.e.*, one which does not arise out of the general
constitution of my species; but if my conception is determined by the
constitution of my species, the distinction between what an object is in
itself, and what it is for me ceases; for this conception is itself an
absolute one. The measure of the species is the absolute measure, law,
and criterion of man. And, indeed, religion has the conviction that its
conceptions, its predicates of God, are such as every man ought to
have, and must have, if he would have the true ones—that they are the
conceptions necessary to human nature; nay, further, that they are
objectively true, representing God as he is. To every religion the gods
of *other* religions are only notions concerning God, but its own conception of God is to it God himself, the true God—God such as he is in
himself. Religion is satisfied only with a complete Deity, a God
without reservation; it will not have a mere phantasm of God; it
demands God himself. Religion gives up its own existence when it
gives up the nature of God; it is no longer a truth when it renounces
the possession of the true God. Scepticism is the arch-enemy of
religion; but the distinction between object and conception—
between God as he is in himself, and God as he is for me—is a sceptical
distinction, and therefore an irreligious one.

That which is to man the self-existent, the highest being, to which
he can conceive nothing higher—that is to him the Divine Being.
How then should he inquire concerning this being, what he is in
himself? If God were an object to the bird, he would be a winged
being: the bird knows nothing higher, nothing more blissful, than the
winged condition. How ludicrous would it be if this bird pronounced:
To me God appears as a bird, but what he is in himself I know not. To
the bird the highest nature is the bird-nature; take from him the
conception of this, and you take from him the conception of the
highest being. How, then, could he ask whether God in himself were
winged? To ask whether God is in himself what he is for me, is to ask
whether God is God, is to lift oneself above one's God, to rise up
against him.

Wherever, therefore, this idea, that the religious predicates are only
anthropomorphisms, has taken possession of a man, there has doubt,
has unbelief, obtained the mastery of faith. And it is only the incon-
sequence of faint-heartedness and intellectual imbecility which does
not proceed from this idea to the formal negation of the predicates,
and from thence to the negation of the subject to which they relate. If
thou doubtest the objective truth of the predicates, thou must also
doubt the objective truth of the subject whose predicates they are. If
thy predicates are anthropomorphisms, the subject of them is an

anthropomorphism too. If love, goodness, personality, &c., are human attributes, so also is the subject which thou presupposest, the existence of God, the belief that there is a God, an anthropomorphism—a presupposition purely human. Whence knowest thou that the belief in a God at all is not a limitation of man's mode of conception? Higher beings—and thou supposest such—are perhaps so blest in themselves, so at unity with themselves, that they are not hung in suspense between themselves and a yet higher being. To know God and not oneself to be God, to know blessedness and not oneself to enjoy it, is a state of disunity, of unhappiness. Higher beings know nothing of this unhappiness; they have no conception of that which they are not.

Thou believest in love as a divine attribute because thou thyself lovest; thou believest that God is a wise, benevolent being because thou knowest nothing better in thyself than benevolence and wisdom; and thou believest that God exists, that therefore he is a subject—whatever exists is a subject, whether it be defined as substance, person, essence, or otherwise—because thou thyself existest, art thyself a subject. Thou knowest no higher human good than to love, than to be good and wise; and even so thou knowest no higher happiness than to exist, to be a subject; for the consciousness of all reality, of all bliss, is for thee bound up in the consciousness of being a subject, of existing. God is an existence, a subject to thee, for the same reason that he is to thee a wise, a blessed, a personal being. The distinction between the divine predicates and the divine subject is only this, that to thee the subject, the existence, does not appear an anthropomorphism, because the conception of it is necessarily involved in thy own existence as a subject, whereas the predicates do appear anthropomorphisms, because their necessity—the necessity that God should be conscious, wise, good, &c.,—is not an immediate necessity, identical with the being of man, but is evolved by his self-consciousness, by the activity of his thought. I am a subject, I exist, whether I be wise or unwise, good or bad. To exist is to man the first datum; it constitutes the very idea of the subject; it is presupposed by the predicates. Hence man relinquishes the predicates, but the existence of God is to him a settled, irrefragable, absolutely certain, objective truth. But, nevertheless, this distinction is merely an apparent one. The necessity of the subject lies only in the necessity of the predicate. Thou art a subject only in so far as thou art a human subject; the certainty and reality of thy existence lie only in the certainty and reality of thy human attributes. What the subject is lies only in the predicate; the predicate is the *truth* of the subject—the subject only the personified, existing predicate, the predicate conceived as existing. Subject and predicate are distinguished only as existence and essence. The negation of the predicates is therefore the negation of the subject. What remains of the human subject when abstracted from the human attributes? Even in the language of common life the divine predicates—Providence, Omniscience, Omnipotence—are put for the divine subject.

The certainty of the existence of God, of which it has been said that it is as certain, nay, more certain to man than his own existence, depends only on the certainty of the qualities of God—it is in itself no immediate certainty. To the Christian the existence of the Christian God only is a certainty; to the heathen that of the heathen God only. The heathen did not doubt the existence of Jupiter, because he took no offence at the nature of Jupiter, because he could conceive of God under no other qualities, because to him these qualities were a certainty, a divine reality. The reality of the predicate is the sole guarantee of existence.

Whatever man conceives to be true, he immediately conceives to be real (that is, to have an objective existence), because, originally, only the real is true to him—true in opposition to what is merely conceived, dreamed, imagined. The idea of being, of existence, is the original idea of truth; or, originally, man makes truth dependent on existence, subsequently, existence dependent on truth. Now God is the nature of man regarded as absolute truth,—the truth of man; but God, or, what is the same thing, religion, is as various as are the conditions under which man conceives this his nature, regards it as the highest being. These conditions, then, under which man conceives God, are to him the truth, and for that reason they are also the highest existence, or rather they are existence itself; for only the emphatic, the highest existence, is existence, and deserves this name. Therefore, God is an existent, real being, on the very same ground that he is a particular, definite being; for the qualities of God are nothing else than the essential qualities of man himself, and a particular man is what he is, has his existence, his reality, only in his particular conditions. Take away from the Greek the quality of being Greek, and you take away his existence. On this ground it is true that for a definite positive religion—that is, relatively—the certainty of the existence of God is *immediate*; for just as involuntarily, as necessarily, as the Greek was a Greek, so necessarily were his gods Greek beings, so necessarily were they real, existent beings. Religion is that conception of the nature of the world and of man which is essential to, *i.e.*, identical with, a man's nature. But man does not stand above this his necessary conception; on the contrary, it stands above him; it animates, determines, governs him. The necessity of a proof, of a middle term to unite qualities with existence, the possibility of a doubt, is abolished. Only that which is apart from my own being is capable of being doubted by me. How then can I doubt of God, who is my being? To doubt of God is to doubt of myself. Only when God is thought of abstractly, when his predicates are the result of philosophic abstraction, arises the distinction or separation between subject and predicate, existence and nature—arises the fiction that the existence or the subject is something else than the predicate, something immediate, indubitable, in distinction from the predicate, which is held to be doubtful. But this is only a fiction. A God who has abstract predicates has also an abstract existence. Existence, being, varies with varying qualities.

The identity of the subject and predicate is clearly evidenced by the progressive development of religion, which is identical with the progressive development of human culture. So long as man is in a mere state of nature, so long is his god a mere nature-god—a personification of some natural force. Where man inhabits houses, he also encloses his gods in temples. The temple is only a manifestation of the value which man attaches to beautiful buildings. Temples in honour of religion are in truth temples in honour of architecture. With the emerging of man from a state of savagery and wildness to one of culture, with the distinction between what is fitting for man and what is not fitting, arises simultaneously the distinction between that which is fitting and that which is not fitting for God. God is the idea of majesty, of the highest dignity: the religious sentiment is the sentiment of supreme fitness. The later more cultured artists of Greece were the first to embody in the statues of the gods the ideas of dignity, of spiritual grandeur, of imperturbable repose and serenity. But why were these qualities in their view attributes, predicates of God? Because they were in themselves regarded by the Greeks as divinities. Why did those artists exclude all disgusting and low passions? Because they perceived them to be unbecoming, unworthy, unhuman, and consequently ungodlike. The Homeric gods eat and drink;—that implies eating and drinking is a divine pleasure. Physical strength is an attribute of the Homeric gods: Zeus is the strongest of the gods. Why? Because physical strength, in and by itself, was regarded as something glorious, divine. To the ancient Germans the highest virtues were those of the warrior; therefore, their supreme god was the god of war, Odin,—war, 'the original or oldest law'. Not the attribute of the divinity, but the divineness or deity of the attribute, is the first true Divine Being. Thus what theology and philosophy have held to be God, the Absolute, the Infinite, is not God; but that which they have held not to be God is God: namely, the attribute, the quality, whatever has reality. Hence he alone is the true atheist to whom the predicates of the Divine Being,—for example, love, wisdom, justice,—are nothing; not he to whom merely the subject of these predicates is nothing. And in no wise is the negation of the subject necessarily also a negation of the predicates considered in themselves. These have an intrinsic, independent reality; they force their recognition upon man by their very nature; they are self-evident truths to him; they prove, they attest themselves. It does not follow that goodness, justice, wisdom, are chimæras because the existence of God is a chimæra, nor truths because this is a truth. The idea of God is dependent on the idea of justice, of benevolence; a God who is not benevolent, not just, not wise, is no God; but the converse does not hold. The fact is not that a quality is divine because God has it, but that God has it because it is in itself divine; because without it God would be a defective being. Justice, wisdom, in general every quality which constitutes the divinity of God, is determined and known by itself independently, but the idea of God is determined by the qualities which have thus been previously judged to be worthy of the divine nature; only in the case in which I identify God and justice, in which I think of God immediately as the reality of the idea of justice, is the idea of God self-determined. But if God as a subject is the determined, while the quality, the predicate, is the determining, then in truth the rank of the godhead is due not to the subject, but to the predicate.

Not until several, and those contradictory, attributes are united in one being, and this being is conceived as personal—the personality being thus brought into especial prominence—not until then is the origin of religion lost sight of, is it forgotten that what the activity of the reflective power has converted into a predicate distinguishable or separable from the subject, was originally the true subject. Thus the Greeks and Romans deified accidents as substances; virtues, states of mind, passions, as independent beings. Man, especially the religious man, is to himself the measure of all things, of all reality. Whatever strongly impresses a man, whatever produces an unusual effect on his mind, if it be only a peculiar, inexplicable sound or note, he personifies as a divine being. Religion embraces all the objects of the world: everything existing has been an object of religious reverence; in the nature and consciousness of religion there is nothing else than what lies in the nature of man and in his consciousness of himself and of the world. Religion has no material exclusively its own. In Rome even the passions of fear and terror had their temples. The Christians also made mental phenomena into independent beings, their own feelings into qualities of things, the passions which governed them into powers which governed the world, in short, predicates of their own nature, whether recognised as such or not, into independent subjective existences. Devils, cobolds, witches, ghosts, angels, were sacred truths as long as the religious spirit held undivided sway over mankind.

Feuerbach goes on to argue that the infinite plenitude or multitude of predicates ascribed to God is only really the infinite abundance of different individuals.

Now, when it is shown that what the subject is lies entirely in the
attributes of the subject; that is, that the predicate is the true subject;
it is also proved that if the divine predicates are attributes of the
human nature, the subject of those predicates is also of the human
nature. But the divine predicates are partly general, partly personal.
The general predicates are the metaphysical, but these serve only as
external points of support to religion; they are not the characteristic
definitions of religion. It is the personal predicates alone which constitute the essence of religion—in which the Divine Being is the object of
religion. Such are, for example, that God is a Person, that he is the
moral Lawgiver, the Father of mankind, the Holy One, the Just, the
Good, the Merciful. It is, however, at once clear, or it will at least be
clear in the sequel, with regard to these and other definitions, that,
especially as applied to a personality, they are purely human definitions, and that consequently man in religion—in his relation to God—
is in relation to his own nature; for to the religious sentiment these
predicates are not mere conceptions, mere images, which man forms
of God, to be distinguished from that which God is in himself, but
truths, facts, realities. Religion knows nothing of anthropomorphisms; to it they are not anthropomorphisms. It is the very essence of
religion, that to it these definitions express the nature of God. They are
pronounced to be images only by the understanding, which reflects on
religion, and which while defending them yet before its own tribunal
denies them. But to the religious sentiment God is a real Father, real
Love and Mercy; for to it he is a real, living, personal being, and
therefore his attributes are also living and personal. Nay, the definitions which are the most sufficing to the religious sentiment are
precisely those which give the most offence to the understanding, and
which in the process of reflection on religion it denies. Religion is
essentially emotion; hence, objectively also, emotion is to it necessarily of a divine nature. Even anger appears to it an emotion not unworthy of God, provided only there be a religious motive at the
foundation of this anger.

But here it is also essential to observe, and this phenomenon is an
extremely remarkable one, characterising the very core of religion,
that in proportion as the divine subject is in reality human, the greater
is the apparent difference between God and man; that is, the more, by
reflection on religion, by theology, is the identity of the divine and
human denied, and the human, considered as such, is depreciated.[2]
The reason of this is, that as what is positive in the conception of the

divine being can only be human, the conception of man, as an object of consciousness, can only be negative. To enrich God, man must become poor; that God may be all, man must be nothing. But he desires to be nothing in himself, because what he takes from himself is not lost to him, since it is preserved in God. Man has his being in God; why then should he have it in himself? Where is the necessity of positing the same thing twice, of having it twice? What man withdraws from himself, what he renounces in himself, he only enjoys in an incomparably higher and fuller measure in God.

Feuerbach concludes the chapter by arguing that people ascribe to God the very things which they sacrifice or feel are impossible for themselves. But then in religious worship they receive back into themselves the rejected nature.

1 *De Genesi ad Litteram* 1. v. ch. 16.
2 'Between Creator and creature no similarity can be expressed without noting a greater dissimilarity between them' (Fourth Lateran Council, canon 2). The last distinction between man and God, between the finite and infinite nature, to which the religious speculative imagination soars, is the distinction between Something and Nothing, Ens and Non-Ens; for only in Nothing is all community with other beings abolished.

● From *The Essence of Christianity*, trans. George Eliot, Chapter 1, § 2.

21

Kierkegaard
Revelation and Authority

Søren Kierkegaard was born in Copenhagen in 1813, and died there in 1855. In his brief life he produced a stream of pseudonymous works, of which the *Philosophical Fragments* and *Concluding Unscientific Postscript* are the most significant philosophically. Later he produced several more directly Christian works, for instance *Purity of Heart* and *The Works of Love*. The essay below was originally part of *The Book on Adler* which Kierkegaard wrote in 1846–47 but never published. He published the essay separately in 1849 as one of the *Two Minor Ethico-Religious Treatises*. The book was occasioned by the case of Adolph Peter Adler, a Danish priest who claimed a series of special revelations and who was deposed by his bishop in 1845. The case sparked off a series of reflections by Kierkegaard on the subject of revelation. In them he raises some favourite themes discussed elsewhere: the tendency of thinkers in the nineteenth century (particularly Hegel and his followers) to reduce Christianity to a set of ideas and theories, thus forgetting about the 'existing individual'; the paradox of the Incarnation, when the Eternal God came into existence in time; the contemporaneousness of true believers with Christ, who is an offence to the world; and the barrenness and time-serving of official Christianity. His reflections on authority and revelation show that although Kierkegaard writes of truth as subjectivity, he also insists on an objective historical element in Christianity.

Of the Difference Between a Genius and an Apostle

What, exactly, have the errors[1] of exegesis and philosophy done in order to confuse Christianity, and how have they confused Christianity? Quite briefly and categorically, they have simply forced back the sphere of paradox-religion[2] into the sphere of aesthetics, and in consequence have succeeded in bringing Christian terminology to such a pass that terms which, so long as they remain within their sphere, are qualitative categories, can be put to almost any use as clever expressions. If the sphere of paradox-religion is abolished, or explained away in aesthetics, an Apostle becomes neither more nor less than a genius, and then—good night, Christianity! *Esprit* and the Spirit, revelation and originality, a call from God and genius, all end by meaning more or less the same thing.

That is how the errors of science and learning have confused Christianity. The confusion has spread from learning to the religious discourse, with the result that one not infrequently hears priests, *bona fide*, in all learned simplicity, prostituting Christianity. They talk in exalted terms of St Paul's brilliance and profundity, of his beautiful similes and so on—that is mere aestheticism. If St Paul is to be regarded as a genius, then things look black for him, and only clerical ignorance would ever dream of praising him in terms of aesthetics, because it has no standard, but argues that all is well so long as one says something good about him. This kind of good-natured and well-intentioned thoughtlessness is due to the fact that the individual in question is not disciplined by qualitative dialectic. If he were he would have learnt that to say something good of an apostle, when it is inapposite, does him no service, for as a result he is acclaimed for what in this case is a matter of indifference, and admired as something which essentially he is not, and then what he is is quite forgotten. This kind of thoughtless eloquence is quite as likely to celebrate St Paul as a stylist and an artist in words or, better still, since it is after all well known that he was also engaged in a craft, as a tent-maker whose masterly work surpassed that of all upholsterers before and since—for as long as one says something good about St Paul all is well. As a genius St Paul cannot be compared with either Plato or Shakespeare, as a coiner of beautiful similes he comes pretty low down in the scale, as a stylist his name is quite obscure—and as an upholsterer: well, I frankly admit I have no idea how to place him. The point is that it is always better to treat stupid solemnity as a joke and then the really serious thing becomes apparent, the fact that St Paul is an Apostle. As an Apostle St Paul has no connexion whatsoever with Plato or Shakespeare, with stylists or upholsterers, and none of them (Plato no more than Shakespeare or Harrison the upholsterer) can possibly be compared with him.

A genius and an apostle are qualitatively different, they are definitions which each belong in their own spheres; *the sphere of immanence, and the sphere of transcendence:*

(1) *Genius may, therefore, have something new to bring forth, but what it brings forth disappears again as it becomes assimilated by the human race, just as the difference 'genius' disappears as soon as one thinks of eternity; the Apostle has, paradoxically, something new to bring, the newness of which, precisely because it is essentially paradoxical, and not an anticipation in relation to the development of the race, always remains, just as an Apostle remains an Apostle in all eternity, and no eternal immanence puts him on the same level as other men, because he is essentially, paradox-*

ically different. (2) Genius is what it is of itself, i.e. through that which it is in itself; an Apostle is what he is by his divine authority. (3) Genius has only an immanent teleology; the Apostle is placed as absolute paradoxical teleology.

All thought breathes in immanence, whereas faith and the paradox are a qualitative sphere unto themselves. As between man and man, *qua* man, all differences are immanent, vanishing before essential and eternal thought, a factor which is certainly valid for the moment, but disappears in the essential equality of eternity. Genius is, as the word itself shows, immediateness (*ingenium*, that which is inborn, primative, *primus*, original, *origo*, &c.), it is a natural qualification, genius *is born*. Even long before there can be any question as to how far genius is prepared to relate its particular gifts to God, it is genius, and it remains genius even if it does not do so. It is possible that genius may so change that it develops into what it is *kata dunamin*, so as to acquire conscious possession of itself. If one uses the expression 'paradox' in order to denote the something new which a genius may have to bring forth, it is only used in an inessential sense of the transitory paradox of the anticipation thus condensed into a paradox which, however, disappears again later. In his first communication a genius may be paradoxical, but the more he comes to himself, the more completely will the paradox disappear. A genius may be a century ahead of his time, and therefore appear to be a paradox, but ultimately the race will assimilate what was once a paradox in such a way that it is no longer paradoxical.

It is otherwise with an Apostle. The word itself indicates the difference. An Apostle is not born; an Apostle is a man called and appointed by God, receiving a mission from him. An Apostle does not develop in such a way that he successively becomes what he is *kata dunamin*. For to become an Apostle is not preceded by any potential possibility; essentially every man is equally near to becoming one. An Apostle can never come to himself in such a way that he becomes conscious of his apostolic calling as a factor in the development of his life. Apostolic calling is a paradoxical factor, which from first to last in his life stands paradoxically outside his personal identity with himself as the definite person he is. A man may perhaps have reached years of discretion long ago, when suddenly he is called to be an Apostle. As a result of this call he does not become more intelligent, does not receive more imagination, a greater acuteness of mind and so on; on the contrary, he remains himself and by that paradoxical fact he is sent on a particular mission by God. By this paradoxical fact the Apostle is made paradoxically different from all other men for all eternity. The new which he may have to bring forth is the essential paradox. However long it may be proclaimed in the world it remains essentially and equally new, equally paradoxical, and no immanence can assimilate it. The Apostle did not behave like the man marked out by natural gifts who is born before his time; he was perhaps what we call a simple man, but by a paradoxical fact he was called to proclaim this new thing. Even if thought were to think that it could assimilate the doctrine, it cannot assimilate the way in which the doctrine came into the world; for the essential paradox is the protest against immanence. But the way in which a doctrine of this kind came into the world is qualitatively decisive, and it can only be ignored by deceit or by thoughtlessness.

(2) Genius is appreciated purely aesthetically, according to the measure of its content, and its specific weight; an Apostle is what he is through having divine authority. *Divine authority is, qualitatively, the decisive factor.* It is not by evaluating the content of the doctrine aesthetically or intellectually that I should or could reach the result: *ergo*, the man who proclaimed the doctrine was called by a revelation; *ergo*, he is an Apostle. The very reverse is the case: the man who is called by a revelation and to whom a doctrine is entrusted, argues from the fact that it is a revelation, from his authority. I have not got to listen to St Paul because he is clever, or even brilliantly clever; I am to bow before St Paul because he has divine authority; and in any case it remains St Paul's responsibility to see that he produces that impression, whether anybody bows before his authority or not. St Paul must not appeal to his cleverness, for in that case he is a fool; he must not enter into a purely aesthetic or philosophical discussion of the content of the doctrine, for in that case he is side-tracked. No, he must appeal to his divine authority and, while willing to lay down his life and everything, by that very means *prevent* any aesthetic impertinence and any direct philosophic approach to the form and content of the doctrine. St Paul has not to recommend himself and his doctrine with the help of beautiful similes; on the contrary, he should say to the individual: 'Whether the comparison is beautiful or whether it is worn and threadbare is all one, you must realize that what I say was entrusted to me by a revelation, so that it is God Himself or the Lord Jesus Christ who speaks, and you must not presumptuously set about criticizing the form. I cannot and dare not compel you to obey, but through your relation to God in your conscience I make you eternally responsible to God, eternally responsible for your relation to this doctrine, by having proclaimed it as revealed to me, and consequently proclaimed it with divine authority'.

Authority is the decisive quality. Or is there perhaps no difference, even within the relativity of human existence, and even though it disappears in immanence, between the king's command and the word of a poet or a thinker? And what is that difference if not that the king's command has authority and prohibits all aesthetic and critical impertinence as to the form and the content? But neither the poet nor the thinker has authority, even within his own sphere of relativity; their statements are judged on purely aesthetic and philosophic grounds according to the value of the form and the content. The cause of the fundamental confusion in Christianity is surely that as a result of scepticism people are uncertain whether there is a God, and furthermore, that rebelling against all authorities they forget the meaning and dialectic of authority. A king is present physically and one can physically assure oneself of the fact, and should it become necessary he can give one decided physical proof that he is there. But God is not present in that sense. Scepticism has used this fact in order to put God on the same level as all those who have no authority, on the same level as genius, poets and thinkers, whose sayings are judged from a purely aesthetic or philosophic point of view; and then, if the thing is well said, the man is a genius—and if it is unusually well said, then God said it!

In that way God is spirited away. What is he to do? If God stops a man on the road, and calls him with a revelation and sends him armed with divine authority among men, they say to him: from whom dost thou come? He answers: from God. But now God cannot help his messenger physically like a king, who gives him soldiers or policemen, or his ring or his signature, which is known to all; in short, God cannot help men by providing them with physical certainty that an Apostle is an Apostle—which would, moreover, be nonsense. Even miracles, if the Apostle has that gift, give no physical certainty; for the miracle is the object of faith. Moreover, it is nonsense to require *physical* certainty that an Apostle is an Apostle (the paradoxical qualification of a spiritual relationship), just as it is nonsense to require a *physical* certainty that God exists, since God is *spirit*. The Apostle, then, says he comes from God. The others answer: Very well, then, let us see whether the content of your teaching is divine, in which case we will accept it, along with the fact that it was revealed to you. In that way both God and the Apostle are fooled. The divine authority of the one called should in fact be the sure protection which safeguards the teaching, and preserves it at the majestic distance of the divine from impertinent curiosity, instead of which the doctrine has to submit to being criticized and sniffed at—in order that people may discover whether it was a revelation or not; and probably in the meanwhile God and the Apostle have to wait at the gate, or in the porter's lodge, till the learned upstairs have settled the matter. The man who is called ought, according to divine ordinance, to use his divine authority in order to be rid of all the impertinent people who will not obey, but want no reason; and instead of that men have, at a single go, transformed the

Apostle into an examinee who appears on the market with a new teaching.

What, then, is authority? Is it the profundity, the excellence, the cleverness of the doctrine? Not at all! If authority simply expressed in a higher potency, or reduplicated, the fact that the doctrine is profound, then there is no such thing as authority; for in that case if the learner were to assimilate this doctrine completely and entirely through the understanding, then there would cease to be any difference between the teacher and the learner. Authority is, on the contrary, something which remains unchanged, which one cannot acquire even by understanding the doctrine perfectly. *Authority is a specific quality which, coming from elsewhere, becomes qualitatively apparent when the content of the message or of the action is posited as indifferent.* Let us take an example, as simple as possible, where the situation is nevertheless made clear. When a man with authority says to a man, go! and when a man who has not the authority says, go! the expression (go!) and its content are identical; aesthetically it is, if you like, equally well said, but the authority makes the difference. If authority is not 'the other' (*to heteron*),[3] if it is in any sense merely a higher potency within the identity, then there is no such thing as authority. If a teacher is enthusiastically conscious that he has expressed the doctrine which he is proclaiming at the sacrifice of all else, this consciousness may well give him determination, but it does not give him authority. His life as a proof of the rightness of the teaching is not 'the other' (*to heteron*); it is a simple reduplication. The fact that he lives according to the doctrine does not prove that it is right, but only that because he is convinced of the righteousness of his teaching he therefore lives according to it. On the other hand, whether a police official is a rascal or an upright man—as soon as he is on duty he has authority.

In order to throw more light on the concept authority, so important for the sphere of the paradox-religious, I will elaborate the dialectic of authority.

Authority is inconceivable within the sphere of immanence, or else it can only be thought of as something transitory. In so far as one may speak of authority in political, social, and disciplinary connexions, or of using authority, authority is only a transitory factor, a passing thing which either vanishes later in time, or vanishes in so far as time and earthly life are transitory factors which disappear with all their differentiations. The only difference which can be *conceived* as the basis for the relations between man and man *qua* man is the difference within the identity of immanence, that is to say essential equality. The individual man cannot be *conceived* as differing from all other men by a specific quality (otherwise all thought would cease, as in fact it quite consistently does in the sphere of paradox-religion and of faith). All the human differences among men *qua* men vanish before thought as factors within the whole and within the quality of identity. For the moment it is my duty to respect and obey the difference, but religiously I may feel myself edified by the certainty that the differences disappear in eternity, those that single me out no less than those which weigh me down. As a subject it is my duty to honour and obey the king with undivided heart, but religiously I may feel strengthened by the thought that, essentially, I am a citizen of heaven and that should I ever meet the king after death I shall no longer be bound to him by the ties of obedience of a subject.

Such is the position as between man and man *qua* man. But between God and man there is an eternal, essential, qualitative difference which cannot, at the risk of presumption, be allowed to disappear in the blasphemous thought that, though certainly different in the transitory moment of time, so that man ought to obey and to pray God in this life, nevertheless the difference will, in eternity, vanish in an essential identity, so that in eternity God and man, like king and servant, become equals.

Between God and man, then, there is and remains an eternal, essential, qualitative difference. *The paradox-religious relationship* (which, quite rightly, cannot be thought, but only believed) *appears when God appoints a particular man to divine authority*, in relation, be it carefully noted, to that which God has entrusted to him. The man thus called is no longer related as man to man *qua* man; his relationship to other men is not that of a qualitative difference (such as genius, exceptional gifts, position, &c.), he is related paradoxically by having a specific quality which no immanence can resolve in the equality of eternity; for it is essentially paradoxical and *after* thought (not before, anterior to thought), contrary to thought. If a man thus called has a doctrine to bring forth according to a divine command, and another man, let us suppose, of himself and by himself discovered the same thing: then in all eternity the two things would not become equal; for the first man is different from every other man by virtue of his paradoxically specific quality (divine authority), and different from the immanently essential equality which is at the basis of all other human differences. The qualification 'an Apostle' belongs in the transcendental sphere, the sphere of paradox-religion which, quite consistently, also has a qualitatively different expression for the relation of other men to an Apostle: namely, they are related to him in faith, whereas thought is and breathes and has its being in immanence. But faith is not a transitory qualification, any more than the Apostle's paradoxical qualification was transitory. Between man and man *qua* man, then, no *established* or continuous authority was *con-*

ceivable; it was something transitory. But for the sake of the essential consideration of authority, however, we may dwell for a moment upon a few examples of so-called, and in temporal conditions true, forms of authority. A king, it is assumed, has authority. Nevertheless, there is something disturbing in the idea of a king who is witty or an artist. The explanation of this is, surely, that one naturally lays the stress on his royal authority and so by comparison looks upon the more general human marks of distinction as something transitory, as something fortuitous, inessential and disturbing. A government department is regarded as having authority within its orbit. And yet it would be disturbing if its ordinances were really clever, witty, and profound. Here again the explanation is that, quite rightly, all the accent falls qualitatively on the authority. To ask whether a king is a genius—with the intention, if such were the case, of obeying him, is in reality *lèse-majesté*; for the question conceals a doubt as to whether one intends to submit to authority. To be prepared to obey a government department if it can be clever is really to make a fool of it. To honour one's father because he is intelligent is impiety.

However, as has already been said, between man and man *qua* man authority, when it exists, is something transitory, and eternity does away with all forms of worldly authority. But now, with regard to the transcendental sphere, let us take an example, as simple as possible and for that very reason as striking as can be. When Christ says, 'There is an eternal life'; and when a theological student says, 'There is an eternal life': both say the same thing, and there is no more deduction, development, profundity, or thoughtfulness in the first expression than in the second; both statements are, judged aesthetically, equally good. And yet there is an eternal qualitative difference between them! Christ, as God-Man, is in possession of the specific quality of authority which eternity can never mediate, just as in all eternity Christ can never be put on the same level as essential human equality. Christ taught, therefore, with authority. To ask whether Christ is profound is blasphemy, and is an attempt (whether conscious or not) to destroy Him surreptitiously; for the question conceals a doubt concerning His authority, and this attempt to weigh Him up is impertinent in its directness, behaving as though He were being examined, instead of which it is to Him that all power is given in heaven and upon earth.

Yet, nowadays, it is seldom, very seldom, that one hears or reads a religious discourse which is framed correctly. The better among them often dabble a little in what one might call unconscious or well-meant rebellion, by defending and upholding Christianity with all their strength—with the wrong categories. Let me take an example, the first that comes to hand. I prefer to choose a German because then I know that no one, not even the most stupid, not even the most wrong-headed, could imagine that I am writing about a matter which in my belief is infinitely important—in order to point to some clergyman or other. Bishop Sailer,[4] in a homily for the Fifth Sunday in Lent, preaches on the text John viii. 47–51. He chooses these two verses: 'He that is of God heareth God's word', and 'If a man keep my sayings, he shall never die', and continues: 'in these words of the Lord three great mysteries are solved, mysteries over which men have racked their brains from the beginning of time'. There we have it. The word 'mystery', and particularly the 'three great mysteries', and then in the next phase 'over which men have racked their *brains*', immediately leads one's thoughts on to the profound in an intellectual sense; pondering, searching, speculation. Yet how can a simple apodictic statement be profound, an apodictic statement which is only what it is because so and so has said it; a statement which is not to be understood or fathomed, but simply believed? How can any man imagine that a mystery is solved, in a learned speculative way, by a direct statement, by an assertion? The question is, after all: Is there an eternal life? The answer: There is an eternal life. What, in heaven's name, is profound about that? If Christ had not said it, and if Christ was not who He said He was, then if the statement itself is profound, it must be possible to discover its profundity. Let us take the example of Herr Petersen, the theological student, who also says, 'There is an eternal life'. Would it ever strike any one to tax him with profundity on account of a direct statement? The decisive thing is not the statement, but the fact that it was Christ who said it; but the confusing thing is that, as though in order to tempt people to believe, they talk about profundity. In order to speak correctly a Christian priest would have to say, quite simply: We have Christ's word for it that there is an eternal life; and that settles the matter. There is no question here of racking one's brains or philosophizing, but simply that Christ said it, not as a profound thinker but with divine authority. Let us go further, let us suppose that a man believes in eternal life on Christ's word. In that case he believes without any fuss about being profound and searching and philosophical and 'racking his brains'. On the other hand, take the case of a man who racks his brains and ruminates profoundly on the question of immortality: would he not be justified in denying that this direct statement is a profound answer to the question? What Plato says on immortality really is profound, reached after deep study; but then poor Plato has no authority whatsoever.

In the meanwhile, the thing is this. Doubt and superstition, which make of faith a vain thing, have among other things also made men shy of obedience, of bowing before authority. This rebelliousness worms its way even into the thought of better people, perhaps unbeknown to them, and so begins all the extravagance, which at bottom is only treachery, about the profundity and the beauty which one can but faintly perceive. And so if one had to describe the Christian-religious discourse as it is now heard with a single definite predicate, one would have to say it was *affected*. Normally in referring to a priest's affectation, one means the way he dresses, or gets himself up, or that he talks in a sugary voice, or that he rolls his Rs like a foreigner, wrinkles his brow, or uses violent gestures and ridiculous poses. All this, however, is of less importance, though it is desirable that he should not do so. But the pernicious thing is when the whole train of his thought is affected, when the price of its orthodoxy is an emphasis in an entirely wrong place, when he calls for faith in Christ, when he preaches faith in Him on grounds which simply cannot be the object of faith. If a son were to say, 'I obey my father, not because he is my father but because he is a genius, or because his orders are always profoundly intelligent', then that filial obedience is affected. The son accentuates something entirely wrong, he emphasizes the intellectual aspect, the profundity in a *command*, whereas a command is, of course, indifferent to that qualification. The son wishes to obey by virtue of the father's intellectual profundity; and to *obey* by virtue thereof is just what is not possible, for his critical attitude as to whether the command is profound undermines the obedience. And so, too, it is affectation to speak of adopting Christianity and believing Christ because of the great profundity of the doctrine. By putting the accent in entirely the wrong place one only makes a show of orthodoxy. The whole of modern philosophy is therefore affected, because it has done away with *obedience* on the one hand, and *authority* on the other, and then, in spite of everything, claims to be orthodox. A priest who is quite correct in his discourse would, when quoting the words of Christ, have to speak in this way: 'These words were spoken by Him to whom, according to His own statement, is given all power in heaven and on earth. You who hear me must consider within yourselves whether you will bow before his authority or not, accept and believe the words or not. But if you do not wish to do so, then for heaven's sake do not go and accept the words because they are clever or profound or wonderfully beautiful, for that is a mockery of God'. For, once the command of authority, of the specific paradox-authority, is posited, then all relationships are qualitatively changed, then the kind of acceptance which was previously allowable and desirable becomes a crime and presumptuous.

But now how can an Apostle prove that he has authority? If he could prove it *physically*, then he would not be an Apostle. He has no other proof than his own statement. That has to be so; for otherwise the believer's relationship to him would be direct instead of being paradoxical. In the transitory conditions of authority between man and man *qua* man, authority will normally be physically recognizable by power. An Apostle has no other proof than his own statement, and at the most his willingness to suffer anything for the sake of that statement. His words in this respect will be short: 'I am called by God; do with me what you will, scourge me, persecute me, but my last words are my first: I am called by God, and I make you eternally responsible for what you do against me'. Let us suppose that an Apostle were really to have power in the worldly sense, had great influence and powerful connexions, the forces with which one is victorious over men's opinions and judgements—then if he used them he would *eo ipso* have lost his cause. By using power he would have defined his efforts as essentially identical with those of other men, and yet an Apostle is only what he is through his paradoxical heterogeneity, through having divine authority, which he can possess absolutely and unchanged even if he is looked upon by men, as St Paul says, as less than the filth they walk upon.

(3) *Genius has only an immanent teleology; the Apostle is absolutely, paradoxically, teleologically placed.*

If a man can be said to be situated absolutely teleologically, then he is an Apostle. The doctrine communicated to him is not a task which he is given to ponder over, it is not given him for his own sake, he is, on the contrary, on a mission and has to proclaim the doctrine and use authority. Just as a man, sent into the town with a letter, has nothing to do with its contents, but has only to deliver it; just as a minister who is sent to a foreign court is not responsible for the content of the message, but has only to convey it correctly; so, too, an Apostle has really only to be faithful in his service, and to carry out his task. Therein lies the essence of an Apostle's life of self-sacrifice, even if he were never persecuted, in the fact that he is 'poor, yet making many rich', that he never dares take the time or the quiet or carefreeness in order to grow rich. Intellectually speaking he is like a tireless housewife who herself hardly has time to eat, so busy is she preparing food for others. And even though at first he might have hoped for a long life, his life to the very end will remain unchanged, for there will always be new people to whom to proclaim the doctrine. Although a revelation is a paradoxical factor which surpasses man's understanding, one can nevertheless understand this much, which has, moreover, proved to be the case everywhere: that a man is called by a revelation to go out in the world, to proclaim the Word, to act and to suffer, to a life of uninterrupted activity as the Lord's messenger. But that a man should be called by a revelation to sit back and enjoy his possessions undisturbed, in active literary *far niente*, momentarily clever, and afterwards as publisher and editor of the uncertainties of his cleverness; that is something approaching blasphemy.[5]

It is otherwise with genius; it has only an immanent teleology, it develops itself, and while developing itself this self-development projects itself as its work. It thus receives importance, perhaps even great importance, but it is not teleologically situated in regard to the world and to others. Genius lives in itself; and, humorously, might live withdrawn and self-satisfied, without for that reason taking its gifts in vain, so long as it develops itself earnestly and industriously, following its own genius, regardless of whether others profit by it or not. Genius is therefore in no sense inactive, and works within itself perhaps harder than a dozen business men put together, but none of its achievements have any exterior *telos*. That is at once the humanity and the pride of genius: the humanity lies in the fact that it does not define itself teleologically in relation to any other man, as though there were any one who needed it; its pride lies in the fact that it immanently relates itself to itself. It is modest of the nightingale not to require any one to listen to it; but it is also proud of the nightingale not to care whether any one listens to it or not. The dialectic of genius will give particular offence in our times, where the masses, the many, the public, and other such abstractions contrive to turn everything topsy-turvy. The honoured public, the domineering masses, wish genius to express that it exists for their sake; they only see one side of the dialectic of genius, take offence at its pride and do not perceive that the same thing is also modesty and humility. The honoured public and the domineering masses would therefore also take the existence of an Apostle in vain. For it is certainly true that he exists absolutely for the sake of others, is sent out for the sake of others; but it is not the masses and not mankind and not the public, not even the highly educated public, which is his lord and master—but God; and the Apostle is one who has divine authority to command both the masses and the public.

The humorous self-sufficiency of genius is the unity of a modest resignation in the world and a proud elevation above the world: of being an unnecessary superfluity and a precious ornament. If the genius is an artist, then he accomplishes his work of art, but neither he nor his work of art has a *telos* outside him. Or he is an author, who abolishes every teleological relation to his environment and humor-ously defines himself as a poet. Lyrical art has certainly no *telos* outside it: and whether a man writes a short lyric or folios, it makes no difference to the quality of the nature of his work. The lyrical author is only concerned with his production, enjoys the pleasure of producing, often perhaps only after pain and effort; but he has nothing to do with others, he does not write *in order that*: in order to enlighten men or in order to help them along the right road, in order to bring about something; in short, he does not write *in order that*. The same is true of every genius. No genius has an *in order that*; the Apostle has, absolutely and paradoxically, an *in order that*.

1 The errors, moreover, are not confined to heterodoxy but are also found in hyper-orthodoxy. They are in fact those of thoughtlessness.
2 [i.e. Christianity.]
3 Perhaps it will occur to some readers, as it occurs to me, to recall in connexion with this examination of 'authority' the 'Edifying Discourses' of Magister Kierkegaard, where he stresses the fact so clearly, by repeating word for word on each occasion, that 'they are not sermons, because the author is without authority to preach'. Authority is a specific quality either of an Apostolic calling or of ordination. To preach simply means to use authority; and that is exactly what is completely and utterly forgotten in these times.
4 [J. M. Sailer (1751–1832), Bishop of Regensburg, tutor of Ludwig I of Bavaria.]
5 [A reference to Adler.]

● From S. Kierkegaard, *The Present Age* and *Of the Difference between a Genius and an Apostle*, trans. A. Dru (London, 1962), pp. 103–127.

22

James
Religious Experience

William James was born in 1842, the brother of the novelist, Henry James. He graduated in medicine at Harvard, where he became Professor of Philosophy and, later, of Psychology. In philosophy he developed the ideas of C. S. Peirce and became an important representative of Pragmatism. He wrote on religion in *The Will to Believe* (1897) and *The Varieties of Religious Experience*, which were Gifford Lectures delivered in Edinburgh in 1901–02.

The *Varieties* discusses mysticism, conversion, saintliness and other related topics, giving many case-studies and attacking attempts to explain them away in purely medical or psychological terms. In the final lecture he addresses himself to the question of why people want something more than a psychological account of religious experience, and what such a further explanation might be. In the first half of the lecture (not printed here) James avers that in private and personal phenomena, such as religious experience, we are dealing with what is *most* real, and criticizes as shallow any scientific approach which would restrict itself to the public and the impersonal.

Lecture 20: Conclusions

Let us agree, then, that Religion, occupying herself with personal destinies and keeping thus in contact with the only absolute realities which we know, must necessarily play an eternal part in human history. The next thing to decide is what she reveals about those destinies, or whether indeed she reveals anything distinct enough to be considered a general message to mankind. We have done as you see, with our preliminaries, and our final summing up can now begin.

I am well aware that after all the palpitating documents which I have quoted, and all the perspectives of emotion-inspiring institution and belief that my previous lectures have opened, the dry analysis to which I now advance may appear to many of you like an anti-climax, a tapering-off and flattening out of the subject, instead of a crescendo of interest and result. I said awhile ago that the religious attitude of Protestants appears poverty-stricken to the Catholic imagination. Still more poverty-stricken, I fear, may my final summing up of the subject appear at first to some of you. On which account I pray you now to bear this point in mind, that in the present part of it I am expressly trying to reduce religion to its lowest admissible terms, to that minimum, free from individualistic excrescences, which all religions contain as their nucleus, and on which it may be hoped that all religious persons may agree. That established, we should have a result which might be small, but would at least be solid; and on it and round it the ruddier additional beliefs on which the different individuals make their venture might be grafted, and flourish as richly as you please. I shall add my own over-belief (which will be, I confess, of a somewhat pallid kind, as befits a critical philosopher), and you will, I hope, also add your over-beliefs, and we shall soon be in the varied world of concrete religious constructions once more. For the moment, let me dryly pursue the analytic part of the task.

Both thought and feeling are determinants of conduct, and the same conduct may be determined either by feeling or by thought. When we survey the whole field of religion, we find a great variety in the thoughts that have prevailed there; but the feelings on the one hand and the conduct on the other are almost always the same, for Stoic, Christian, and Buddhist saints are practically indistinguishable in their lives. The theories which Religion generates, being thus variable, are secondary; and if you wish to grasp her essence, you must look to the feelings and the conduct as being the more constant elements. It is between these two elements that the short circuit exists on which she carries on her principal business, while the ideas and symbols and other institutions form loop-lines which may be perfections and improvements, and may even some day all be united into one harmonious system, but which are not to be regarded as organs with an indispensable function, necessary at all times for religious life to go on. This seems to me the first conclusion which we are entitled to draw from the phenomena we have passed in review.

The next step is to characterize the feelings. To what psychological order do they belong?

The resultant outcome of them is in any case what Kant calls a 'sthenic' affection, an excitement of the cheerful, expansive, 'dynamogenic' order which, like any tonic, freshens our vital powers. In almost every lecture, but especially in the lectures on Conversion and on Saintliness, we have seen how this emotion overcomes temperamental melancholy and imparts endurance to the Subject, or a zest, or a meaning, or an enchantment and glory to the common objects of life. The name of 'faith-state', by which Professor Leuba designates it, is a good one.[1] It is a biological as well as a psychological condition, and Tolstoy is absolutely accurate in classing faith among the forces *by which men live*. The total absence of it, anhedonia, means collapse.

The faith-state may hold a very minimum of intellectual content. We saw examples of this in those sudden raptures of the divine presence, or in such mystical seizures as Dr Bucke described. It may be a mere vague enthusiasm, half spiritual, half vital, a courage, and a feeling that great and wondrous things are in the air.[2]

When, however, a positive intellectual content is associated with a faith-state, it gets invincibly stamped in upon belief,[3] and this explains the passionate loyalty of religious persons everywhere to the minutest details of their so widely differing creeds. Taking creeds and faith-state together, as forming 'religions', and treating these as purely subjective phenomena, without regard to the question of their 'truth', we are obliged, on account of their extraordinary influence upon action and endurance, to class them amongst the most important biological functions of mankind. Their stimulant and anæsthetic effect is so great that Professor Leuba, in a recent article,[4] goes so far as to say that so long as men can *use* their God, they care very little who he is, or even whether he is at all. 'The truth of the matter can be put', says Leuba, 'in this way: *God is not known, he is not understood; he is used*—sometimes as meat-purveyor, sometimes as moral support, sometimes as friend, sometimes as an object of love. If he proves himself useful, the religious consciousness asks for no more than that. Does God really exist? How does he exist? What is he? are so many irrelevant questions. Not God, but life, more life, a larger, richer, more satisfying life, is, in the last analysis, the end of religion. The love of life, at any and every level of development, is the religious impulse.'[5]

At this purely subjective rating, therefore, Religion must be considered vindicated in a certain way from the attacks of her critics. It would seem that she cannot be a mere anachronism and survival, but must exert a permanent function, whether she be with or without intellectual content, and whether, if she have any, it be true or false.

We must next pass beyond the point of view of merely subjective utility, and make inquiry into the intellectual content itself.

First, is there, under all the discrepancies of the creeds, a common nucleus to which they bear their testimony unanimously?

And second, ought we to consider the testimony true?

I will take up the first question first, and answer it immediately in the affirmative. The warring gods and formulas of the various religions do indeed cancel each other, but there is a certain uniform deliverance in which religions all appear to meet. It consists of two parts:—

1. An uneasiness; and

2. Its solution.

1. The uneasiness, reduced to its simplest terms, is a sense that there is *something wrong about us* as we naturally stand.

2. The solution is a sense that *we are saved from the wrongness* by making proper connection with the higher powers.

In those more developed minds which alone we are studying, the wrongness takes a moral character, and the salvation takes a mystical tinge. I think we shall keep well within the limits of what is common to all such minds if we formulate the essence of their religious experience in terms like these:—

The individual, so far as he suffers from his wrongness and criticises it, is to that extent consciously beyond it, and in at least possible touch with something higher, if anything higher exist. Along with the wrong part there is thus a better part of him, even though it may be but a most helpless germ. With which part he should identify his real being is by no means obvious at this stage; but when stage 2 (the stage of solution or salvation) arrives,[6] the man identifies his real being with the germinal higher part of himself; and does so in the following way. *He becomes conscious that this higher part is conterminous and continuous with a* MORE *of the same quality, which is operative in the universe outside of him, and which he can keep in working touch with, and in a fashion get on board of and save himself when all his lower being has gone to pieces in the wreck.*

It seems to me that all the phenomena are accurately describable in these very simple general terms.[7] They allow for the divided self and the struggle; they involve the change of personal centre and the surrender of the lower self; they express the appearance of exteriority of the helping power and yet account for our sense of union with it;[8] and they fully justify our feelings of security and joy. There is probably no autobiographic document, among all those which I have quoted, to which the description will not well apply. One need only add such specific details as will adapt it to various theologies and various personal temperaments, and one will then have the various experiences reconstructed in their individual forms.

So far, however, as this analysis goes, the experiences are only psychological phenomena. They possess, it is true, enormous biological worth. Spiritual strength really increases in the subject when he has them, a new life opens for him, and they seem to him a place of conflux where the forces of two universes meet; and yet this may be nothing but his subjective way of feeling things, a mood of his own fancy, in spite of the effects produced. I now turn to my second question: What is the objective 'truth' of their content?[9]

The part of the content concerning which the question of truth most pertinently arises is that 'MORE of the same quality' with which our own higher self appears in the experience to come into harmonious working relation. Is such a 'more' merely our own notion, or does it really exist? If so, in what shape does it exist? Does it act, as well as exist? And in what form should we conceive of that 'union' with it of which religious geniuses are so convinced?

It is in answering these questions that the various theologies perform their theoretic work, and that their divergencies most come to light. They all agree that the 'more' really exists; though some of them hold it to exist in the shape of a personal god or gods, while others are satisfied to conceive it as a stream of ideal tendency embedded in the eternal structure of the world. They all agree, moreover, that it acts as well as exists, and that something really is effected for the better when you throw your life into its hands. It is when they treat of the experience of 'union' with it that their speculative differences appear most clearly. Over this point pantheism and theism, nature and second birth, works and grace and karma, immortality and reincarnation, rationalism and mysticism, carry on inveterate disputes.

At the end of my lecture on Philosophy I held out the notion that an impartial science of religions might sift out from the midst of their discrepancies a common body of doctrine which she might also formulate in terms to which physical science need not object. This, I said, she might adopt as her own reconciling hypothesis, and recommend it for general belief. I also said that in my last lecture I should have to try my own hand at framing such an hypothesis.

The time has now come for this attempt. Who says 'hypothesis' renounces the ambition to be coercive in his arguments. The most I can do is, accordingly, to offer something that may fit the facts so easily that your scientific logic will find no plausible pretext for vetoing your impulse to welcome it as true.

The 'more', as we called it, and the meaning of our 'union' with it, form the nucleus of our inquiry. Into what definite description can these words be translated, and for what definite facts do they stand? It would never do for us to place ourselves offhand at the position of a particular theology, the Christian theology, for example, and proceed immediately to define the 'more' as Jehovah, and the 'union' as his imputation to us of the righteousness of Christ. That would be unfair to other religions, and, from our present standpoint at least, would be an over-belief.

We must begin by using less particularized terms; and, since one of the duties of the science of religions is to keep religion in connection with the rest of science, we shall do well to seek first of all a way of describing the 'more', which psychologists may also recognize as real.

The *subconscious self* is nowadays a well-accredited psychological entity; and I believe that in it we have exactly the mediating term required. Apart from all religious considerations, there is actually and literally more life in our total soul than we are at any time aware of. The exploration of the transmarginal field has hardly yet been seriously undertaken, but what Mr Myers said in 1892 in his essay on the Subliminal Consciousness[10] is as true as when it was first written: 'Each of us is in reality an abiding psychical entity far more extensive than he knows—an individuality which can never express itself completely through any corporeal manifestation. The Self manifests through the organism; but there is always some part of the Self unmanifested; and always, as it seems, some power of organic expression in abeyance or reserve'. Much of the content of this larger background against which our conscious being stands out in relief is insignificant. Imperfect memories, silly jingles, inhibitive timidities, 'dissolutive' phenomena of various sorts, as Myers calls them, enters into it for a large part. But in it many of the performances of genius seem also to have their origin; and in our study of conversion, of mystical experiences, and of prayer, we have seen how striking a part invasions from this region play in the religious life.

Let me then propose, as an hypothesis, that whatever it may be on its *farther* side, the 'more' with which in religious experience we feel ourselves connected is on its *hither* side the subconscious continuation of our conscious life. Starting thus with a recognized psychological fact as our basis, we seem to preserve a contact with 'science' which the ordinary theologian lacks. At the same time the theologian's contention that the religious man is moved by an external power is vindicated, for it is one of the peculiarities of invasions from the subconscious region to take on objective appearances, and to suggest to the Subject an external control. In the religious life the control is felt as 'higher'; but since on our hypothesis it is primarily the higher faculties of our own hidden mind which are controlling, the sense of union with the power beyond us is a sense of something, not merely apparently, but literally true.

This doorway into the subject seems to me the best one for a science of religions, for it mediates between a number of different points of view. Yet it is only a doorway, and difficulties present themselves as soon as we step through it, and ask how far our transmarginal consciousness carries us if we follow it on its remoter side. Here the over-beliefs begin: here mysticism and the conversion-rapture and Vedantism and transcendental idealism bring in their monistic interpretations and tell us that the finite self rejoins the absolute self, for it was always one with God and identical with the soul of the world.[11] Here the prophets of all the different religions come with their visions, voices, raptures, and other openings, supposed by each to authenticate his own peculiar faith.

Those of us who are not personally favored with such specific revelations must stand outside of them altogether and, for the present at least, decide that, since they corroborate incompatible theological doctrines, they neutralize one another and leave no fixed results. If we follow any one of them, or if we follow philosophical theory and embrace monistic pantheism on non-mystical grounds, we do so in the exercise of our individual freedom, and build out our religion in the way most congruous with our personal susceptibilities. Among these susceptibilities intellectual ones play a decisive part. Although the religious question is primarily a question of life, of living or not living in the higher union which opens itself to us as a gift, yet the spiritual excitement in which the gift appears a real one will often fail to be aroused in an individual until certain particular intellectual beliefs or ideas which, as we say, come home to him, are touched.[12] These ideas will thus be essential to that individual's religion;—which is as much as to say that over-beliefs in various directions are absolutely indispensable, and that we should treat them with tenderness and tolerance so long as they are not intolerant themselves. As I have elsewhere written, the most interesting and valuable things about a man are usually his over-beliefs.

Disregarding the over-beliefs, and confining ourselves to what is common and generic, we have in *the fact that the conscious person is continuous with a wider self through which saving experiences come*,[13] a positive content of religious experience which, it seems to me, *is literally and objectively true as far as it goes*. If I now proceed to state my own hypothesis about the farther limits of this extension of our personality, I shall be offering my own over-belief—though I know it will appear a sorry under-belief to some of you—for which I can only bespeak the same indulgence which in a converse case I should accord to yours.

The further limits of our being plunge, it seems to me, into an altogether other dimension of existence from the sensible and merely 'understandable' world. Name it the mystical region, or the supernatural region, whichever you choose. So far as our ideal impulses originate in this region (and most of them do originate in it, for we find them possessing us in a way for which we cannot articulately account), we belong to it in a more intimate sense than that in which we belong to the visible world, for we belong in the most intimate sense wherever our ideals belong. Yet the unseen region in question is not merely ideal, for it produces effects in this world. When we commune with it, work is actually done upon our finite personality, for we are turned into new men, and consequences in the way of conduct follow in the natural world upon our regenerative change.[14] But that which produces effects within another reality must be termed a reality itself, so I feel as if we had no philosophic excuse for calling the unseen or mystical world unreal.

God is the natural appellation, for us Christians at least, for the supreme reality, so I will call this higher part of the universe by the name of God.[15] We and God have business with each other; and in opening ourselves to his influence our deepest destiny is fulfilled. The universe, at those parts of it which our personal being constitutes, takes a turn genuinely for the worse or for the better in proportion as each one of us fulfills or evades God's demands. As far as this goes I probably have you with me, for I only translate into schematic language what I may call the instinctive belief of mankind: God is real since he produces real effects.

The real effects in question, so far as I have as yet admitted them, are exerted on the personal centres of energy of the various subjects, but the spontaneous faith of most of the subjects is that they embrace a wider sphere than this. Most religious men believe (or 'know', if they be mystical) that not only they themselves, but the whole universe of beings to whom the God is present, are secure in his parental hands. There is a sense, a dimension, they are sure, in which we are *all* saved, in spite of the gates of hell and all adverse terrestrial appearances. God's existence is the guarantee of an ideal order that shall be permanently preserved. This world may indeed, as science assures us, some day burn up or freeze; but if it is part of his order, the old ideals are sure to be brought elsewhere to fruition, so that where God is, tragedy is only provisional and partial, and shipwreck and dissolution are not the absolutely final things. Only when this farther step of faith concerning God is taken, and remote objective consequences are predicted, does religion, as it seems to me, get wholly free from the first immediate subjective experience, and bring a *real hypothesis* into play. A good hypothesis in science must have other properties than those of the phenomenon it is immediately invoked to explain, otherwise it is not prolific enough. God, meaning only what enters into the religious man's experience of union, falls short of being an hypothesis of this more useful order. He needs to enter into wider cosmic relations in order to justify the subject's absolute confidence and peace.

That the God with whom, starting from the hither side of our own extra-marginal self, we come at its remoter margin into commerce should be the absolute world-ruler, is of course a very considerable over-belief. Over-belief as it is, though, it is an article of almost every one's religion. Most of us pretend in some way to prop it upon our philosophy, but the philosophy itself is really propped upon this faith. What is this but to say that Religion, in her fullest exercise of function, is not a mere illumination of facts already elsewhere given, not a mere passion, like love, which views things in a rosier light. It is indeed that, as we have seen abundantly. But it is something more, namely, a postulator of new *facts* as well. The world interpreted religiously is not the materialistic world over again, with an altered expression; it must have, over and above the altered expression, *a natural constitution* different at some point from that which a materialistic world would have. It must be such that different events can be expected in it, different conduct must be required.

This thoroughly 'pragmatic' view of religion has usually been taken as a matter of course by common men. They have interpolated divine miracles into the field of nature, they have built a heaven out beyond the grave. It is only transcendentalist metaphysicians who think that, without adding any concrete details to Nature, or subtracting any, but by simply calling it the expression of absolute spirit, you make it more divine just as it stands. I believe the pragmatic way of taking religion to be the deeper way. It gives it body as well as soul, it makes it claim, as everything real must claim, some characteristic realm of fact as its very own. What the more characteristically divine facts are, apart from the actual inflow of energy in the faith-state and the prayer-state, I know not. But the over-belief on which I am ready to make my personal venture is that they exist. The whole drift of my education goes to persuade me that the world of our present consciousness is only one out of many worlds of consciousness that exist, and that those other worlds must contain experiences which have a meaning for our life also; and that although in the main their experiences and those of this world keep discrete, yet the two become continuous at certain points, and higher energies filter in. By being faithful in my poor measure to this over-belief, I seem to myself to keep more sane and true. I *can*, of course, put myself into the sectarian scientist's attitude, and imagine vividly that the world of sensations and of scientific laws and objects may be all. But whenever I do this, I hear that inward monitor of which W. K. Clifford once wrote, whispering the word 'bosh!' Humbug is humbug, even though it bear the scientific name, and the total expression of human experience, as I view it objectively, invincibly urges me beyond the narrow 'scientific' bounds. Assuredly, the real world is of a different temperament—more intricately built than physical science allows. So my objective and my subjective conscience both hold me to the over-belief which I express. Who knows whether the faithfulness of individuals here below to their own poor over-beliefs may not actually help God in turn to be more effectively faithful to his own greater tasks?

Postscript

In writing my concluding lecture I had to aim so much at simplification that I fear that my general philosophic position received so scant a statement as hardly to be intelligible to some of my readers. I therefore add this epilogue, which must also be so brief as possibly to remedy but little the defect. In a later work I may be enabled to state my position more amply and consequently more clearly.

Originality cannot be expected in a field like this, where all the attitudes and tempers that are possible have been exhibited in literature long ago, and where any new writer can immediately be classed under a familiar head. If one should make a division of all thinkers into naturalists and supernaturalists, I should undoubtedly have to go, along with most philosophers, into the supernaturalist branch. But there is a crasser and a more refined supernaturalism, and it is to the refined division that most philosophers at the present day belong. If not regular transcendental idealists, they at least obey the Kantian direction enough to bar out ideal entities from interfering causally in the course of phenomenal events. Refined supernaturalism is universalistic supernaturalism; for the 'crasser' variety 'piecemeal' supernaturalism would perhaps be the better name. It went with that older theology which to-day is supposed to reign only among uneducated people, or to be found among the few belated professors of the dualisms which Kant is thought to have displaced. It admits miracles and providential leadings, and finds no intellectual difficulty in mixing the ideal and the real worlds together by interpolating influences from the ideal region among the forces that causally determine the real world's details. In this the refined supernaturalists think that it muddles disparate dimensions of existence. For them the world of the ideal has no efficient causality, and never bursts into the world of phenomena at particular points. The ideal world, for them, is not a world of facts, but only of the meaning of facts; it is a point of view for judging facts. It appertains to a different '-ology', and inhabits a different dimension of being altogether from that in which existential propositions obtain. It cannot get down upon the flat level of experience and interpolate itself piecemeal between distinct portions of nature, as those who believe, for example, in divine aid coming in response to prayer, are bound to think it must.

Notwithstanding my own inability to accept either popular Christianity or scholastic theism, I suppose that my belief that in communion with the Ideal new force comes into the world, and new departures are made here below, subjects me to being classed among the supernaturalists of the piecemeal or crasser type. Universalistic supernaturalism surrenders, it seems to me, too easily to naturalism. It takes the facts of physical science at their face-value, and leaves the laws of life just as naturalism finds them, with no hope of remedy, in case their fruits are bad. It confines itself to sentiments about life as a whole, sentiments which may be admiring and adoring, but which need not be so, as the existence of systematic pessimism proves. In this universalistic way of taking the ideal world, the essence of practical religion seems to me to evaporate. Both instinctively and for logical reasons, I find it hard to believe that principles can exist which make no difference in facts.[16] But all facts are particular facts, and the whole interest of the question of God's existence seems to me to lie in the consequences for particulars which that existence may be expected to entail. That no concrete particular of experience should alter its complexion in consequence of a God being there seems to me an incredible proposition, and yet it is the thesis to which (implicitly at any rate) refined supernaturalism seems to cling. It is only with experience *en bloc*, it says, that the Absolute maintains relations. It condescends to no transactions of detail.

I am ignorant of Buddhism and speak under correction, and merely in order the better to describe my general point of view; but as I apprehend the Buddhistic doctrine of Karma, I agree in principle with that. All supernaturalists admit that facts are under the judgment of higher law; but for Buddhism as I interpret it, and for religion generally so far as it remains unweakened by transcendentalistic metaphysics, the word 'judgment' here means no such bare academic verdict or platonic appreciation as it means in Vedantic or modern absolutist systems; it carries, on the contrary, *execution* with it, is *in rebus* as well as *post rem*, and operates 'causally' as partial factor in the total fact. The universe becomes a gnosticism[17] pure and simple on any other terms. But this view that judgment and execution go together is that of the crasser supernaturalist way of thinking, so the present volume must on the whole be classed with the other expressions of that creed.

I state the matter thus bluntly, because the current of thought in academic circles runs against me, and I feel like a man who must set his back against an open door quickly if he does not wish to see it closed and locked. In spite of its being so shocking to the reigning intellectual tastes, I believe that a candid consideration of piecemeal supernaturalism and a complete discussion of all its metaphysical bearings will show it to be the hypothesis by which the largest number of legitimate requirements are met. That of course would be a program for other books than this; what I now say sufficiently indicates to the philosophic reader the place where I belong.

If asked just where the differences in fact which are due to God's existence come in, I should have to say that in general I have no hypothesis to offer beyond what the phenomenon of 'prayerful communion', especially when certain kinds of incursion from the subconscious region take part in it, immediately suggests. The appearance is that in this phenomenon something ideal, which in one sense is part of ourselves and in another sense is not ourselves, actually exerts an influence, raises our centre of personal energy, and produces regenerative effects unattainable in other ways. If, then, there be a wider world of being than that of our every-day consciousness, if in it there be forces whose effects on us are intermittent, if one facilitating condition of the effects be the openness of the 'subliminal' door, we have the elements of a theory to which the phenomena of religious life lend plausibility. I am so impressed by the importance of these phenomena that I adopt the hypothesis which they so naturally suggest. At these places at least, I say, it would seem as though transmundane energies, God, if you will, produced immediate effects within the natural world to which the rest of our experience belongs.

The difference in natural 'fact' which most of us would assign as the first difference which the existence of a God ought to make would, I imagine, be personal immortality. Religion, in fact, for the great majority of our own race *means* immortality, and nothing else. God is the producer of immortality; and whoever has doubts of immortality is written down as an atheist without farther trial. I have said nothing in my lectures about immortality or the belief therein, for to me it seems a secondary point. If our ideals are only cared for in 'eternity', I do not see why we might not be willing to resign their care to other hands than ours. Yet I sympathize with the urgent impulse to be present ourselves, and in the conflict of impulses, both of them so vague yet both of them noble, I know not how to decide. It seems to me that it is eminently a case for facts to testify. Facts, I think, are yet lacking to prove 'spirit-return', though I have the highest respect for the patient labors of Messrs Myers, Hodgson, and Hyslop, and am somewhat impressed by their favorable conclusions. I consequently leave the matter open, with this brief word to save the reader from a possible perplexity as to why immortality got no mention in the body of this book.

The ideal power with which we feel ourselves in connection, the 'God' of ordinary men, is, both by ordinary men and by philosophers, endowed with certain of those metaphysical attributes which in the lecture on philosophy I treated with such disrespect. He is assumed as a matter of course to be 'one and only' and to be 'infinite'; and the notion of many finite gods is one which hardly any one thinks it worth while to consider, and still less to uphold. Nevertheless, in the interests of intellectual clearness, I feel bound to say that religious experience, as we have studied it, cannot be cited as unequivocally supporting the infinitist belief. The only thing that it unequivocally testifies to is that we can experience union with *something* larger than ourselves and in that union find our greatest peace. Philosophy, with its passion for unity, and mysticism with its monoideistic bent, both 'pass to the limit' and identify the something with a unique God who is the all-inclusive soul of the world. Popular opinion, respectful to their authority, follows the example which they set.

Meanwhile the practical needs and experiences of religion seem to me sufficiently met by the belief that beyond each man and in a fashion continuous with him there exists a larger power which is friendly to him and to his ideals. All that the facts require is that the power should be both other and larger than our conscious selves. Anything larger will do, if only it be large enough to trust for the next step. It need not be infinite, it need not be solitary. It might conceivably even be only a larger and more godlike self, of which the present self would then be but the mutilated expression, and the universe might conceivably be a collection of such selves, of different degrees of inclusiveness, with no absolute unity realized in it at all.[18] Thus would a sort of polytheism return upon us—a polytheism which I do not on this occasion defend, for my only aim at present is to keep the testimony of religious experience clearly within its proper bounds.

Upholders of the monistic view will say to such a polytheism (which, by the way, has always been the real religion of common people, and is so still to-day) that unless there be one all-inclusive God, our guarantee of security is left imperfect. In the Absolute, and in the Absolute only, *all* is saved. If there be different gods, each caring for his part, some portion of some of us might not be covered with divine protection, and our religious consolation would thus fail to be complete. It goes back to what was said on pages 129–131 [of James's lectures], about the possibility of there being portions of the universe that may irretrievably be lost. Common sense is less sweeping in its demands than philosophy or mysticism have been wont to be, and can suffer the notion of this world being partly saved and partly lost. The ordinary moralistic state of mind makes the salvation of the world conditional upon the success with which each unit does its part. Partial and conditional salvation is in fact a most familiar notion when taken in the abstract, the only difficulty being to determine the details. Some men are even disinterested enough to be willing to be in the unsaved remnant as far as their persons go, if only they can be persuaded that their cause will prevail—all of us are willing whenever our activity-excitement rises sufficiently high. I think, in fact, that a final philosophy of religion will have to consider the pluralistic hypothesis more seriously than it has hitherto been willing to consider it. For practical life at any rate, the *chance* of salvation is enough. No fact in human nature is more characteristic than its willingness to live on a chance. The existence of the chance makes the difference, as Edmund Gurney says, between a life of which the keynote is resignation and a life of which the keynote is hope.[19] But all these statements are unsatisfactory from their brevity, and I can only say that I hope to return to the same questions in another book.

1 [Leuba], *American Journal of Psychology*, vii. 345.
2 Example: Henri Perreyve writes to Gratry: 'I do not know how to deal with the happiness which you aroused in me this morning. It overwhelms me; I want to *do* something, yet I can do nothing and am fit for nothing. ... I would fain do *great things*'. Again, after an inspiring interview, he writes: 'I went homewards, intoxicated with joy, hope, and strength. I wanted to feed upon my happiness in solitude, far from all men. It was late; but, unheeding that, I took a mountain path and went on like a madman, looking at the heavens, regardless of earth. Suddenly an instinct made me draw hastily back—I was on the very edge of a precipice, one step more and I must have fallen. I took fright and gave up my nocturnal promenade'. A. Gratry: *Henri Perreyve*, London, 1872, pp. 92, 89.

This primacy, in the faith-state, of vague expansive impulse over direction is well expressed in Walt Whitman's lines (*Leaves of Grass*, 1872, p. 190):—

O to confront night, storms, hunger, ridicule, accidents, rebuffs, as the trees and animals do. ...
Dear Camerado! I confess I have urged you onward with me, and still urge you, without the least idea what is our destination,
Or whether we shall be victorious, or utterly quell'd and defeated.

This readiness for great things, and this sense that the world by its importance, wonderfulness, etc., is apt for their production, would seem to be the undifferentiated germ of all the higher faiths. Trust in our own dreams of ambition, or in our country's expansive destinies, and faith in the providence of God, all have their source in that onrush of our sanguine impulses, and in that sense of the exceedingness of the possible over the real.

3 Compare Leuba: *Loc. cit.*, pp. 346–349.
4 'The Contents of Religious Consciousness' in *The Monist*, xi, 536, July 1901.
5 *Loc. cit.*, pp. 571, 572, abridged. See, also, this writer's extraordinarily true criticism of the notion that religion primarily seeks to solve the intellectual mystery of the world. Compare what W. Bender says (in his *Wesen der Religion*, Bonn, 1888, pp. 85, 38): 'Not the question about God, and not the inquiry into the origin and purpose of the world is religion, but the question about Man. All religious views of life are anthropocentric'. 'Religion is that activity of the human impulse towards self-preservation by means of which Man seeks to carry his essential vital purposes through against the adverse pressure of the world by raising himself freely towards

the world's ordering and governing powers when the limits of his own strength are reached.' The whole book is little more than a development of these words.

6　Remember that for some men it arrives suddenly, for others gradually, whilst others again practically enjoy it all their life.

7　The practical difficulties are: 1, to 'realize the reality' of one's higher part; 2, to identify one's self with it exclusively; and 3, to identify it with all the rest of ideal being.

8　'When mystical activity is at its height, we find consciousness possessed by the sense of a being at once *excessive* and *identical* with the self: great enough to be God; interior enough to be *me*. The "objectivity" of it ought in that case to be called *excessivity*, rather, or exceedingness.' [E.] Récéjac: *Essai sur les fondements de la conscience mystique*, 1897, p. 46.

9　The word 'truth' is here taken to mean something additional to bare value for life, although the natural propensity of man is to believe that whatever has great value for life is thereby certified as true.

10　*Proceedings of the Society for Psychical Research*, vol. vii. p. 305. For a full statement of Mr Myers's views, I may refer to his posthumous work, 'Human Personality in the Light of Recent Research', which is already announced by Messrs Longmans, Green & Co. as being in press. Mr Myers for the first time proposed as a general psychological problem the exploration of the subliminal region of consciousness throughout its whole extent, and made the first methodical steps in its topography by treating as a natural series a mass of subliminal facts hitherto considered only as curious isolated facts, and subjecting them to a systematized nomenclature. How important this exploration will prove, future work upon the path which Myers has opened can alone show. Compare my paper: 'Frederic Myers's Services to Psychology', in the said *Proceedings*, part xlii., May, 1901.

11　One more expression of this belief, to increase the reader's familiarity with the notion of it:—

'If this room is full of darkness for thousands of years, and you come in and begin to weep and wail, "Oh, the darkness", will the darkness vanish? Bring the light in, strike a match, and light comes in a moment. So what good will it do you to think all your lives, "Oh, I have done evil, I have made many mistakes"? It requires no ghost to tell us that. Bring in the light, and the evil goes in a moment. Strengthen the real nature, build up yourselves, the effulgent, the resplendent, the ever pure, call that up in every one whom you see. I wish that every one of us had come to such a state that even when we see the vilest of human beings we can see the God within, and instead of condemning, say, "Rise, thou effulgent One, rise thou who art always pure, rise thou birthless and deathless, rise almighty, and manifest your nature". . . . This is the highest prayer that the Advaita teaches. This is the one prayer: remembering our nature. . . .

'Why does man go out to look for a God? . . . It is your own heart beating, and you did not know, you were mistaking it for something external. He, nearest of the near, my own self, the reality of my own life, my body and my soul.—I am Thee and Thou art Me. That is your own nature. Assert it, manifest it. Not to become pure, you are pure already. You are not to be perfect, you are that already. Every good thought which you think or act upon is simply tearing the veil, as it were, and the purity, the Infinity, the God behind, manifests itself—the eternal Subject of everything, the eternal Witness in this universe, your own Self. Knowledge is, as it were, a lower step, a degradation. We are It already; how to know It?' Swami Vivekananda: *Addresses*, No. XII., *Practical Vedanta*, part iv. pp. 172, 174, London, 1897; and *Lectures*, *The Real and the Apparent Man*, p. 24, abridged.

12 For instance, here is a case where a person exposed from her birth to Christian ideas had to wait till they came to her clad in spiritistic formulas before the saving experience set in:—

'For myself I can say that spiritualism has saved me. It was revealed to me at a critical moment of my life, and without it I don't know what I should have done. It has taught me to detach myself from worldly things and to place my hope in things to come. Through it I have learned to see in all men, even in those most criminal, even in those from whom I have most suffered, undeveloped brothers to whom I owed assistance, love, and forgiveness. I have learned that I must lose my temper over nothing, despise no one, and pray for all. Most of all I have learned to pray! And although I have still much to learn in this domain, prayer ever brings me more strength, consolation, and comfort. I feel more than ever that I have only made a few steps on the long road of progress; but I look at its length without dismay, for I have confidence that the day will come when all my efforts shall be rewarded. So Spiritualism has a great place in my life, indeed it holds the first place there.' Flournoy Collection.

13 'The influence of the Holy Spirit, exquisitely called the Comforter, is a matter of actual experience, as solid a reality as that of electro-magnetism.' W. C. Brownell, *Scribner's Magazine*, vol. xxx. p. 112.

14 That the transaction of opening ourselves, otherwise called prayer, is a perfectly definite one for certain persons, appears abundantly in the preceding lectures. I append another concrete example to reinforce the impression on the reader's mind:—

'Man can learn to transcend these limitations [of finite thought] and draw power and wisdom at will. ... The divine presence is known through experience. The turning to a higher plane is a distinct act of consciousness. It is not a vague, twilight or semi-conscious experience. It is not an ecstasy; it is not a trance. It is not super-consciousness in the Vedantic sense. It is not due to self-hypnotization. It is a perfectly calm, sane, sound, rational, common-sense shifting of consciousness from the phenomena of sense-perception to the phenomena of seership, from the thought of self to a distinctively higher realm. ... For example, if the lower self be nervous, anxious, tense, one can in a few moments compel it to be calm. This is not done by a word simply. Again I say, it is not hypnotism. It is by the exercise of power. One feels the spirit of peace as definitely as heat is perceived on a hot summer day. The power can be as surely used as the sun's rays can be focused and made to do work, to set fire to wood.' *The Higher Law*, vol. iv. pp. 4, 6, Boston, August, 1901.

15 Transcendentalists are fond of the term 'Over-soul', but as a rule they use it in an intellectualist sense, as meaning only a medium of communion. 'God' is a causal agent as well as a medium of communion, and that is the aspect which I wish to emphasize.

16 Transcendental idealism, of course, insists that its ideal world makes *this* difference, that facts *exist*. We owe it to the Absolute that we have a world of fact at all. 'A world' of fact!—that exactly is the trouble. An entire world is the smallest unit with which the Absolute can work, whereas to our finite minds work for the better ought to be done within this world, setting in at single points. Our difficulties and our ideals are all piecemeal affairs, but the Absolute can do no piecework for us; so that all the interests which our poor souls compass raise their heads too late. We should have spoken earlier, prayed for another world absolutely, before this world was born. It is strange, I have heard a friend say, to see this blind corner into which Christian thought has worked itself at last, with its God who can raise no particular weight whatever, who can help us with no private burden, and who is on the side of our enemies as much as he is on our own. Odd evolution from the God of David's psalms!

17 See my *Will to Believe and other Essays in popular Philosophy*, 1897, p. 165.

18 Such a notion is suggested in my Ingersoll Lecture *On Human Immortality*, Boston and London, 1899.

19 *Tertium Quid*, 1887, p. 99. See also pp. 148, 149.

● From the *Varieties of Religious Experience* (New York, 1902), Lecture 20 and Postscript.

23

Wisdom
Verification and Interpretation

John Wisdom was born in 1904 and educated at Cambridge, where he was deeply influenced by Ludwig Wittgenstein (1889–1951). He later took up the chair in philosophy at Cambridge which Wittgenstein had held. His paper 'Gods' was first published in the *Proceedings of the Aristotelian Society* for 1944–45, at a time when religion was dismissed by many philosophers on the grounds that religious statements are unverifiable. Wisdom is concerned to show that an 'appeal to the facts' is no simple matter, whether in religion or in other fields, such as law, art and science. He developed his ideas later in some of the essays in *Paradox and Discovery* (1965), especially 'The Logic of God' and 'Religious Belief'.

Gods

1. *The existence of God is not an experimental issue in the way it was.* An atheist or agnostic might say to a theist 'You still think there are spirits in the trees, nymphs in the streams, a God of the world'. He might say this because he noticed the theist in time of drought pray for rain and make a sacrifice and in the morning look for rain. But disagreement about whether there are gods is now less of this experimental or betting sort than it used to be. This is due in part, if not wholly, to our better knowledge of why things happen as they do.

It is true that even in these days it is seldom that one who believes in God has no hopes or fears which an atheist has not. Few believers now expect prayer to still the waves, but some think it makes a difference to people and not merely in ways the atheist would admit. Of course with people, as opposed to waves and machines, one never knows what they won't do next, so that expecting prayer to make a difference to them is not so definite a thing as believing in its mechanical efficacy. Still, just as primitive people pray in a business-like way for rain, so some people still pray for others with a real feeling of doing something to help. However, in spite of this persistence of an experimental element in some theistic belief, it remains true that Elijah's method on

Mount Carmel of settling the matter of what god or gods exist would be far less appropriate today than it was then.

2. *Belief in gods is not merely a matter of expectation of a world to come.* Someone may say 'The fact that a theist no more than an atheist expects prayer to bring down fire from heaven or cure the sick does not mean that there is no difference between them as to the facts, it does not mean that the theist has no expectations different from the atheist's. For very often those who believe in God believe in another world and believe that God is there and that we shall go to that world when we die'.

This is true, but I do not want to consider here expectations as to what one will see and feel after death nor what sort of reasons these logically unique expectations could have. So I want to consider those theists who do not believe in a future life, or rather, I want to consider the differences between atheists and theists insofar as these differences are not a matter of belief in a future life.

3. *What are these differences? And is it that theists are superstitious or that atheists are blind?* A child may wish to sit awhile with his father and he may, when he has done what his father dislikes, fear punishment and feel distress at causing vexation, and while his father is alive he may feel sure of help when danger threatens and feel that there is sympathy for him when disaster has come. When his father is dead he will no longer expect punishment or help. Maybe for a moment an old fear will come or a cry for help escape him, but he will at once remember that this is no good now. He may feel that his father is no more until perhaps someone says to him that his father is still alive though he lives now in another world and one so far away that there is no hope of seeing him or hearing his voice again. The child may be told that nevertheless his father can see him and hear all he says. When he has been told this the child will still fear no punishment nor expect any sign of his father, but now, even more than he did when his father was alive, he will feel that his father sees him all the time and will dread distressing him and when he has done something wrong he will feel separated from his father until he has felt sorry for what he has done. Maybe when he himself comes to die he will be like a man who expects to find a friend in the strange country where he is going, but even when this is so, it is by no means all of what makes the difference between a child who believes that his father lives still in another world and one who does not.

Likewise one who believes in God may face death differently from one who does not, but there is another difference between them besides this. This other difference may still be described as belief in another world, only this belief is not a matter of expecting one thing rather than another here or hereafter, it is not a matter of a world to come but of a world that now is, though beyond our senses.

We are at once reminded of those other unseen worlds which some philosophers 'believe in' and others 'deny', while non-philosophers unconsciously 'accept' them by using them as models with which to 'get the hang of' the patterns in the flux of experience. We recall the timeless entities whose changeless connections we seek to represent in symbols, and the values which stand firm amidst our flickering satisfaction and remorse, and the physical things which, though not beyond the corruption of moth and rust, are yet more permanent than the shadows they throw upon the screen before our minds. We recall, too, our talk of souls and of what lies in their depths and is manifested to us partially and intermittently in our own feelings and the behaviour of others. The hypothesis of mind, of other human minds and of animal minds, is reasonable because it explains for each of us why certain things behave so cunningly all by themselves unlike even the most ingenious machines. Is the hypothesis of minds in flowers and trees reasonable for like reasons? Is the hypothesis of a world mind reasonable for like reasons—someone who adjusts the blossom to the bees, someone whose presence may at times be felt—in a garden in high summer, in the hills when clouds are gathering, but not, perhaps, in a cholera epidemic?

4. *The question 'Is belief in gods reasonable?' has more than one source.* It is clear now that in order to grasp fully the logic of belief in divine minds we need to examine the logic of belief in animal and human minds. But we cannot do that here and so for the purposes of this discussion about divine minds let us acknowledge the reasonableness of our belief in human minds without troubling ourselves about its logic. The question of the reasonableness of belief in divine minds then becomes a matter of whether there are facts in nature which support claims about divine minds in the way facts in nature support our claims about human minds.

In this way we resolve the force behind the problem of the existence of gods into two components, one metaphysical and the same which prompts the question 'Is there *ever any* behaviour which gives reason to believe in *any* sort of mind?' and one which finds expression in 'Are there other mind-patterns in nature beside the human and animal patterns which we can all easily detect, and are these other mind-patterns superhuman?'

Such overdetermination of a question syndrome is common. Thus, the puzzling questions 'Do dogs think?' 'Do animals feel?' are partly metaphysical puzzles and partly scientific questions. They are not purely metaphysical; for the reports of scientists about the poor performances of cats in cages and old ladies' stories about the remarkable performances of their pets are not irrelevant. But nor are these questions purely scientific; for the stories never settle them and therefore they have other sources. One other source is the metaphysical source we have already noticed, namely, the difficulty about getting behind an animal's behaviour to its mind, whether it is a non-human animal or a human one.

But there's a third component in the force behind these questions, these disputes have a third source, and it is one which is important in the dispute which finds expression in the words 'I believe in God', 'I do not'. This source comes out well if we consider the question 'Do flowers feel?' Like the questions about dogs and animals this question about flowers comes partly from the difficulty we sometimes feel over inference from *any* behaviour to thought or feeling and partly from ignorance as to what behaviour is to be found. But these questions, as opposed to a like question about human beings, come also from hesitation as to whether the behaviour in question is *enough* mind-like, that is, is it enough similar to or superior to human behaviour to be called 'mind-proving'? Likewise, even when we are satisfied that human behaviour shows mind and even when we have learned whatever mind-suggesting things there are in nature which are not explained by human and animal minds, we may still ask 'But are these things sufficiently striking to be called a mind-pattern? Can we fairly call them manifestations of a divine being?'

'The question', someone may say, 'has then become merely a matter of the application of a name. And "What's in a name?"'

5. *But the line between a question of fact and a question or decision as to the application of a name is not so simple as this way of putting things suggests.* The question 'What's in a name?' is engaging because we are inclined to answer both 'Nothing' and 'Very much'. And this 'Very much' has more than one source. We might have tried to comfort Heloïse by saying 'It isn't that Abelard no longer loves you, for this man isn't Abelard'; we might have said to poor Mr Tebrick in Mr Garnett's *Lady into Fox* 'But this is no longer Silvia'. But if Mr Tebrick replied 'Ah, but it is!' this might come not at all from observing facts about the fox which we have not observed, but from noticing facts about the fox which we had missed, although we had in a sense observed all that Mr Tebrick had observed. It is possible to have before one's eyes all the items of a pattern and still to miss the pattern. Consider the following conversation:

'And I think Kay and I are pretty happy. We've always been happy.'

Bill lifted up his glass and put it down without drinking.

'Would you mind saying that again?' he asked.

'I don't see what's so queer about it. Taken all in all, Kay and I have really been happy.'

'All right', Bill said gently, 'Just tell me how you and Kay have been happy.'

Bill had a way of being amused by things which I could not understand.

'It's a little hard to explain', I said. 'It's like taking a lot of numbers that don't look alike and that don't mean anything until you add them all together.'

I stopped, because I hadn't meant to talk to him about Kay and me.

'Go ahead', Bill said. 'What about the numbers.' And he began to smile.

'I don't know why you think it's so funny', I said. 'All the things that two people do together, two people like Kay and me, add up to something. There are the kids and the house and the dog and all the people we have known and all the times we've been out to dinner. Of course, Kay and I do quarrel sometimes but when you add it all together, all of it isn't as bad as the parts of it seem. I mean, maybe that's all there is to anybody's life.'

Bill poured himself another drink. He seemed about to say something and checked himself. He kept looking at me.[1]

Or again, suppose two people are speaking of two characters in a story which both have read[2] or of two friends which both have known, and one says 'Really she hated him', and the other says 'She didn't, she loved him'. Then the first may have noticed what the other has not although he knows no incident in the lives of the people they are talking about which the other doesn't know too, and the second speaker may say 'She didn't, she loved him' because he hasn't noticed what the first noticed, although he can remember every incident the first can remember. But then again he may say 'She didn't, she loved him' not because he hasn't noticed the patterns in time which the first has noticed but because though he has noticed them he doesn't feel he still needs to emphasize them with 'Really she hated him'. The line between using a name because of how we feel and because of what we have noticed isn't sharp. 'A difference as to the facts', 'a discovery', 'a revelation', these phrases cover many things. Discoveries have been made not only by Christopher Columbus and Pasteur, but also by Tolstoy and Dostoievsky and Freud. Things are revealed to us not only by the scientists with microscopes, but also by the poets, the prophets, and the painters. What is so isn't merely a matter of 'the facts'. For sometimes when there is agreement as to the facts there is still argument as to whether defendant did or did not 'exercise reasonable care', was or was not 'negligent'.

And though we shall need to emphasize how much 'There is a God' evinces an attitude to the familiar,[3] we shall find in the end that it also evinces some recognition of patterns in time easily missed and that, therefore, difference as to there being any gods is in part a difference as to what is so and therefore as to the facts, though not in the simple ways which first occurred to us.

6. *Let us now approach these same points by a different road.*

6.1. *How it is that an explanatory hypothesis, such as the existence of God, may start by being experimental and gradually become something quite different can be seen from the following story:*

Two people return to their long neglected garden and find among the weeds a few of the old plants surprisingly vigorous. One says to the other 'It must be that a gardener has been coming and doing something about these plants'. Upon inquiry they find that no neighbour has ever seen anyone at work in their garden. The first man says to the other 'He must have worked while people slept'. The other says 'No, someone would have heard him and besides, anybody who cared about the plants would have kept down these weeds'. The first man says 'Look at the way these are arranged. There is purpose and a feeling for beauty here. I believe that someone comes, someone invisible to mortal eyes. I believe that the more carefully we look the more we shall find confirmation of this'. They examine the garden ever so carefully and sometimes they come on new things suggesting that a gardener comes and sometimes they come on new things suggesting the contrary and even that a malicious person has been at work. Besides examining the garden carefully they also study what happens to gardens left without attention. Each learns all the other learns about this and about the garden. Consequently, when after all this, one says 'I still believe a gardener comes' while the other says 'I don't', their different words now reflect no difference as to what they have found in the garden, no difference as to what they would find in the garden if they looked further and no difference about how fast untended gardens fall into disorder. At this stage, in this context, the gardener hypothesis has ceased to be experimental, the difference between one who accepts and one who rejects it is now not a matter of the one expecting something the other does not expect. What is the difference between them? The one says 'A gardener comes unseen and unheard. He is manifested only in his works with which we are all familiar', the other says 'There is no gardener' and with this difference in what they say about the gardener goes a difference in how they feel towards the garden, in spite of the fact that neither expects anything of it which the other does not expect.

But is this the whole difference between them—that the one calls the garden by one name and feels one way towards it, while the other calls it by another name and feels in another way towards it? And if this is what the difference has become then is it any longer appropriate to ask 'Which is reasonable?'

And yet surely such questions *are* appropriate when one person says to another 'You still think the world's a garden and not a wilderness, and that the gardener has not forsaken it' or 'You still think there are nymphs of the streams, a presence in the hills, a spirit of the world'. Perhaps when a man sings 'God's in His heaven' we need not take this as more than an expression of how he feels. But when Bishop Gore or Dr Joad write about belief in God and young men read them in order to settle their religious doubts the impression is not simply that of persons choosing exclamations with which to face nature and the 'changes and chances of this mortal life'. The disputants speak as if they are concerned with a matter of scientific fact, or of trans-sensual, trans-scientific and metaphysical fact, but still of fact and still a matter about which reasons for and against may be offered, although no scientific reasons in the sense of field surveys for fossils or experiments on delinquents are to the point.

6.2. *Now can an interjection have a logic?* Can the manifestation of an attitude in the utterance of a word, in the application of a name, have a logic? When all the facts are known how can there still be a question of fact? How can there still be a question? Surely as Hume says '. . . after every circumstance, every relation is known, the understanding has no further room to operate'.[4]

6.3. When the madness of these questions leaves us for a moment *we can all easily recollect disputes which though they cannot be settled by experiment are yet disputes in which one party may be right and the other wrong* and in which both parties may offer reasons and the one better reasons than the other. *This may happen in pure and applied mathematics and logic.* Two accountants or two engineers provided with the same data may reach different results and this difference is resolved not by collecting further data but by going over the calculations again. Such differences indeed share with differences as to what will win a race, the honour of being among the most 'settlable' disputes in the language.

6.4. *But it won't do to describe the theistic issue as one settlable by such calculation*, or as one about what can be deduced in this *vertical* fashion from the facts we know. No doubt dispute about God has sometimes, perhaps especially in mediaeval times, been carried on in this fashion. But nowadays it is not and we must look for some other analogy, some other case in which a dispute is settled, but not by experiment.

6.5. *In courts of law* it sometimes happens that opposing counsel are agreed as to the facts and are not trying to settle a question of further fact, are not trying to settle whether the man who admittedly had quarrelled with the deceased did or did not murder him, but are concerned with whether Mr *A* who admittedly handed his long-trusted clerk signed blank checks did or did not exercise reasonable care, whether a ledger is or is not a document,[5] whether a certain body was or was not a public authority.

In such cases we notice that the process of argument is not a *chain* of demonstrative reasoning. It is a presenting and re-presenting of those features of the case which *severally cooperate* in favour of the conclusion, in favour of saying what the reasoner wishes said, in favour of calling the situation by the name by which he wishes to call it. The reasons are like the legs of a chair, not the links of a chain. Consequently although the discussion is a priori and the steps are not a matter of experience, the procedure resembles scientific argument in that the reasoning is not *vertically* extensive but *horizontally* extensive—it is a matter of the cumulative effect of several independent premises, not of the repeated transformation of one or two. And because the premises are severally inconclusive the process of deciding the issue becomes a matter of weighing the cumulative effect of one group of severally inconclusive items against the cumulative effect of another group of severally inconclusive items, and thus lends itself to description in terms of conflicting 'probabilities'. This encourages the feeling that the issue is one of fact—that it is a matter of guessing from the premises at a further fact, at what is to come. But this is a muddle. *The dispute does not cease to be a priori because it is a matter of the cumulative effect of severally inconclusive premises.* The logic of the dispute is not that of a chain of deductive reasoning as in a mathematic calculation. But nor is it a matter of collecting from several inconclusive items of information an expectation as to something further, as when a doctor from a patient's symptoms guesses at what is wrong, or a detective from many clues guesses the criminal. It has its own sort of logic and its own sort of end—the solution of the question at issue is a decision, a ruling by the judge. But it is not an arbitrary decision, though the rational connections are neither quite like those in vertical deductions nor like those in inductions in which from many signs we guess at what is to come; and though the decision manifests itself in the application of a name it is no more merely the application of a name than is the pinning on of a medal merely the pinning on of a bit of metal. Whether a lion with stripes is a tiger or a lion is, if you like, merely a matter of the application of a name. Whether Mr So-and-So of whose conduct we have so complete a record did or did not exercise reasonable care is not merely a matter of the application of a name or, if we choose to say it is, then we must remember that with this name a game is lost and won and a game with very heavy stakes. With the judges' choice of a name for the facts goes an attitude, and the declaration, the ruling, is an exclamation evincing that attitude. But *it is an exclamation which not only has a purpose but also has a logic*, a logic surprisingly like that of 'futile', 'deplorable', 'graceful', 'grand', 'divine'.

6.6 *Suppose two people are looking at a picture or natural scene.* One says 'Excellent' or 'Beautiful' or 'Divine'; the other says 'I don't see it'. He means he doesn't see the beauty. And this reminds us of how we felt the theist accuse the atheist of blindness and the atheist accuse the theist of seeing what isn't there. And yet surely each sees what the other sees. It isn't that one can see part of the picture which the other can't see. So the difference is in a sense not as to the facts. And so it cannot be removed by one disputant discovering to the other what so far he hasn't seen. It isn't that the one sees the picture in a different light and so, as we might say, sees a different picture. Consequently the difference between them cannot be resolved by putting the picture in a different light. And yet surely this is just what can be done in such a case—not by moving the picture but by talk perhaps. To settle a dispute as to whether a piece of music is good or better than another we listen again, with a picture we look again. Someone perhaps points to emphasize certain features and we see it in a different light. Shall we call this 'field work' and 'the last of observation' or shall we call it 'reviewing the premises' and 'the beginning of deduction (horizontal)'?

If in spite of all this we choose to say that a difference as to whether a thing is beautiful is not a factual difference, we must be careful to remember that there is a procedure for settling these differences and that this consists not only in reasoning and redescription as in the legal case, but also in a more literal re-setting-before with re-looking or re-listening.

6.7. *And if we say, as we did at the beginning, that when a difference as to the existence of a God is not one as to future happenings then it is not experimental and therefore not as to the facts, we must not forthwith assume that there is no right and wrong about it*, no rationality or irrationality, no appropriateness or inappropriateness, no procedure which tends to settle it, *nor even that this procedure is in no sense a discovery of new facts.* After all even in science this is not so. Our two gardeners, even when they had reached the stage when neither expected any experimental result which the other did not, might yet have continued the dispute, each presenting and re-presenting the features of the garden favouring his hypothesis, that is, fitting his model for describing the accepted fact; each emphasizing the pattern he wishes to emphasize. True, in science, there is seldom or never a pure instance of this sort of dispute, for nearly always with difference of hypothesis goes some difference of expectation as to the facts. But scientists argue about rival hypotheses with a vigour which is not exactly proportioned to difference in expectations of experimental results.

The difference as to whether a God exists involves our feelings more than most scientific disputes and in this respect is more like a difference as to whether there is beauty in a thing.

7. *The Connecting Technique.* Let us consider again the technique used in revealing or proving beauty, in removing a blindness, in inducing an attitude which is lacking, in reducing a reaction that is inappropriate. Besides running over in a special way the features of the picture, tracing the rhythms, making sure that this and that are not only seen but noticed, and their relation to each other—besides all this—there are other things we can do to justify our attitude and alter that of the man who cannot see. For features of the picture may be brought out by setting beside it other pictures; just as the merits of an argument may be brought out, proved, by setting beside it other arguments, in which striking but irrelevant features of the original are changed and relevant features emphasized; just as the merits and demerits of a line of action may be brought out by setting beside it other actions. To use Susan Stebbing's example: Nathan brought out for David certain features of what David had done in the matter of Uriah the Hittite by telling him a story about two sheep-owners. This is the kind of thing we very often do when someone is 'inconsistent' or 'unreasonable'. This is what we do in referring to other cases in law. The paths we need to trace from other cases to the case in question are often numerous and difficult to detect and the person with whom we are discussing the matter may well draw attention to connections which, while not incompatible with those we have tried to emphasize, are of an opposite inclination. *A* may have noticed in *B* subtle and hidden likenesses to an angel and reveal these to *C*, while *C* has noticed in *B* subtle and hidden likenesses to a devil which he reveals to *A*.

Imagine that a man picks up some flowers that lie half withered on a table and gently puts them in water. Another man says to him 'You believe flowers feel'. He says this although he knows that the man who helps the flowers doesn't expect anything of them which he himself doesn't expect; for he himself expects the flowers to be 'refreshed' and to be easily hurt, injured, I mean, by rough handling, while the man who puts them in water does not expect them to whisper 'Thank you'. The skeptic says 'You believe flowers feel' because something about the way the other man lifts the flowers and puts them in water suggests an attitude to the flowers which he feels inappropriate although perhaps he would not feel it inappropriate to butterflies. He feels that this attitude to flowers is somewhat crazy *just as it is sometimes felt that a lover's attitude is somewhat crazy even when this is not a matter of his having false hopes about how the person he is in love with will act.* It is often said in such cases that reasoning is useless. But the very person who says this feels that the lover's attitude is crazy, is inappropriate like some dreads and hatreds, such as some horrors of enclosed places. And often one who says 'It is useless to reason' proceeds at once to reason with the lover, nor is this reasoning always quite without effect. We may draw the lover's attention to certain things done by her he is in love with and trace for him a path to these from things done by others at other times[6] which have disgusted and infuriated him. And by this means we may weaken his admiration and confidence, make him feel it unjustified and arouse his suspicion and contempt and make him feel our suspicion and contempt reasonable. It is possible, of course, that he has already noticed the analogies, the connections, we point out and that he has accepted them—that is, he has not denied them nor passed them off. He has recognized them and they have altered his attitude, altered his love, but he still loves. We then feel that perhaps it is we who are blind and cannot see what he can see.

8. *Connecting and Disconnecting.* But before we confess ourselves thus inadequate there are other fires his admiration must pass through. For when a man has an attitude which it seems to us he should not have or lacks one which it seems to us he should have, then not only do we suspect that he is not influenced by connections which we feel should influence him and draw his attention to these, but also we suspect he is influenced by connections which should not influence him and draw his attention to these. It may, for a moment, seem strange that we should draw his attention to connections which we feel should not influence him, and which, since they do influence him, he has in a sense already noticed. But we do—such is our confidence in 'the light of reason'.

Sometimes the power of these connections comes mainly from a man's mismanagement of the language he is using. This is what happens in the Monte Carlo fallacy, where by mismanaging the laws of chance a man passes from noticing that a certain colour or number has not turned up for a long while to an improper confidence that now it soon will turn up. In such cases our showing up of the false connections is a process we call 'explaining a fallacy in reasoning'. To remove fallacies in reasoning we urge a man to call a spade a spade, ask him what he means by 'the State' and having pointed out ambiguities and vaguenesses ask him to reconsider the steps in his argument.

9. *Unspoken Connections. Usually, however, wrongheadedness or wrongheartedness in a situation, blindness to what is there or seeing what is not, does not arise merely from mismanagement of language but is more due to connections which are not mishandled in language, for the reason that they are not put into language at all.* And often these misconnections

too, weaken in the light of reason, if only we can guess where they lie and turn it on them. Insofar as these connections are not presented in language the process of removing their power is not a process of correcting the mismanagement of language. But it is still akin to such a process; for though it is not a process of setting out fairly what has been set out unfairly, it is a process of setting out fairly what has not been set out at all. And we must remember that the line between connections ill-presented or half-presented in language and connections operative but not presented in language, or only hinted at, is not a sharp one.

Whether or not we call the process of showing up these connections 'reasoning to remove bad unconscious reasoning' or not, it is certain that in order to settle in ourselves what weight we shall attach to someone's confidence or attitude we not only ask him for his reasons but also look for unconscious reasons both good and bad; that is, for reasons which he can't put into words, isn't explicitly aware of, is hardly aware of, isn't aware of at all—perhaps it's long experience which he *doesn't* recall which lets him know a squall is coming, perhaps it's old experience which he *can't* recall which makes the cake in the tea mean so much and makes Odette so fascinating?[7]

I am well aware of the distinction between the question 'What reasons are there for the belief that S is P?' and the question 'What are the sources of beliefs that S is P?' There are cases where investigation of the rationality of a claim which certain persons make is done with very little inquiry into why they say what they do, into the causes of their beliefs. This is so when we have very definite ideas about what is really logically relevant to their claim and what is not. Offered a mathematical theorem we ask for the proof; offered the generalization that parental discord causes crime we ask for the correlation coefficients. But even in this last case, if we fancy that only the figures are reasons, we underestimate the complexity of the logic of our conclusion; and yet it is difficult to describe the other features of the evidence which have weight and there is apt to be disagreement about the weight they should have. In criticizing other conclusions, and especially conclusions which are largely the expression of an attitude, we have not only to ascertain what reasons there are for them but also to decide what things are reasons and how much. This latter process of sifting reasons from causes is part of the critical process for every belief, but in some spheres it has been done pretty fully already. In these spheres we don't need to examine the actual processes to belief and distil from them a logic. But in other spheres this remains to be done. Even in science or on the stock exchange or in ordinary life we sometimes hesitate to condemn a belief or a hunch[8] merely because those who believe it cannot offer the sort of reasons we had hoped for.

And now suppose Miss Gertrude Stein finds excellent the work of a new artist while we see nothing in it. We nervously recall, perhaps, how pictures by Picasso, which Miss Stein admired and others rejected, later came to be admired by many who gave attention to them, and we wonder whether the case is not a new instance of her perspicacity and our blindness. But if, upon giving all our attention to the work in question, we still do not respond to it, and we notice that the subject matter of the new pictures is perhaps birds in wild places and learn that Miss Stein is a bird-watcher, then we begin to trouble ourselves less about her admiration.

It must not be forgotten that our attempt to show up misconnections in Miss Stein may have an opposite result and reveal to us connections we had missed. Thinking to remove the spell exercised upon his patient by the old stories of the Greeks, the psychoanalyst may himself fall under that spell and find in them what his patient has found and, incidentally, what made the Greeks tell those tales.

10. *Now what happens, what should happen, when we inquire in this way into the reasonableness, the propriety of belief in gods?* The answer is: A double and opposite-phased change. Wordsworth writes:

> . . . And I have felt
> A presence that disturbs me with the joy
> Of elevated thoughts; a sense sublime
> Of something far more deeply interfused,
> Whose dwelling is the light of setting suns,
> And the round ocean and the living air,
> And the blue sky, and in the mind of man:
> A motion and a spirit, that impels
> All thinking things, all objects of all thought,
> And rolls through all things. . . .[9]

We most of us know this feeling. But is it well placed like the feeling that here is first-rate work, which we sometimes rightly have even before we have fully grasped the picture we are looking at or the book we are reading? Or is it misplaced like the feeling in a house that has long been empty that someone secretly lives there still. Wordsworth's feeling *is* the feeling that the world is haunted, that something watches in the hills and manages the stars. The child feels that the stone tripped him when he stumbled, that the bough struck him when it flew back in his face. He has to learn that the wind isn't buffeting him, that there is not a devil in it, that he was wrong, that his attitude was inappropriate. And as he learns that the wind wasn't hindering him so he also learns it wasn't helping him. But we know how, though he learns, his attitude lingers. It is plain that Wordsworth's feeling is of this family.

Belief in gods, it is true, is often very different from belief that stones are spiteful, the sun kindly. For the gods appear in human form and from the waves and control these things and by so doing reward and punish us. But varied as are the stories of the gods, they have a family likeness and we have only to recall them to feel sure of the other main sources which cooperate with animism to produce them.

What are the stories of the gods? What are our feelings when we believe in God? They are feelings of awe before power, dread of the thunderbolts of Zeus, confidence in the everlasting arms, unease beneath the all-seeing eye. They are feelings of guilt and inescapable vengeance, of smothered hate and of a security we can hardly do without. We have only to remind ourselves of these feelings and the stories of the gods and goddesses and heroes in which these feelings find expression to be reminded of how we felt as children to our parents and the big people of our childhood. Writing of a first telephone call from his grandmother, Proust says:

> . . . it was rather that this isolation of the voice was like a symbol, a presentation, a direct consequence of another isolation, that of my grandmother, separated for the first time in my life, from myself. The orders or prohibitions which she addressed to me at every moment in the ordinary course of my life, the tedium of obedience or the fire of rebellion which neutralized the affection that I felt for her were at this moment eliminated. . . . 'Granny!' I cried to her . . . but I had beside me only that voice, a phantom, as unpalpable as that which would come to revisit me when my grandmother was dead. 'Speak to me!' but then it happened that, left more solitary still, I ceased to catch the sound of her voice. My grandmother could no longer hear me . . . I continued to call her, sounding the empty night, in which I felt that her appeals also must be straying. I was shaken by the same anguish which, in the distant past, I had felt once before, one day when, a little child, in a crowd, I had lost her.

Giorgio de Chirico, writing of Courbet, says:

> The word yesterday envelops us with its yearning echo, just as, on waking, when the sense of time and the logic of things remain a while confused, the memory of a happy hour we spent the day before may sometimes linger reverberating within us. At times we think of Courbet and his work as we do of our own father's youth.

When a man's father fails him by death or weakness how much he needs another father, one in the heavens with whom is 'no variableness nor shadow of turning'.

We understood Mr Kenneth Grahame, when he wrote of the Golden Age we feel we have lived in under the Olympians. Freud says: 'The ordinary man cannot imagine this Providence in any other form but that of a greatly exalted father, for only such a one could understand the needs of the sons of men, or be softened by their prayers and be placated by the signs of their remorse. The whole thing is so patently infantile, so incongruous with reality. . .'. 'So incongruous with reality'! It cannot be denied.

But here a new aspect of the matter may strike us.[10] For the very facts which make us feel that now we can recognize systems of superhuman, subhuman, elusive beings for what they are—the persistent projections of infantile phantasies—include facts which make these systems less fantastic. What are these facts? They are patterns in human reactions which are well described by saying that we are as if there were hidden within us powers, persons, not ourselves and stronger than ourselves. That this is so may perhaps be said to have been common knowledge yielded by ordinary observation of people,[11] but we did not know the degree in which this is so until recent study of extraordinary cases in extraordinary conditions had revealed it. I refer, of course, to the study of multiple personalities and the wider studies of psychoanalysts. Even when the results of this work are reported to us, that is not the same as tracing the patterns in the details of the cases on which the results are based; and even that is not the same as taking part in the studies oneself. One thing not sufficiently realized is that some of the things shut within us are not bad but good.

Now the gods, good and evil and mixed, have always been mysterious powers outside us rather than within. But they have also been within. It is not a modern theory but an old saying that in each of us a devil sleeps. Eve said: 'The serpent beguiled me'. Helen says to Menelaus:

> . . . And yet how strange it is!
> I ask not thee; I ask my own sad thought,
> What was there in my heart, that I forgot
> My home and land and all I loved, to fly
> With a strange man? Surely it was not I,
> But Cypris there![12]

Elijah found that God was not in the wind, nor in the thunder, but in a still small voice. The kingdom of Heaven is within us, Christ insisted, though usually about the size of a grain of mustard seed, and he prayed that we should become one with the Father in Heaven.

New knowledge made it necessary either to give up saying 'The sun is sinking' or to give the words a new meaning. In many contexts we preferred to stick to the old words and give them a new meaning which was not entirely new but, on the contrary, *practically* the same as the old. The Greeks did not speak of the dangers of repressing instincts but they did speak of the dangers of thwarting Dionysos, of neglecting Cypris for Diana, of forgetting Poseidon for Athena. We have eaten of the fruit of a garden we can't forget though we were never there, a garden we still look for though we can never find it. Maybe we look for too simple a likeness to what we dreamed. Maybe we are not as free as we fancy from the old idea that Heaven is a happy hunting ground, or a city with streets of gold. Lately Mr Aldous Huxley has recommended our seeking not somewhere beyond the sky or late in time but a timeless state not made of the stuff of this world, which he rejects, picking it into worthless pieces. But this sounds to me still too much a looking for another place, not indeed one filled with sweets but instead so empty that some of us would rather remain in the Lamb or the Elephant, where, as we know, they stop whimpering with another bitter and, so far from sneering at all things, hang pictures of winners at Kempton and stars of the 'nineties. Something good we have for each other is freed there, and in some degree and for awhile the miasma of time is rolled back without obliging us to deny the present.

The artists who do most for us don't tell us only of fairylands. Proust, Manet, Breughel, even Botticelli and Vermeer show us reality. And yet they give us for a moment exhilaration without anxiety, peace without boredom. And those who, like Freud, work in a different way against that which too often comes over us and forces us into deadness or despair,[13] also deserve critical, patient, and courageous attention. For they, too, work to release us from human bondage into human freedom.

Many have tried to find ways of salvation. The reports they bring back are always incomplete and apt to mislead even when they are not in words but in music or paint. But they are by no means useless; and not the worst of them are those which speak of oneness with God. But insofar as we become one with Him He becomes one with us. St John says He is in us as we love one another.

This love, I suppose, is not benevolence but something that comes of the oneness with one another of which Christ spoke.[14] Sometimes it momentarily gains strength.[15] Hate and the Devil do too. And what is oneness without otherness?

1 J. P. Marquand, *H. M. Pulham, Esq.* (New York: Little, Brown & Co., 1941), p. 320.
2 E.g., Havelock Ellis's autobiography.
3 'Persuasive Definitions', *Mind* (July 1938), by Charles Leslie Stevenson,

should be read here. [Also his *Ethics and Language* (New Haven, Conn.: Yale University Press), 1945.]

4 Hume, *An Enquiry Concerning the Principles of Morals*, Appendix I.

5 *The Times*, March 2, 1945. Also in *The Times* of June 13, 1945, contrast the case of Hannah v. Peel with that of the cruiser cut in two by a liner. In the latter case there is not agreement as to the facts. See also the excellent articles by Dr Glanville L. Williams in the *Law Quarterly Review*, 'Language and the Law' (January and April 1945) and 'The Doctrine of Repugnancy' (October 1943, January 1944, and April 1944). The author, having set out how arbitrary are many legal decisions, needs now to set out how far from arbitrary they are—if his readers are ready for the next phase in the dialectic process.

6 Thus, like the scientist, the critic is concerned to show up the irrelevance of time and space.

7 Proust, *Swann's Way*, Vol. I, 58, Vol. II. Phoenix Edition.

8 Here I think of Mr Stace's interesting reflections in *Mind* (January 1945), 'The Problem of Unreasoned Beliefs'.

9 *Tintern Abbey.*

10 I owe to the late Dr Susan Isaacs the thought of this different aspect of the matter, of this connection between the heavenly Father and 'the good father' spoken of in psychoanalysis.

11 Consider Tolstoy and Dostoievsky—I do not mean, of course, that their observation was ordinary.

12 Euripides, *The Trojan Women*, Gilbert Murray's translation. Roger Hinks in *Myth and Allegory in Ancient Art* writes (p. 108): 'Personifications made their appearance very early in Greek poetry. . . . It is out of the question to call these terrible beings "abstractions". . . . They are real demons to be worshipped and propitiated. . . . These beings we observe correspond to states of mind. The experience of man teaches him that from time to time his composure is invaded and overturned by some power from outside, panic, intoxication, sexual desire'.

> What use to shoot off guns at unicorns?
> Where one horn's hit another fierce horn grows.
> These beasts are fabulous, and none were born
>   Of woman who could lay a fable low.
> *The Glass Tower*, Nicholas Moore, p. 100.

13 Matthew Arnold, *Summer Night*.

14 John 16:21.

15 'The Harvesters' in *The Golden Age*, Kenneth Grahame.

• From *Philosophy and Psycho-analysis* (Oxford, 1953), Chapter 10.